Turkey in Africa

Turkey in Africa

Turkey's Strategic Involvement in Sub-Saharan Africa

Federico Donelli

BLOOMSBURY ACADEMIC
LONDON · NEW YORK · OXFORD · NEW DELHI · SYDNEY

BLOOMSBURY ACADEMIC
Bloomsbury Publishing Plc
50 Bedford Square, London, WC1B 3DP, UK
1385 Broadway, New York, NY 10018, USA
29 Earlsfort Terrace, Dublin 2, Ireland

BLOOMSBURY, BLOOMSBURY ACADEMIC and the Diana logo
are trademarks of Bloomsbury Publishing Plc

First published in Great Britain, 2021
This paperback edition published 2022

A catalogue record for this book is available from the British Library.

A catalog record for this book is available from the Library of Congress.

ISBN: HB: 978-0-7556-3697-6
PB: 978-0-7556-3701-0
ePDF: 978-0-7556-3699-0
eBook: 978-0-7556-3698-3

Typeset by Deanta Global Publishing Services, Chennai, India

To find out more about our authors and books visit www.bloomsbury.com and
sign up for our newsletters.

Contents

Acknowledgements

I want to express my gratitude to the many colleagues with whom I shared this long research journey through a continuous exchange of insights and ideas, from which I benefited both professionally and personally. Among the many people to whom I am grateful, I especially want to thank my friend and trusted advisor Brendon J. Cannon. Second, I want to thank the many people in Turkey who have over the course of many years contributed to designing and improving the structure and content of the book. Between them, without taking anything away from all the others, a warm thanks to Muzaffer Şenel, a true friend. Third, I want to thank my academic supervisors of the Department of Political Science at the University of Genoa: Professor Giampiero Cama and Professor Elisabetta Tonizzi. Without their constant guidance, I would have probably gotten lost. Thanks also to my mentor and friend Professor Carlo Degli Abbati for the long talks and for helping me in moments of discouragement. My thanks also to the two anonymous reviewers, whose comments and critics have strengthened the book and my arguments. Finally, my most heartfelt thanks go to my family and particularly to my wife Monica. This book would not have been possible without her support.

Introduction

The post-conflict system promoted by the US administration at the end of the Second World War, based on integrated security and guaranteed by a system of alliances and commercial openness, has undergone a process of adaptation over the past seventy years. At the end of the Cold War, the international system became, effectively, a global order. Several emerging actors or latecomers soon became the main beneficiaries of this system. The rising powers have been favoured especially by the opening to the global market, which has allowed them to grow rapidly and without any disruption. This trend has enabled them to fill the gap with more industrialized economies. Yet, the impressive economic performance has prompted emerging players to claim a greater role in global governance, partly challenging American hegemony. As a result, since the beginning of the new millennium a distinctive feature of global order developments has been the rise of emerging powers that have adopted non-military forms of soft balancing such as economic, diplomatic and multilateral action.

Asserting their new-found influence, these countries seek a reorientation of power towards multipolarity. It is a widespread belief among scholars that the next few years will be characterized by a trend towards a multipolar system in which the gradual downsizing of the Western countries' power will correspond to the increase of the emerging powers. Articulated through an economically led diplomacy, the emerging powers have demanded a new set of international norms, a new trade agenda and equitable representation in the multilateral arena. The dynamics will make the 'regime change' of global governance not a long shot.[1] In parallel to their increasing roles in international politics, the emerging powers have begun to take on an active role in the international development and humanitarian aid landscape through multilayered foreign policy strategies. Among the causes of such a general trend is the transformation of the world economy that has generated an unprecedented demand for energy resources, making Africa a geopolitical competitive arena. The increased

---

[1] Stephen, Matthew D. 2017. 'Emerging Powers and Emerging Trends in Global Governance'. *Global Governance* 23 (3):483–502.

global competition has reached its peak in sub-Saharan Africa (SSA) due to its enormous natural wealth, including vast deposits of precious minerals such as diamonds, gold and tantalum.

The huge resources are considered a primary source for fostering the growth of both traditional and rising economies. This demand for raw materials from emerging economies appears to be almost inexhaustible, which will lead them to increase their presence in Africa and strengthen their ties with the continent. The rising engagement of non-Western actors like China, India, Russia, Japan and Brazil, mainly in the economic field, has affected African relations with traditional Western partners on one hand, and it has led them to rethink African future development, on the other. Therefore, the new multipolar balance, although not yet defined, has given back centrality to the continent defeating a belief, assumed for a long time as true, that the position of Africa, and in particular SSA, would be irrelevant in the international arena as a politically empty space.[2] The involvement of the emerging powers in Africa has not only brought the continent back to the centre of international attention but also given new impetus to the traditional powers which, instead of withdrawing, have rethought the way of relating with the African countries. The growing interest has led the global powers to compete with each other in order to win pre-emptive rights over resources, energy and other natural wealth found in abundance in the African continent. This phenomenon has been described by some scholars and analysts as a 'new race' to Africa or a 'new scramble' for Africa.[3] Thus, the competitive and cooperative dynamics of the current multipolar system have been substantiated on the African continent. Nowadays, Africa increasingly appears to be an arena in which old and new extra-regional actors compete to gain important positions, driven by both economic interests and the desire to reflect, at least within the regional framework, the reshuffling of the global political hierarchy.

In an environment where Africa's role in international politics is increasing and all traditional and emerging powers are in competition over access to the abundant natural resources of African countries, Turkey is also seeking to enhance its engagement in the continent. In this context, Turkey is a very young extra-regional player; indeed, it has only been operating continuously and effectively since 2005, designated in Turkey as the 'Year of Africa'. In the

[2]   Morgenthau, Hans J. 1948. *Politics Among Nations: The Struggle for Power and Peace.* New York: Alfred Kopf. Cfr. Mangala, Jack, ed. 2010. *Africa and the New World Era: From Humanitarianism to a Strategic View.* New York: Palgrave Macmillan.

[3]   Carmody, Pádraig. 2011. *The New Scramble for Africa.* Cambridge: Polity Press.

last fifteen years Turkey has earned a special place among the extra-regional partners, becoming part of the emerging powers that have strengthened their ties with African countries. However, Turkish policy towards the African continent has presented characteristics that are distinct both from the traditional Western powers and from the other emerging players. Since the end of the 1990s Turkey's relations with Africa have shown an increasing revival, gaining momentum following the rise to power of the post-Islamist Justice and Development Party (JDP). In order to encourage this development, a change was necessary in the Turkish geographical imagination of both its own country, today conceived as an Afro-Eurasian state, and Africa, no longer considered a poor and backward place but as a fecund ground full of opportunities. Thus, Turkey's opening to Africa also had a profound psychological effect on Turkish policymakers and society. Since then the Ankara government has launched several initiatives with African states and assumed the role of a strategic partner within regional fora, such as the African Union, and intergovernmental organizations such as the United Nations and the Organization of Islamic Cooperation (OIC). The active Turkish involvement in the Somali crisis that started in 2011 has deepened Turkey's presence in SSA, changing the nature of the Turkish role in the whole continent. Nowadays, Turkey's presence in the region has particular characteristics that differentiate it from other external powers. The current partnership agenda goes along with the idea of the Ankara consensus that is both an alternative approach to African sustainability problems and a useful political discourse to foster Turkish ambitions as an emerging global power.

The traditional 'consensus' formulae are unable to explain the peculiar set of prescriptions that Turkey promotes in SSA based on its own development experience, which – mainly in light of the gradual democratic regression – could be considered a mix of democratic liberalism (Washington consensus) and authoritarian capitalism (Beijing consensus). Besides, the notion of the Ankara consensus lends itself to include and synthesize Turkish public narrative in which the traditional South-South Cooperation rhetoric is mixing with Islamic humanitarianism and third-world discourses.

I.1 Overview and structure of the book

The book is based on the assumptions that the current reshuffle in the global balance will inevitably lead to changes in the framework of institutions, norms, rules and values on which the international society is based. A further outcome of these developments is the recovered centrality of the single regions and of the regional actors that operate within them. The present and future structures of the emerging international system depend, to a large extent, on the internal dynamics of the individual regions. In other words, it is impossible to understand the new international order without taking into account the role played by the individual regions within it. At the same time, it is impossible to explain the internal dynamics of the individual regional systems without grasping the complexity of the dense interconnections between the international system dimension and the domestic sphere of the actors involved. Among the latter, an increasing role is being played by the emerging powers. In addition to acquiring a primary position or the leadership in their respective regional contexts, these powers also operate beyond their borders with the aim of achieving a global relevance. This is the case of Turkey, which, since the new millennium, has adopted a multidirectional foreign policy with the aim of diversifying its political and commercial relations. Like other emerging powers, such as China and India, Turkey has also chosen to invest significantly in Africa through a distinct approach.

Drawing critically on the informal diplomacy literature and on the studies of Turkey–Africa relations, this book provides a comprehensive and conceptually rich analysis of the Turkish rapprochement with SSA that has made Turkey a relevant and unconventional actor in the region. Further, almost two decades after the launch of the engagement agenda in SSA, this study attempts to analyse and conceptualize the characteristics, benefits, challenges and limits of Turkish policy in the region. The rationale is based on the awareness that Africa, in particular SSA, has witnessed a transition from dependence on former colonial powers to dependence on emerging powers such as Turkey. Therefore, behind the so-called 'new scramble of Africa' there is a deeper shift in the extra-regional actors' leverage that will unquestionably influence the future of the region. Considering the rising saliency of Turkey's involvement in SSA, there is a need for greater attention from scholars on a few pertinent questions: What are the main factors that drive Turkey's engagement? What does the Ankara consensus mean and which narrative fosters it? How does Turkey apply in an original manner the multitrack approach with the involvement of non-state actors? What are the limits and weaknesses of Turkey's policy?

To answer these research questions and to discuss the main stages of Turkish involvement in Africa, this book presents its arguments in six chapters, as outlined next.

The first chapter seeks to clarify the so-called 'new scramble for Africa' in the broader context of change that has affected the entire international system.

The end of the Cold War opened a phase of transition distinguished by a brief unipolar period that gradually blurred into a multipolarity, which had been emancipated from the US leadership. The US global leadership has been partially disputed by the rise of counter-hegemonic powers such as China and Russia. The global competition has shifted to regional contexts including Africa, whose centrality is determined by its abundance of raw materials. In addition to global powers, however, there has been an increase in the presence of middle and rising powers including Turkey.

The second chapter provides a historical overview of Turkey's relations with Africa in the run-up to the political rise of the JDP and its leader Recep Tayyip Erdoğan in 2002. To provide a clearer picture of the subject, the chapter is divided into three parts, each of which deals with a specific phase of Turkey's history. The first section concerns relations during the Ottoman period; the second with the decades after the birth of the Republic; and finally the third section presents the basis of Turkish foreign policy characterized by the presence of Turgut Özal, who tried to promote a new phase of relations with Africa. The three periods shared the Turkish conception of Africa as a continent divided, with North Africa being perceived as closer geographically while the rest of the region was neglected and considered dangerous.

On the basis of these considerations, the third chapter highlights how the launch of the open policy towards Africa has necessarily required a profound psychological change in Turkish foreign policymakers – a shift favoured by the wider changes triggered by the rise of the JDP and the emergence of a new establishment. After analysing the new Turkish strategic approach to Africa, conceived as a whole region full of wealth and opportunities, the chapter revisits the main stages of Turkish involvement, especially towards SSA. The year 2011 has been a turning point for both JDP's political experience and its policy towards other regions, including Africa.

As such, the fourth chapter focuses on the interweaving of domestic, regional and systemic factors that have led to a change in Turkish foreign policy and the beginning of a new phase in Africa, defined by the consolidation of relations with African countries on a horizontal partnership. The growing engagement in African political affairs, in particular in the Horn of Africa (HOA), has been coupled with the ambition to share its own formula or way towards growth and development: the Ankara consensus. An element of continuity in Turkish policy towards Africa during the JDP period has been the presence of non-state actors, public and private, operating on the ground, strengthening bilateral relations and the image of Turkey in the African eyes.

The fifth chapter analyses in detail the actors involved, highlighting the particular inter-agencies' coordination method. Among the non-state actors involved in the multitrack policy there was also the Gülen movement, which has developed Turkish public diplomacy for years, but after the split with the JDP government (2014) and the failed coup attempt (2016), it effectively became a deeply rooted anti-state lobby in Africa.

Finally, before the conclusions, the sixth chapter highlights an ongoing process that involves the area in which Turkey has invested most in recent years, namely the HOA. Following the so-called Arab Spring (2011), with the outbreak of the Yemeni civil war, the Horn has become a geographical appendix of the rivalries among Middle Eastern powers. The growing influence of regional powers, above all the United Arab Emirates (UAE) and the Kingdom of Saudi Arabia (KSA), has had direct effects on local dynamics, generating instability and increasing the risk of sectarianization.

The concluding chapter takes stock of Turkish action in Africa, highlighting current and future limits and criticalities. In addition to filling the existing gaps in the literature, the aim of the book is to provide scholars, practitioners and the public, increasingly interested in the politics and security of Africa, a different reading about the role that extra-regional emerging powers have the ambition to play in the continent, also within the field of development.

I.2 The extant literature and the nature of African studies in Turkey

The last two decades have witnessed a greater exploration of African issues within Turkish academia, with the field of African studies in Turkey now gaining more academic priority. At the same time, Turkish and non-Turkish research on Turkey's role in Africa has also increased – a new phenomenon, undoubtedly related to the recent political opening of the Ankara government towards the African continent. The study of Turkey's relations with African countries and the research on African topics during the Republican era have been strongly conditioned by Turkish elite political orientation and strategic considerations. As will be discussed in the next chapter, the Turkish elites have for decades considered the African continent to be an area of limited interest and minimal importance in their foreign policy agenda. Consequently, since 1998, the revival of Turkish interest in Africa has favoured the rapid spread of new studies and research. However, compared to other regional areas – such as the Middle East,

Europe, Central Asia, the Balkans – the existing literature on Africa is still very limited and mostly composed of reports and policy papers from think tanks and research centres somehow linked to ministries.

During the last Ottoman period, in the second half of the nineteenth century, the first studies on Africa were published. Among these, a prominent place was occupied by the travel diaries (*seyahatname*) of key figures and officials of the empire. Thanks to the valuable work of Zekeriya Kurşun, who has listed the Turkish studies on Africa, we know that the initial studies included the reports of Ömer Lütfi's *Ümitburnu Seyahatnamesi* (1876); Ömer Kamil Paşa's *Sudan-ı Mısri* (1886–7); Mehmed Muhsin's *Afrika Delili* (1894); Mehmet Ekrem's *Afrika Seyahatnamesi* (1895–6); Sadık el-Müeyyed Paşa's *Habeş Seyahatnamesi* (1904); Mehmet Mihri's *Sudan Seyahatnamesi* (1910); Mahmud Naci and Mehmet Nuri's *Trablusgarp* (1914) and Halil Halit's *Cezayir Hatıratından* (1906).[4]

The interest in African issues lost its appeal in the early years of the Turkish Republic when the Republican elites sought to distance the new state from its Ottoman past. Relations with African countries, like their own imperial past, began to represent a dead weight for the policymakers of the young republic engaged in rebuilding the country in the wake of Western civilization. The long history of relations that linked many African peoples to the heirs of the Ottoman Empire were ignored and gradually removed from the Turkish press and literature. Therefore, when the African countries began to gain independence at the end of the 1960s, there was barely any publication on African studies in Turkey, whether on African history, culture, economics or the fight against colonialism. One of the very rare publications, *Yarının Kıtası Africa* (1959), was the article by the journalist Abdi İpekçi published after a tour to several African countries. The book, reflecting the dominant Turkish narrative, treated African events and African people as something exotic, subtly emphasizing the distance from Turkey. The approach adopted by İpekçi, as by the elite, was very much influenced by Western Orientalism.

Just as Africa had quickly become a region ignored by Turkish politics, so too had it become a completely neglected area of study in Turkish academia. Likewise, the first faint attempts of political openness towards Africa – in the mid-1960s and in the second half of the 1970s – were followed by increased interest and publications with the aim of filling a knowledge gap. Indeed, the earlier few publications like *Kara Afrika* (1971) by Hıfzı Topuz and *Afrika*

[4] Kurşun, Zekeriya, ed. 2013. *Osmanlı'dan Günümüze Afrika Bibliyografyası*. İstanbul: Ortadoğu ve Afrika Araştırmacıları Derneği Yayınları.

Ulusal Kurtuluş Mücadeleleri (1977) by Türkkaya Ataöv have sought to inform academics who had little knowledge of Africa by providing general information on the continent. Ataöv's book was the first attempt at a comprehensive and detailed study on African countries. Its publication in the late 1970s coincided with Turkish attempts to pursue a different African policy, especially by providing financial assistance to African countries. During this period, various foreign African studies ranging from religion, philosophy, history to politics were also translated into Turkish, including the works of the most important anti-colonial thinkers and politicians such as Frantz Fanon, Amilcar Cabral and Nelson Mandela. The military coup of 1980 negatively affected the interest of Turkish academia in African studies and the development of research on the topic. The almost total zeroing of university cadres and staff along with strict military control over research activities drastically reduced the area studies.

Only with the end of the Cold War, the partial failure to become the leader of the Turkic world, and the difficulties in the process of joining the European Union at the Luxembourg Summit (1997), Turkey shifted its attention towards Africa, which was enshrined by the adoption of the Opening to Africa Policy (1998). However, the economic crisis and internal political instability delayed the effective launch of a new policy towards Africa for a few years. Coherent and consistent policy implementation was finally possible when Turkey's JDP replaced a three-party coalition following the 2002 election. Therefore, it was only after 2005 that the efforts made by the new ruling party, JDP, opened a new phase in relations between Turkey and African countries and with them revitalized academic interest. The inattention to Africa prevalent in Turkish academia began to be replaced in a short time. Behind this new impulse there were sometimes purely academic reasons of contributing to a less developed area of study, but sometimes there were pragmatic reasons for government agencies to collect data on Africa. For this reason, a key role in the growth of interest in Africa was played by several think tanks most of which received government contributions to develop specific projects. These strategic research centres or advocacy tanks have provided important analysis and insights into the region and have offered policy recommendations to government officials through the regular publication of reports, articles, analyses and policy papers. The first wave of studies concentrated on Turkish–African political and economic relations and on the political economy of Turkey's engagement with Africa relations began to spread simultaneously. An interesting aspect of the early studies is that, like the political rhetoric of the new JDP policymakers, elements hitherto ostracized as historical and cultural affinities acquired considerable relevance. The emphasis placed on Turkey's Ottoman heritage by the new political elite has conditioned the new studies, such as Ahmet Kavas's *Osmanlı-Afrika İlişkileri* (2006), which provides important insights into the history of the Ottoman engagement with Africa with a focus on the spread of Islam in the continent.

To summarize, from 1998 to the present day, the period that the present study focuses on, the literature on Turkish–African relations can be divided into two major groups: the first comprising mainly Turkish scholars who have produced works on Africa in various fields such as cinema, poetry, media, geography, education, migration, politics, religion, history, security, tourism, economics, nature and animals;[5] and the second group comprising various articles on Turkish initiatives published either in academic journals or as policy papers by international scholars, most of which provide detailed information on Turkey's recent engagement with Africa.[6]

The correlation between foreign policy initiatives and scholarly work is not a specificity of the Turkish case but, conversely, Turkey is in line with a trend shared by other states, including major powers such as Russia, China and the United States. In the United States, for example, as pointed out by David Wiley, security concerns have made African studies increasingly militarized and, following 9/11, some government institutions have provided large amounts of funding for Africanist scholars to provide information on Africa critical to national security.[7] More recently, China's growing involvement in Africa has been matched by a proliferation of studies of the continent. The Chinese

---

[5] See for example Şakı Aydın, Oya. 2005. 'Afrika'da Sinema Serüveni ve Cinéma Beur Akımı'. *Galatasaray Üniversitesi İleti-ş-im Dergisi* 2:89–103; Memiş, Hasan, Mehmet Kara and Lütfü Tayfur. 2010. 'Yoksulluk, Yapısal Uyum Programları ve Sahra Altı Afrika Ülkeleri'. *Mustafa Kemal Üniversitesi Sosyal Bilimler Enstitüsü Dergisi* 7 (14):325–46; Özçomak, Suphi M. and Ayhan Demirci. 2010. 'Afrika Birliği Ülkelerinin Sosyal ve Ekonomik Göstergeleri Arasındaki İlişkinin Kanonik Korelasyon Analizi ile İncelenmesi'. *Atatürk Üniversitesi Sosyal Bilimler Enstitüsü Dergisi* 14 (1):361–74; Özoran, Beris Artan. 2014. 'Güney Afrika'da Halkla İlişkiler: Farklı bir Yol Arayışına Vaka Analizi Yoluyla Bakmak'. *İletişim Kuram ve Araştırma Dergisi* 38:74–95.

[6] For example, see Özkan, Mehmet. 2010. 'What Drives Turkey's Involvement in Africa?' *Review of African Political Economy* 37 (126):533–40; Wheeler, Tom. 2011. 'Ankara to Africa: Turkey's Outreach since 2005'. *South African Journal of International Affairs* 18 (1):43–62; Bacik, Gökhan and Afacan, Isa 2013. 'Turkey Discovers Sub-Saharan Africa: The Critical Role of Agents in the Construction of Turkish Foreign-Policy Discourse'. *Turkish Studies* 14 (3):483–502; Rudincová, Kateřina. 2014. 'New Player on the Scene: Turkish Engagement in Africa'. *Bulletin of Geography. Socio-economic Series* (25):197–213; Cannon, Brendon J. 2016. 'Turkey in Kenya and Kenya in Turkey: Alternatives to the East/West Paradigm in Diplomacy, Trade and Security'. *Africa Journal of Political Science and International Relations* 10 (5):56–65; Donelli, Federico. 2017. 'A Hybrid Actor in the Horn of Africa: An Analysis of Turkey's Involvement in Somalia'. In *The Horn of Africa since the 1960s: Local and International Politics Intertwined*, edited by Aleksi Ylönen and Jan Záhořík, 158–70. London: Routledge; Langan, Mark. 2017. 'Virtuous Power Turkey in Sub-Saharan Africa: The "Neo-Ottoman" Challenge to the European Union'. *Third World Quarterly* 38 (6):1399–414.

[7] Martin, William G. 2011. 'The Rise of African Studies (USA) and the Transnational Study of Africa'. *African Studies Review* 54 (1):59–83; Wiley, David. 2012. 'Militarizing Africa and African Studies and the U.S. Africanist Response'. *African Studies Review* 55 (2):147–61.

government has allocated substantial amounts of resources to gather more information on African countries and to better shape its foreign policy towards them by contributing to the establishment and activities of various specialized research centres such as the Chinese Association of African Studies and the Chinese Academy of Social Sciences.[8] These samples, like the Turkish case, highlight the mutual correlation between the policies of the states towards Africa and the growth of African studies within them, with government institutions providing funding to scholars to gather practical information on particular regions and areas of study critical to policy priorities, and academics collecting information that are sometimes politically motivated, and sometimes for purely academic purposes, in order to increase awareness about underdeveloped areas of study. What makes the Turkish case different from the others, however, is that political elites have also influenced the public perception of Africa for many years. Indeed, it should be noted that until the beginning of the new millennium, Africa was not considered a whole geographical entity but, rather, a broken body with two distinct and, paradoxically, separate parts. Both the northern part of the continent and SSA have distinctive historical, cultural, religious, political and ecological characteristics. Being under the Ottoman rule for centuries, North African countries shared a common history, religion and traditions with the Ottoman Empire and its successor, the Turkish Republic. The geographical imagination promoted by the Kemalist elite during the early years of the Republic included those countries in the wide Middle East and North Africa region. Accordingly, the historical and political events of countries such as Egypt, Libya and even Sudan have been studied by Middle Eastern experts. Therefore, as evidenced by the study of Elem Eyrice Tepeciklioğlu, the Maghreb region has long been studied by Turkish academics though not under the label of African studies.[9] As will be discussed in Chapter 3, even before it could develop its economic and diplomatic relations with African countries, Turkey had to promote among state officials, the academic world and the whole public opinion a new geographical perception or geographical imagination of the African continent and specifically of SSA.

Until recently, the literature about the strategic orientation of Turkey had paid no attention to its southern dimension, namely towards Africa or Latin

[8] Princeton, Lyman. 2006. 'China's Involvement in Africa: A View from the US'. *South African Journal of International Affairs* 13 (1):129–38. doi: 10.1080/10220460609556790; Li, Anshan. 2010. 'African Studies in China: A Historiographical Survey'. In *Chinese and African Perspectives on China in Africa*, edited by Axel Harneit-Sievers, Stephen Marks and Sanusha Naidu, 2–24. Kampala: Pambazuka Press.

[9] Eyrice Tepeciklioğlu, Elem. 2016. 'African Studies in Turkey'. *Uluslararası İlişkiler* 13 (50):3–19.

America. Indeed, a review of the key textbooks about the central events of the Turkish foreign policy shows that the 'Third World' or the 'Global South' is almost absent. There are only a couple of publications that explore the relations of Turkey with the third world in the midst of the Cold War,[10] and – after the Cold War – the Global South.[11] Actually, there is very little information about the Turkish position towards the decolonization process, the links between Turkish social and political leftist movements and national liberation movements in the non-Arab world, and the Turkish multilateral policy towards the main topics of the Global South's international agenda before the JDP years. Nonetheless, in the last decade, there had been a new interest in the increasing ties of Turkey with the Global South in different regions and policy areas. Especially, Turkey's new policies towards Africa has gained the attention of experts and analysts while the significant developmental and humanitarian efforts in such diverse places as Somalia have enhanced the role of Turkey as a responsible partner in the world efforts to achieve more effective results in the quest for regional and global governance.[12] Even though such a topic has gained the attention of the international academia, Turkey's growing engagement in SSA is rarely addressed and analysed. Moreover, at the moment, there is no single book or monograph that analyses Turkish involvement in the region in depth. At the same time, the existing literature lacks a comprehensive study that analyses Turkey as an emerging extra-regional actor on the African continent in a similar way to other emerging players such as China, India or

[10] Bölükbaşı, Suha. 1988. *The Superpowers and the Third World: Turkish-American Relations and Cyprus*. Maryland: University Press of America; Sönmezoğlu, Faruk. 1994. *Türk Dış Politikasının Analizi*, 441–81. Istanbul: Der Yayınları.

[11] Apaydin, Fulya. 2012. 'Overseas Development Aid Across the Global South: Lessons from the Turkish Experience in Sub-Saharan Africa and Central Asia'. *European Journal of Development Research* 24 (2):261–82.

[12] Hasan, Yusuf Fadl. 2007. 'Some Aspects of Turco-African Relations with Special Reference to the Sudan'. *Middle East and African Studies* 2; Özkan, Mehmet. 2012. 'Turkiye'nin Afrika'da Artan Rolu: Pratik Cabalar ve Soylem Arayislari'. Ortadoğu Analiz 4 (46):19–28; Özkan, Mehmet. 2018. 'Africa's Place in Turkey's Foreign Policy: From Doubts to Normalization'. *Africa e Orienti* 20 (1–2):41–53; Özkan, 'What Drives Turkey's Involvement in Africa?', 533–40; Özkan, Mehmet. 2011. 'Turkey's "New" Engagements in Africa and Asia: Scope, Content and Implications'. *Perceptions – Journal of International Affairs* 16 (3):115–37; Özkan, Mehmet. 2013. 'Turkey's Religious and Socio-Political Depth in Africa: "Emerging Powers in Africa"'. *LSE IDEAS Special Report* 16:45–50; Özkan, Mehmet. 2014. *Turkey's Involvement in Somalia: Assessments of a State-Building in Progress*. Ankara: SETA Publications; Mbabia, Oliver. 2011. 'Ankara en Afrique: stratégies d expansion'. *Outre-Terre* 3 (29):107–19; Wheeler, 'Ankara to Africa: Turkey's Outreach since 2005', 43–62; Bacik and Afacan, 'Turkey Discovers Sub-Saharan Africa', 483–502; Akpınar, Pınar 2013. 'Turkey's Peacebuilding in Somalia: The Limits of Humanitarian Diplomacy'. *Turkish Studies* 14 (4):735–57; Rudincová, 'New Player on the Scene', 197–213; Abdirahman, Ali. 2013. 'Turkey's Foray into Africa: A New Humanitarian Power?' *Insight Turkey* 13 (4):65–73; Ipek, Volkan. 2017. 'Turkey's Foreign Policy towards Sub-Saharan Africa'. In *Turkish Foreign Policy*, edited by Ercan P. Gözen, 217–35. London: Palgrave Macmillan; Langan, 'Virtuous Power Turkey in Sub-Saharan Africa'.

Brazil. Based on this consideration, the book aims to examine the various steps that have characterized Turkey's involvement in the African context since the new millennium. To better understand the magnitude of the change that began in 2005, the volume will also provide a brief overview of the historical relations between Turkey and the African continent from the Ottoman period to the 2000s. While that section (Chapter 2) may appear to be a superfluous description of events not of relevance to the subject of this study, it is an essential component of current Turkish foreign policy in Africa. History and, more specifically, the Ottoman past has a double significance in the current Turkish discourse on Africa. From a domestic point of view, it is functional to brand the difference with the policies of the past decades, which have been considered too cautious and unambitious. From the international point of view, the imperial past is used, on the one hand, to legitimize the JDP government's ambition to restore the international centrality of the state and, on the other hand, to mark a difference with both traditional and emerging extra-regional actors. These elements are especially visible in the narrative that accompanies Turkish politics in Africa. Therefore, the analysis of Turkish foreign policy in Africa should not disregard the scrutiny of all those factors – material and non-material – that shape it.

This book aims to fill the gap in the extant literature through the comprehensive study of Turkish involvement in Africa, in particular in SSA, within a theoretical framework of International Relations (IR). As mentioned earlier, while not neglecting the historical perspective necessary to understand the impact of the effort undertaken by Turkey in the last two decades, the research fits into the existing area studies literature as an IR subfield. Ever since the JDP came to power in 2002, a growing number of IR scholars have argued that Turkey has been developing into a more self-confident and assertive regional power that is increasingly pushing its own foreign policy interests and demands.[13]Primarily due to the theoretical neorealist approach that these scholars apply, most of them tend to ignore domestic factors which, in fact, provide the main context for decisions on foreign policy.[14] On the other hand, following the constructivist approach, few scholars have pointed out the importance of the ideational factor

---

[13] For a review of the different approaches used in the study of Turkish foreign policy under JDP, see Yalvaç, Faruk. 2014. 'Approaches to Turkish Foreign Policy: A Critical Realist Analysis'. *Turkish Studies* 15 (1):117–38.

[14] Hale, William. 2000. *Turkish Foreign Policy, 1774-2000*. Portland, London: Frank Cass; Candar, Cengiz and Fuller Graham E. 2001. 'Grand Geopolitics for a New Turkey'. *Mediterranean Quarterly* 12 (1):22–38; Yilmaz, Muzaffer Ercan. 2010. 'Conceptual Framework of Turkish Foreign Policy in the AK Party Era'. *Turkish Review* 1 (1):68–73; Keyman, E. Fuat. 2010. 'Globalization, Modernity and Democracy: Turkish Foreign Policy 2009 and Beyond'. *Perceptions* 15 (3–4):1–20.

without considering the saliency of the state's relative power in terms of resources and capabilities.[15] The same approaches have been used for the analysis of Turkish involvement in Africa. However, both approaches present some limits, because they don't comprehend the uninterrupted twining between external and internal factors that have influenced Turkey's foreign policy behaviour in the last two decades. In other words, for this case study, neorealism and constructivism prove to be not completely suitable for analysing the 'intermestic' dimension in which Turkey has been operating since the end of the Cold War. For this reason, drawing from the dualist interpretation of the nexus between domestic and international politics, this book aims to fill the literature gap, arguing that Turkish foreign policy outputs not only are a result of bargaining between domestic and international constraints but also reflect a shift in variables related to the intrastate level.

How does Turkey place itself in the African context to local and external stakeholders? What were the multilevel factors that have led to the Turkish opening to Africa? What are the distinctive traits of Turkey's strategy towards the continent? What are the Turkish state and non-state actors involved in the African context and how are they framed within the African agenda? These are just some of the research questions that the study is trying to answer. The main arguments of the study are that Turkey represents a new reality in the African context that can compete with other emerging middle powers. Unlike other emerging powers that have set their relations with Africa solely on an economic-commercial dimension, Turkey has developed a multidimensional framework of engagement characterized by the use of government and non-government actors and by the exploitation of its historical and cultural peculiarities. During the last two decades, the approach followed towards African countries aimed at encouraging win-win solutions to the continent's many challenges has allowed Turkey to carve out areas of increasing presence and influence. Furthermore, research argues that the determinants of Turkey's expanding interest in African issues are the result of explanatory variables on different levels (international, regional, state, individual).

---

[15] Bozdaglioglu, Yucel and Max Novick, eds. 2003. *Turkish Foreign Policy and Turkish Identity: A Constructivist Approach*. New York: Routledge; Sözen, Ahmet. 2010. 'A Paradigm Shift in Turkish Foreign Policy: Transition and Challenges'. *Turkish Studies* 11 (1):103–23; Atalay, Zeynep. 2013. 'Civil Society as Soft Power: Islamic NGOs and Turkish Foreign Policy'. In *Turkey between Nationalism and Globalization*, edited by Riva Kastoryano, 165–86. New York: Routledge.

I.3 Analytical framework

The change of international context has led to an inevitable adjustment of the tools and approaches best suited to understand the political dynamics. Since the mid-1990s, most observers have suggested that the line between domestic and international politics is not just blurry but also quickly disappearing because of globalization.[16] Some have called it 'intermestic', combining the words to indicate the intertwining of issues and interests. Among them is Bahgat Korany who believes that 'intermestic' is 'a reflection of creeping globalization, characterized by the retreat of exclusive state sovereignty, and the rise instead of the intensity of societal interconnectedness and speedy circulation of ideas, but without wiping out the impact of local features'.[17] Such an interpretation is particularly useful in the understanding of certain regions, such as the Middle East and Africa, considered to be penetrated systems composed of several distinct levels – the global environment, the interstate environment, the trans-state environment and the domestic environment – exposed to a high rate of influence by external actors.[18] Within the IR discipline, new trends of analysis have been developed that have introduced alternative approaches to the study of international politics, so as to be able to understand in a comprehensive way the intertwined and multilayered dynamics. Recent years have witnessed different interpretations of the changing dynamics of international politics. Among these, an interpretative paradigm of great importance is neoclassical realism (NCR). This research presents a realist approach to IR; notably it uses the neoclassical theory considered as the most suitable for a multilayered analysis that includes both the material and the ideational dimensions. In the following chapters, the book tries to expand the existing studies applying a neoclassical realist analytical framework in order to identify the influence of certain domestic constraints and priorities on Turkish foreign policy behaviour. It seeks to offer an interpretation of Turkey's strategic involvement in SSA, one that explicitly combines the entwined material and ideational factors in the manner suggested by NCR. The

---

[16] Kaarbo, Juliet. 2015. 'A Foreign Policy Analysis Perspective on the Domestic Politics Turn in IR Theory'. *International Studies Review* 17:189–216.

[17] Korany, Bahgat. 2010. *The Changing Middle East: A New Look at Regional Dynamics*. Cairo, New York: The American University in Cairo Press; Korany, Bahgat. 2013. 'The Middle East Since the Cold War'. In *International Relations of the Middle East*, edited by Louise Fawcett, 83. Oxford: Oxford University Press.

[18] For example, see Brown, Carl L. 1984. *International Politics in the Middle East: Old Rules, Dangerous Game*. Princeton: Princeton University Press; Ehteshami, Anoushirvan. 2014. 'Middle East Middle Powers: Regional Role, International Impact'. *Uluslararası İlişkiler* 11 (42):29–49; Clapham, Christopher. 1996. *Africa and the International System: The Politics of State Survival*. Cambridge: Cambridge University Press.

purpose is to improve the dominant neorealist and constructivist analysis of Turkey's foreign policy, thereby demonstrating the value of a neoclassical realist interpretation to explain the recent developments towards Africa. The book's theoretical aims are to show how the realist perspective does not necessarily neglect ideational factors and the non-material dimensions of power but, rather, includes them as intervening variables useful to broaden explanatory factors or *explanans*.

As an emerging school of foreign policy, NCR is among the newest branches of the realist school that has wrought a very productive theoretical debate within the IR field.[19] NCR represents a thriving decade-old research programme, the raison d'être of which is the study of the foreign policy of states, without claims to explaining the broad systemic patterns of recurring outcomes. Different IR scholars refer to NCR using labels such as 'neo-traditional realism'[20] or 'post-classical realism'.[21]

As summarized by Foulon, NCR outstrips 'standard realism's summary of human nature, the anthropomorphism of the state (classical realism), and the material balance of power that affects states (neorealism)'.[22] Yet, as well as constructivists, neoclassical realists believe that ideas matter – ideology, threat assessment, leaders' perceptions – this is why James argued that NCR is 'realist-inspired constructivism'.[23] The core principles of neorealism with regard to the state, relative power and the primacy of the anarchical material structure are largely shared by neoclassical realists. The overall argument is that systemic factors are the most important to explain international developments over time. In other words, this approach maintains that the relative powers – the resources and capabilities – of the state are the main causal variable of state actions. At the same time, NCR has distanced itself from neorealism because it does not consider anarchy as an independent causal force but, rather, as a permissive condition that gives states considerable latitude in defining their security interests. Neoclassical

[19] Taliaferro, Jeffrey W., Steven E. Lobell and Norrin M. Ripsman. 2009. *Neoclassical Realism, the State and Foreign Policy*, 3–4. Cambridge: Cambridge University Press.

[20] Schweller, Randall L. 2003. 'The Progressiveness of Neoclassical Realism'. In *Progress in International Relations Theory: Appraising the Field*, edited by Colin Elman and Miriam Fendius Elman, 316. London: MIT Press.

[21] Brooks, Stephen G. 1997. 'Dueling Realisms'. *International Organization* 51 (3):445; Schuett, Robert. 2010. *Political Realism, Freud, and Human Nature in International Relations*, 17. Basingstoke: Palgrave Macmillan.

[22] Foulon, Michiel. 2015. 'Neoclassical Realism: Challengers and Bridging Identities'. *International Studies Review* 17:647–48.

[23] James, Patrick. 2009. 'Elaborating on Offensive Realism.' In Rethinking Realism in International Relations: Between Tradition and Innovation, edited by Annette Freyberg-Inan, Ewan Harrison and Patrick James, 245–62. Abingdon: Routledge, p. 259.

realists believe that systemic effects on the state's behaviour vary and are indirect.[24] While it emerges that the system gives incentives to state actors, it is not immediate to its involvement in determining their behaviour.[25] Indeed, there is not 'an immediate or perfect "transmission belt" between structural pressures and the formation of foreign policy behaviour, as the state cannot always directly respond to international incentives'.[26]

The central tenets of NCR, according to Baylis, Smith and Owens, are that foreign policy is the result of international structure, domestic influence and a complex relation between the two.[27] The decision-making unit – be it a leader, a small group or a coalition of actors – is a funnel through which other factors are transmitted and interpreted.[28] Emphasizing the role of state-level factors, strategic assessment and policymakers' perception, NCR offers a two-level theory of foreign policy.[29] Indeed, if the external environment of a state determines the kind of challenges – threats and opportunities – it faces, how the state responds to them varies according to internal factors, notably the level of state formation, the social composition of ruling coalitions, the elite threat perceptions and the capacity of institutions to mobilize power. Particularly, neoclassical realists' recurring topic is the relationship between state leaders or foreign policy elites (FPE) and the people. Indeed, neoclassical realists incorporated the state–society relations model emphasizing the role of state leaders and policymakers' perceptions. From the NCR perspective, state leaders or FPE exist at the intersection of the international and the domestic with their charge of perceptions and misperceptions.[30]

[24] Wohlforth, Curtis. 2008. 'Realism and Foreign Policy.' In Foreign Policy: Theories, Actors, Cases, edited by Steve Smith, Amelia Hadfield and Tim Dunne, 31–48. Oxford: Oxford University Press.

[25] Rathbun, Brian. 2008. 'A Rose by Any Other Name: Neoclassical Realism as the Logical and Necessary Extension of Structural Realism.' Security Studies 17 (2), p. 305.

[26] Neoclassical realist thinkers argue that internal and local factors are intervening or mediating variables that play the role of a string between independent variable (relative power) and dependent variable (foreign policy outcomes). Rose, Gideon. 1998. 'Neoclassical Realism and Theories of Foreign Policy.' World Politics 51 (1), p. 146; Schweller, Randall L. 2004. 'Unanswered Threats: A Neoclassical Realist Theory of Underbalancing.' International Security 29 (2), pp. 164–6.

[27] Baylis, John, Steve Smith and Patricia Owens, eds. 2008. *The Globalization of World Politics*, 99. New York: Oxford University Press Inc.

[28] See for example, Hagan, Joe and Margaret G. Hermann. 2002. *Leaders, Groups, and Coalitions*. Hoboken: Blackwell Publishers.

[29] As the famous Robert Putnam's 'two level game' approach also NCR takes into consideration international and domestic levels of analysis, but there is no ideological closeness. Putnam, Robert D. 1988. 'Diplomacy and Domestic Politics: The Logic of Two-Level Games'. *International Organization* 42 (03):427–60.

[30] Lobell, Steven E. 2009. 'Threat Assessment, the State, and Foreign Policy: A Neoclassical Realist Model'. In *Neoclassical Realism, the State and Foreign Policy*, edited by Jeffrey W. Taliaferro, Steven E. Lobell and Norrin M. Ripsman, 42–74. Cambridge: Cambridge University Press.

Due to these traits, the neoclassical approach has been evaluated as the most suitable for interpreting the motivations, tools and aims of the Turkish policy towards Africa. In particular, what makes the NCR particularly suitable to analyse the case study is its explanatory power, locating causal properties at both structural and unit levels. Conventional multilevel theories view the formulation of foreign policy as a process based on the sum of external factors and domestic or internal constraints, quantitatively stated as $P = E+D$. NCR views the formulation of foreign policy as a correlation of external factors as affected by, or as a function of, certain intervening domestic factors, $P = E(D)$.[31] Yet, without reducing the importance of interests and material factors, the NCR approach helps to understand how the Turkish opening towards Africa has been strongly marked by a profound change of identity that has first involved the foreign policymakers and then the entire Turkish public. The adoption of NCR is justified by the awareness that its theoretical framework offers arguments that can mediate and integrate the neorealist and constructivist approaches. Based on the neorealist approach, NCR underlines the role of the international system as a provider of constraints and opportunities for the foreign policy actions of the state. Unlike neorealism, however, it tackles a complex relationship between the systemic variable and the external performance of states that involves variables at the unitary level such as elite consensus, the relationship between state and society, the vulnerability of the regime, internal coalitions and the role of ideology. Furthermore, NCR, thanks to the use of a multilayered approach – international, regional, state and individual – allows both material and ideational elements to be examined. In other words, it enables the foreign policy choices and behaviour of states to be explained by assessing a plethora of factors and the interaction among these factors. Finally, what also makes this approach particularly suitable for the current international context is that NCR usually focuses on interstate competition rather than cooperation.[32] Although the research adopts the theoretical framework provided by the neoclassical approach, it maintains a flexible and open attitude to integrating this framework with other elements of different theoretical and disciplinary backgrounds – among these, some analytical concepts and categories, such as intermestic and multitrack – drawn from foreign policy analysis and conflict studies.

---

[31] Smith, Steve, Amelia Hadfield and Tim Dunne, eds. 2012. *Foreign Policy: Theories, Actors, Cases.* Oxford: Oxford University Press.

[32] Ripsman, Norrin M. 2017. 'Neoclassical Realism'. In *Oxford Research Encyclopedia of International Studies*, edited by Nukhet Sandal and Renée Marlin-Bennett. Oxford: Oxford University Press.

From a methodological point of view, an original approach has been adopted by mixing qualitative and quantitative methods. The use of secondary sources (general and specialist literature, information from websites of official organizations and reports drawn up by state agencies and think tanks), carried out in a precise and detailed manner, is limited by the small number of studies on the subject. For this reason, bibliographic references are integrated with the use of primary sources (official documents, semi-structured interviews, field observations, content and discourse analysis) collected over the years of research. Observational data has been analysed using different qualitative methods: discourse analysis of relevant policy documents via the software packages, which allow processing of documents in multiple languages; process-tracing method, as a form of within-case analysis, which attempts to trace the links between possible causes and observed outcomes. These are then cross-checked with quantitative data on the Turkish material power capabilities and its power projection towards Africa in terms of direct investments, trade and humanitarian and development aid.

1

The relevance of Africa in a multipolar and decentralized system

The chapter analyses the transformations that have taken place within the international system from the beginning of the new millennium to the modern day. The main argument is that the current global order, defined as irregular multipolarity, has provided a permissive and favourable environment for the emerging powers in quest of greater political and economic protagonism and influence. While the multipolar structure, defined by some scholars as nonpolarity, has opened more windows of opportunity for the emerging powers, it has also contributed to the newly found centrality of the African continent. The latter, thanks to its huge natural and human wealth, has soon become a new arena of global competition. Over the years, a wide range of extra-regional powers, traditional-emerging and great-middle powers have launched a new scramble for Africa, resulting in a multilevel competition in the economic, political and security sectors.

1.1 The irregular and decentralized multipolar world order

Dealing with the international system as a whole means referring to the outcome of the dynamics – political, social and economic – which, being interconnected, determine the distribution of power among the different actors that operate in the international arena. The post-conflict system promoted by the United States at the end of the Second World War was based on the concept of integrated security, guaranteed by a system of alliances and growing economic interdependence based on the commercial market. Over the course of more than sixty years, this structure has undergone a process of adaptation and development, becoming, at the end of the Cold War, a real global order.[1] Several emerging players or latecomers have soon become the main beneficiaries of this globalized system. Encouraged by the opening up of the global market, these emerging players were able to fill – to a large extent – the gap with the more industrialized economies thanks to high and sustained growth rates. After the fall of the Berlin Wall, the liberal order, understood as a set of principles and institutions, which governed the international system since the Second World War in coexistence with Soviet–American bipolarism, which was characterized by the mutual balance of democracy and market, gradually gave way to a neoliberal global order.[2] Within this new global order, the original and, for years, latent tension between the political and economic dimensions, the outcome of liberalism, was progressively resolved in favour of the latter. As a result, liberal democracy was progressively, and more often, sacrificed in the name of the free market.

The 9/11 terrorist attacks on the American soil wiped out an order that seemed to have been finally shaped. The unilateral interventionism embodied in the idea of pre-emptive war promoted by the Bush administration's security policy and substantiated by Afghan and Iraq conflicts marked the beginning of the end of the brief unipolar interlude that had characterized the previous decade. The neoconservative agenda, according to many scholars and analysts,[3] drove US foreign policy during the Bush presidency, was designed to prevent the rise of potential competitors not only by defending the American model of freedom, democracy and free enterprise as in the past but also by actively promoting its spread.[4] This ambitious global project came at a high cost to the United States, both in economic and reputational terms and in terms of human lives. The sizeable investment of resources in non-essential strategic contexts, such as Afghanistan, exposed the United States to the risk of overstretching.[5] In the United States, in fact, the investment of an exceeding amount of resources at the limit of its real capabilities has led to the gradual disengagement from some

[1] Ikenberry, G. John. 1989. 'Rethinking the Origins of American Hegemony'. *Political Science Quarterly* 104 (3):375–400.
[2] Grondin, David and Charles-Philippe David, eds. 2016. *Hegemony or Empire?: The Redefinition of US Power under George W. Bush.* London, New York: Routledge.
[3] Some scholars challenged the idea that neoconservative components had great influence on the Bush administration, pointing out that their role had been overestimated. Among these, see Hurst, Steven. 2005. 'Myths of Neoconservatism: George W. Bush's "Neo-conservative" Foreign Policy Revisited'. *International Politics* 42 (1):75–96.
[4] See, for example, Halper, Stefan and Jonathan Clarke. 2004. *America Alone: The Neo-Conservatives and the Global Order.* Cambridge: Cambridge University Press; Haar, Roberta. 2010. 'Explaining George W. Bush's Adoption of the Neoconservative Agenda after 9/11'. *Politics & Policy* 38 (5):965–90.
[5] Kennedy, Paul. 1987. *The Rise and Fall of the Great Powers: Economic Change and Military Conflict from 1500 to 2000.* New York: Random House.

strategic contexts, leaving a vacuum that has partially been filled by the rise of emerging powers, such as China, and by the Russian resurgence.[6] The Iraq War, moreover, led to a rift between the United States and the 'others', in particular some of the historical European allies (Germany, France), generating the first significant political debate on multipolarism, a counter-hegemonic trend as an alternative to US unilateralism. While the United States was increasing its boots on the ground, causing divisions and misunderstandings within its system of alliances, academia was wondering about the direction taken by the international system. Some scholars began to develop the idea of the 'interregnum', a transition phase from the missed unipolarity and the hoped-for multipolarity.[7]

The asymmetry of power in favour of the United States raised concern in several countries. They were worried that unilateral action by the United States might shape the entire global order according to Washington's preferences, ignoring and threatening their interests and security.[8] Consequently, the 'others', not being able to counterbalance, due to the costs involved, or challenge through anti-hegemonic alliances to avoid provoking the United States, decided to adopt soft balancing' strategies. Scholars define soft balancing as the initiatives aimed at hindering or limiting a great power, without running the risk of a reaction. Such strategies are less serious than the mobilization of military capabilities or the establishment of security alliances against a hegemonic power.[9]

The military interventions in Afghanistan and Iraq, in addition to placing the main global powers on different positions, have provoked criticism from civil society, including that of the United States. In a few months, transnational movements and pacifist counter-narratives spread all over the world. This trend had the merit of sensitizing the world public opinion not only on the events in the conflict zones but also on the transition phase of the international order.

At the end of Bush's term, the United States had accelerated the process intended to reduce their international commitment. During the decade of 2009–18, the US role in the international system has gone from being a primary player or 'global hegemon' (Bush's presidency) to a 'reluctant hegemon' (Obama's presidency), and in recent years it has taken on the role of almost a 'revisionist power' (Trump's presidency). At the same time, the 2008 financial crisis, which

[6] Goldman, Emily O. 2011. *Power in Uncertain Times: Strategy in the Fog of Peace.* Stanford: Stanford University Press.
[7] Sørensen, Georg. 2006. 'What Kind of World Order?: The International System in the New Millennium'. *Cooperation & Conflict* 41 (4):343–63.
[8] Jervis, Robert. 2009. 'Unipolarity: A Structural Perspective'. *World Politics* 61 (1):188–213.
[9] Pape, 'Soft Balancing against the United States'; Paul, T. V. 2005. 'Soft Balancing in the Age of U.S. Primacy'. *International Security* 30 (1):46–71.

involved Western 'economies', favoured the spreading of the idea of a post-American order. Most of the economies of the so-called Global South have gone through soft crises, or 'good crises', overcome by following independent and original paths. Conversely, the West, struggling with a slow and asymmetric growth, has lost legitimacy and credibility in relation to both the emerging players and the poorest countries that no longer or not only look to Western liberalism to regulate, organize and plan their economic growth paths.[10] As a result, emerging state actors have gained greater capacity to exert pressure on traditional powers, claiming greater influence in global governance as well as the possibility of developing and promoting alternative strategies to address global challenges.

The traumas to which the West has been subjected in the first decade of the new millennium have exacerbated the disappointment about the 'end of history' predicted by Fukuyama in 1992.[11] This frustration has fed, on one hand, the tendency of those who saw imminent the 'Western sunset' predicted by Spengler almost a century ago, and rehabilitating, on the other hand, the theories of the 'clash of civilizations'.[12] In this environment, several exponents – scholars and policymakers – of liberal internationalism reflected on the fate of a global order whose structure was and still is shaped by the balances of power dating back to the 1940s and which excludes many key players of current international politics.[13]

Over the years, different interpretations have been provided on the transformation of the global power structure, from the neo-realists centred on the anarchic nature of the system to the hierarchical ones, and of the power transition, focused on the asymmetries of power configured in a pyramidal way.[14] Moreover, it was the same conception of power that changed, from a state-centric to a multi-centric and multidimensional one. The temporary and transitory nature of the international system appeared immediately characterized by a 'strong ambiguity'[15] and marked by the emergence of an 'irregular' multipolarity, in which the United States had preserved a central, albeit not hegemonic, role. As Samuel Huntington brilliantly predicted in 1999, world politics oscillates between unipolarity and multipolarity, a uni-multipolar system with one

[10] Murphy, Craig N. 2010. 'Lessons of a "Good" Crisis: Learning in, and From the Third World'. *Globalizations* 7 (1–2):203–15.
[11] Fukuyama, Francis. 1989. 'The End of History?' *The National Interest* 16:3–18.
[12] Huntington, Samuel P. 1993. 'The Clash of Civilizations'. *Foreign Affairs* 72 (3):22–49.
[13] Ikenberry, John G. and Annie-Marie Slaughter. 2006. *Forging a World of Liberty under Law: U.S. National Security in the 21st Century*. Princeton: Princeton University Press.
[14] Lemke, Douglas. 2002. *Regions of War and Peace*. Cambridge: Cambridge University Press.
[15] Nye Jr, Joseph S. 2011. *The Future of Power*. New York: Public Affairs.

superpower and several major powers – a strange hybrid order, which, according to the well-known political scientist, could be followed by a new era marked not only by multipolarism but also by renewed multilateralism.[16] In contrast to the idea of an inevitable configuration of the global order in a multipolar reality, some scholars have advanced the hypothesis of an international system in which power is more fragmented and dispersed, namely, nonpolarity. Nonpolarity would be a condition characterized not by the simultaneous presence of distinct poles or power concentrations but by a balanced distribution of power in a multiplicity of centres linked together by globalization. The latter with the many interdependencies it has generated – economic, financial, commercial and cultural – plays a central role in this system. As stressed by Haas,

> Today's nonpolar world is not simply a result of the rise of other states and organizations or of the failures and follies of U.S. policy. It is also an inevitable consequence of globalization. Globalization has increased the volume, velocity, and importance of cross-border flows of just about everything, from drugs, e-mails, greenhouse gases, manufactured goods, and people to television and radio signals, viruses (virtual and real), and weapons.[17]

The literature, on both IR and international political economy, agrees that the financial crisis of 2008 has accelerated the process of reconfiguring the global order, economic and political.[18] Furthermore, the same negative effects have affected the United States' choice to revise their international approach, thereby favouring a different distribution of power and the consolidation of China as a major rival.[19]

The developments of the last decade have shown how the international system is still going through a phase of transition from a period characterized by unipolarity, followed by a short interlude of asymmetrical multipolarity (interregnum), to a new era characterized by 'emancipated' multipolarity.[20] In the present-day international context, the United States, while maintaining its

[16] Huntington, Samuel P. 1999. 'The Lonely Superpower'. *Foreign Affairs* 78 (2):35–49.

[17] Haas, Richard. 2008. 'The Age of Nonpolarity: What Will Follow U.S. Dominance'. *Foreign Affairs* 87 (3):44–56.

[18] See, for example, Randall, German. 2009. 'Financial Order and World Politics: Crisis, Change and Continuity'. *International Affairs* 85 (4):669–87; Gamble, Andrew. 2010. 'A New World Order? The Aftermath of the Financial Crisis'. *Political Insight* 1 (1):17–19; Burrows, Mathew J. and Jennifer Harris. 2009. 'Revisiting the Future: Geopolitical Effects of the Financial Crisis'. *The Washington Quarterly* 32 (2):27–38.

[19] Friedberg, Aaron L. 2010. 'Implications of the Financial Crisis for the US–China Rivalry'. *Survival: Global Politics and Strategy* 52 (4):31–54; Nye Jr, Joseph S. 2010. 'American and Chinese Power after the Financial Crisis'. *The Washington Quarterly* 33 (4):143–53.

[20] Pieterse, Jan Nederveen. 2011. 'Global Rebalancing: Crisis and the East-South Turn'. *Development and Change* 42 (1):22–48.

leadership in terms of resources and capabilities, has become aware of the rise of counter-hegemonic powers such as China and Russia.[21] These two countries, albeit with multiple limitations, have enough material capabilities (military, economic and scientific) to counterbalance the US presence in regional and, in some cases, global arenas.[22] Although to different extents, both are also able to project military power beyond their respective territories.[23] Over the last two decades, these two global players have been joined by several emerging powers that have adopted non-military forms of soft balancing such as economic, diplomatic and multilateral action. Their growing economic power together with an increased international activism has shaped the developments of the global order. The proliferation of new multilateral and interregional fora – such as BRICS (Brazil, Russia, India, China, South Africa), IBSA (India, Brazil, South Africa) – has had a visible effect of the enlargement of global stakeholders. These have created new spaces of debate, within which emerging powers, long considered 'junior partners', can make their voices heard on relevant issues, such as the establishment of a different and more equal global governance.[24] These international fora are potentially becoming alternative poles of power.[25] With an almost unanimous consensus among scholars, the next few years will be dominated by a trend towards a multipolar system in which the gradual downsizing of the power of Western states will be matched by the increase in emerging powers[26] – a trend that makes 'regime change' in global governance an option that is no longer so far off.

In the future global order, China will have a special place. China itself is the product of the process of financial and geographical relocation started in the mid-1970s to face the first crisis that involved the capitalist system. China is now proposed as the great rising superpower and potential counter-hegemonic

[21] Schweller, Randall L. and Xiaoyu Pu. 2011. 'After Unipolarity: China's Visions of International Order in An Era of U.S. Decline'. *International Security* 36 (1):41–72.

[22] Mastanduno, Michael. 2019. 'Partner Politics: Russia, China, and the Challenge of Extending US Hegemony after the Cold War'. *Security Studies* 28 (3):479–504.

[23] Pape, Robert A. 2005. 'Soft Balancing against the United States'. *International Security* 30 (1):7–45.

[24] Salzman, Rachel S. 2019. *Russia, BRICS, and the Disruption of Global Order.* Washington: Georgetown University Press.

[25] Regarding the effects of the rise of emerging players on the global governance, there is a wide range of literature, including Antkiewicz, Agata, ed. 2008. *Emerging Powers in Global Governance: Lessons From the Heiligendamm Process.* Waterloo: Wilfrid Laurier University Press; Gray, Kevin and Craig N. Murphy, eds. 2014. *Rising Powers and the Future of Global Governance.* Milton Park: Routledge; Stuenkel, Oliver. 2015. *The BRICS and the Future of Global Order.* Lanham: Lexington Books; Christensen, Steen Fryba and Li Xing, eds. 2016. *Emerging Powers, Emerging Markets, Emerging Societies: Global Responses.* New York: Palgrave Macmillan.

[26] Stephen, 'Emerging Powers and Emerging Trends in Global Governance'.

state.[27] The Chinese neoliberal path of transformation, which differs from the Russian 'shock therapy',[28] has been able to mitigate the effects on the institutional political system through a specific strategy oriented towards intensive exports over which the state maintained a tight productive, financial and monetary control.[29]

By the end of the last century, China's growth faced many material constraints, especially of energy resources. Consequently, Beijing decided to change its approach to the external environment, promoting a policy of internationalization of Chinese companies.[30] Therefore, the desire to provide resources to sustain the country's economic growth has led China to adopt an assertive strategy in the international realm. In 1997, the launch of the 'Go out' or 'Go global' agenda opened a new phase in China's foreign policy and also in the development of the new global order. The multilateral and assertive approach adopted by Beijing, particularly under the leadership of President Xi Jinping, has definitively changed the global balance, dealing a harsh blow to the United States' unipolar design.[31] In a few years, the economic policy combined with a simultaneous development of its own soft power set the basis for an alternative and original vision of development, which soon became a Chinese model known as the 'Beijing consensus'.[32] Many scholars argue that unlike the Washington consensus that is supported by lists of policies to be adopted by countries seeking loans and aid from Bretton Woods Institutions, the Beijing consensus has been devoid of any unilaterally formulated policy reforms to be adhered to by the states. In addition, unlike the Washington consensus, the Beijing consensus does not

---

[27] Arrighi, Giovanni and Beverly J. Silver. 2006. *Caos e governo del mondo. Come cambiano le egemonie e gli equilibri planetari*. Milano: Mondadori Bruno.

[28] For an in-depth analysis of Russian 'shock therapy', see Murrell, Peter. 1993. 'What Is Shock Therapy? What Did It Do in Poland and Russia?' *Post-Soviet Affairs* 9 (2):111–40; Rutland, Peter. 2013. 'Neoliberalism and the Russian Transition'. *Review of International Political Economy* 20 (2):332–62.

[29] Liew, Leong. 2005. 'China's Engagement with Neoliberalism: Path Dependency, Geography and Party Self-Reinvention'. *The Journal of Development Studies* 41 (2):331–52; Wu, Fulong. 2010. 'How Neoliberal Is China's Reform? The Origins of Change during Transition'. *Eurasian Geography and Economics* 51 (5):619–31.

[30] Li, Minqi. 2009. *The Rise of China and the Demise of the Capitalist World-Economy*. New York: Monthly Review Press; Oertel, Janka. 2014. *China and the United Nations: Chinese UN Policy in the Areas of Peace and Development in the Era of Hu Jintao*. Baden-Baden: Nomos & Bloomsbury.

[31] Nien-chung, Chang-Liao. 2016. 'China's New Foreign Policy under Xi Jinping'. *Asian Security* 12 (2):82–91; Kai, Jin. 2017. *Rising China in a Changing World: Power Transitions and Global Leadership*. London: Palgrave Macmillan.

[32] Joshua Cooper Ramo coined the term Beijing consensus in 2004 in his book entitled "The Beijing Consensus" in which he outlined the Chinese ambitious objective to debunk the famous doctrine of the Washington Consensus. See Cooper Ramo, Joshua. 2004. *The Beijing Consensus, Notes on the New Physics of Chinese Power*. London: Foreign Policy Centre.

claim the existence of any values and principles that it promotes as a universal value.[33] Stressed as well by Robel,

> China stays committed to a multipolarity of ideas, in which different models can exist peacefully next to each other. The most obvious effect of recognizing this is its denying universality of one's own approaches especially in its relations with developing countries.[34]

China's unstoppable rise has led to a shift in the global economic centre of gravity eastwards, a change that has also included the political dimension as certified by the 'pivot to Asia' strategy introduced by the Obama administration.[35]

1.2 The new 'scramble' for Africa and the rising of extra-regional middle powers

As argued by Laura Neack in the uncertain and globalized international context, marked by increasing threats and competition, the foreign policy of the actors revolves around maintaining power and seeking power in multiple scenarios.[36]

The new structures of global governance reflect both the political and economic weight of the emerging powers and the fact that the same (powers) represent different geopolitical spheres of the planet. One of the main consequences of the transition phase of the global order – from a missed unipolarity to an irregular and decentralized multipolarity – is the centrality of the regional dimension. Regions will play a central role in the future edifice of international politics. This regained significance is the result of the reversal in the relationship between the regional dimension and global dynamics. In the current international context, regional dynamics tend to progressively gain importance at the expense of the

---

[33] Ambrosio, Thomas. 2012. 'The Rise of the "China Model" and "Beijing Consensus": Evidence of Authoritarian Diffusion?' *Contemporary Politics* 18 (4):381–99; Williamson, John. 2012. 'Is the "Beijing Consensus" Now Dominant?' *Asia Policy* 13:1–16; Yagci, Mustafa. 2016. 'A Beijing Consensus in the Making: The Rise of Chinese Initiatives in the International Political Economy and Implications for Developing Countries'. *Perceptions - Journal of International Affairs* 21 (2):29–56.

[34] Robel, Max. 2010. 'Why the Beijing Consensus Is a Non-Consensus: Implications for Contemporary China-Africa Relations'. *Bulletin of the Centre for East-West Cultural & Economic Studies* 9 (1):18.

[35] Sally, Razeen. 2010. 'The Shift to the East'. *Economic Affairs* 30 (3):94–104; Hughes, James H. 2010. 'China's Place in Today's World'. *The Journal of Social, Political, and Economic Studies* 35 (2):167–223; Layne, Christopher. 2012. 'The Global Power Shift from West to East'. *The National Interest* (119):21–31.

[36] Neack, Laura. 2008. *The New Foreign Policy: Power Seeking in a Globalized Era*. Miami: Rowman & Littlefield Publishers.

global ones.[37] Africa is one of the regional contexts most affected by the global changes that characterized the international system at the end of the Cold War. The global developments of the last decades have given centrality to the African continent, denying the long-accepted conviction that the position of Africa, especially SSA, would be irrelevant in the international arena. Moreover, the perception of Africa as a separate entity from the global context has also been overcome, an irreducible otherness that is completely without any foundation today.[38]

One of the main interests of African scholars is to understand what the new multipolar order will mean for Africa and for the complex path of growth and development that awaits the African people. The debate is very vibrant and is divided between those who believe that the continent has fallen victim to a 2.0 version of nineteenth-century imperialism,[39] and those who, instead, consider the new global order as an opportunity for African countries to address the problems that have limited their economic, social and political development.[40] With the new millennium, security, especially in relation to the phenomenon of Islamic radicalism and the spread of piracy along the eastern coasts, and the global economy have brought Africa back to the centre of international attention. While security issues have led to a joint effort between traditional and emerging powers, economic rivalry or the 'scramble' for Africa has been sparked. In the African continent, 40 to 80 per cent of the world's reserves of metallic and non-metallic minerals can be found. For this reason, the continent has become the main source of raw materials that is essential to ensure the positive performance of traditional economies and support the rapid growth of several developing countries, especially China. This growing interest has led the major global powers to compete with each other in order to gain the rights of first refusal on resources.

Hence the spread of the idea of the 'new scramble' for Africa.[41] The definition evokes the partition of Africa drawn on the map by the European colonial

---

[37] In this regard, see Katzenstein, Peter J. 2005. *A World of Regions: Asia and Europe in the American Imperium*. Ithaca: Cornell University Press; Acharya, Amitav. 2007. 'The Emerging Regional Architecture of World Politics'. *World Politics* 59 (4):629–52.

[38] Brown, William. 2010. 'A Question of Agency: Africa in International Politics'. *Third World Quarterly* 33 (10):1889–908.

[39] One of the most famous works of this current of thought is that of Pádraig Carmody, *The New Scramble for Africa*. See also Mohan, Giles and Marcus Power. 2008. 'New African Choices? The Politics of Chinese Engagement'. *Review of African Political Economy* 35 (115):23–42.

[40] See, for example, Alden, Chris. 2005. 'China in Africa'. *Survival - Global Politics and Strategy* 47 (3):147–64; Zhao, Suisheng. 2014. 'A Neo-Colonialist Predator or Development Partner? China's Engagement and Rebalance in Africa'. *Journal of Contemporary China* 23 (90):1033–52.

[41] In addition to the aforementioned text by Carmody, see also Lee, Margaret C. 2006. 'The 21st Century Scramble for Africa'. *Journal of Contemporary African Studies* 24 (3):303–30; Klare, Michael and Daniel Volman. 2006. 'America, China & the Scramble for Africa's Oil'. *Review of African*

powers during the Berlin Conference of 1884.[42] As with the first scramble for Africa, even today states need raw materials to feed their economies and to ensure the protection of their political and economic power. Now as then, Africa is witnessing a sharp increase in investment and external activism that is in many respects reminiscent of the dynamics that preceded Berlin.[43] In particular, the new scramble for Africa has a dual aspect. On the one hand, a new phase of 'naked imperialism' which, in the name of uncontrolled consumerism, exploits, with aggressive policies, both the resources present on the continent and the native populations and on the other hand, the idea of 'saving Africa' is a facade used to hide the real interests of the extra-regional powers.[44] Although much of the literature on the topic puts China at the forefront of the new scramble, presenting the issue in some cases in terms of a real 'yellow danger' or 'Chinese threat' to Africa, the traditional Western powers remain predominant actors on the continent.[45] One of the deepest implications of the growing weight acquired by the BRICS countries in the African context is the change in the relationship between African countries and traditional Western powers. The involvement of the emerging powers in Africa has not only brought the continent back to the centre of international concern but also given a new stimulus to the traditional powers which, instead of withdrawing, have redesigned the ways of interacting with the continent, renewing their commitment to new development and economic growth programmes.[46] Therefore, many of the competitive and cooperative dynamics of the current decentralized multipolar system find their concrete manifestation on the African continent. Africa increasingly looks like a scenario in which old and new extra-regional players are competing to conquer important positions, driven both by economic interest and by the desire to reflect,

Political Economy 33 (108):297–309; Marton, Peter. 2014. 'New Scramble for Africa; Globalization in Africa: Recolonization or Renaissance?' *Journal of Contemporary African Studies* 32 (1):137–40; Scholvin, Sören, ed. 2015. *A New Scramble for Africa? The Rush for Energy Resources in Sub-Saharan Africa.* Abingdon: Routledge.

[42] On this issue, see Wesseling, Henk L. 1996. *Divide and Rule: The Partition of Africa, 1880–1914.* Westport: Praeger Publishers.

[43] Southall, Roger and Melber Henning, eds. 2009. *A New Scramble for Africa? Imperialism, Investment and Development.* South Africa: University of Kwazulu-Natal Press.

[44] Lee, 'The 21st Century Scramble for Africa'.

[45] Yee, Herbert and Ian Storey, eds. 2002. *The China Threat: Perceptions, Myths and Realities.* London: Routledge Curzon; Navarro, Peter. 2007. *The Coming China Wars: Where they Will Be Fought, How they Can Be Won.* Upper Saddle River: Financial Times Press; Curtis, Lisa. 2008. *China's Expanding Global Influence: Foreign Policy Goals, Practices and Tools.* Washington: The Heritage Foundation; Guerrero, Dorothy-Grace and Firoze Manji, eds. 2008. *China's New Role in Africa and the South.* Oxford: Fahamu; Ayers, Alison J. 2013. 'Beyond Myths, Lies and Stereotypes: The Political Economy of a "New Scramble for Africa"'. *New Political Economy* 18 (2):227–57.

[46] Cornelissen, Scarlett. 2009. 'Awkward Embraces: Emerging and Established Powers and the Shifting Fortunes of Africa's International Relations in the Twenty-First Century'. *Politikon: South African Journal of Political Studies* 36 (1):5–26.

at least in the regional framework, the reshuffling of the global political hierarchy. Over the last decade, several scholars and commentators have described Africa as a continent in rapid rise, basing their arguments on the growth rates of most African countries, on the multiple examples of economic integration and on the improvement of internal governance. In 2011, *The Economist*, a newspaper traditionally sceptical about the African continent, dedicated an entire issue to the rise of Africa, bringing to the centre stage the debate that had already been initiated some time before among Africanists, policymakers and practitioners. However, like those who for decades have described Africa in a 'marginal' position with regard to both the world economy and the international politics, even the validity of the argument of the 'emerging' and 'rising' continent is questionable because it is based on a more general perception than on empirical data related to the global economy.[47] While there is no doubt that several African countries are growing fast, it is also true that the vast majority of the continent's most dynamic sectors – such as minerals, gold, tourism and the development of biofuel – are strongly influenced, if not fully driven, by external interests.[48]

As during the Cold War, Africa continues to remain a region most open to external interferences, dependencies and exploitation.[49] In addition, another factor to be considered is that growth is in no way inclusive and, with the exception of a few rare virtuous experiences (Botswana), the benefits do not reach the populations that are still living in conditions of extreme poverty.[50] As in a cyclical repetition of history, the dependence of African states on industrialized countries is 'reified' rather than reduced. African people are witnessing a growth based on the intensive exploitation of natural resources without a social redistribution of revenues. The latter most often fall into the hands of a few, thereby exacerbating both external dependency and internal inequalities. In the background, the problems generated by the first scramble to Africa remain and have become almost chronic in a continent whose perspectives for development, economic and democratic, remain conditioned and profoundly affected by cyclical humanitarian crises and by the strong, at times violent and almost always irreconcilable, political clashes.

[47] Carpintero, Oscar, Ivan Murray and Josè Bellver. 2016. 'The New Scramble for Africa: BRICS Strategies in a Multipolar World'. *Research in Political Economy* 30:191–226; Taylor, Ian. 2016. 'Dependency Redux: Why Africa Is Not Rising'. *Review of African Political Economy* 43 (147):8–25.

[48] Zamfir, Ionel. 2016. 'Africa's Economic Growth'. *European Parliamentary Research Service.* PE 573.891.

[49] Sylla, Ndongo Samba. 2014. 'From a Marginalised to an Emerging Africa? A Critical Analysis'. *Review of African Political Economy* 41 (1):7–25.

[50] Barnes, Sandra T. 2005. 'Global Flows: Terror, Oil & Strategic Philanthropy'. *Review of African Political Economy* 32 (104/105):235–52.

One of the most interesting aspects of recent developments is the way in which Africa seeks to counteract and address growing international interventionism. In 2016, the main regional body, the African Union (AU), introduced an ambitious 'Agenda 2063' project. The mission of the AU is to promote by 2063, the centenary year of the foundation of the Organization of the African Union, an integrated Africa, politically united and based on the idea of pan-Africanism, prosperous – thanks to inclusive and sustainable development – and in peace – with respect for democracy and human rights – led by the African people and able to represent a dynamic and young force in the global arena.[51] In the goals of the common agenda the most important would be to mitigate the negative effects of the new scramble on the continent. However, despite the AU's stance, there is still no clear, coherent and shared strategy to deal with the growing foreign presence. Furthermore, the agenda's purposes seem difficult to achieve because of the continuous interweaving of endogenous and exogenous factors that paralyse many African countries.[52] Moreover, most of the current African leaders appear to be trapped in the cycle of patronage and endemic corruption that foreign investment partly feeds. There is therefore a lack of shared political will to fight the 'scramble' phenomenon and protect the interests of the continent. At the same time, it is necessary to keep in mind the way in which the different African actors, state and non-state, interact with extra-regional players, state and non-state, attracting them in some cases and even violently rejecting them in others, but still trying to exploit the intervention and influence to achieve their own goals.

---

[51] DeGhetto, Kaitlyn, Jacob R. Gray and Moses N. Kiggundu. 2016. 'The African Union's Agenda 2063: Aspirations, Challenges, and Opportunities for Management Research'. *Africa Journal of Management* 2 (1):93–116.

[52] Ufiem, Maurice Ogbonnaya. 2016. 'Terrorism, Agenda 2063 and the Challenges of Development in Africa'. *South African Journal of International Affairs* 23 (2):185–99.

2

Turkish–African relations

A historical perspective

In the new global context, Africa has therefore regained its international centrality. Many middle-sized powers, including Turkey, had for decades ignored the African continent as a region full of hazards and without political and economic benefits. Such perceptions favoured the crystallization of negative bias towards Africa in the imagination of the Turkish elites and public, as along with the view of a continent split between an Arab North and a backward South (sub-Saharan Africa). This chapter examines in a diachronic way the relations between Turkey and Africa since the Ottoman period. It is divided into three parts. The first section analyses the period of the Ottoman Empire when Africa was essentially the Maghreb, considered an extension of the Turkish Mediterranean domains and the Red Sea coastline. The beginning of European colonialism and the simultaneous Ottoman decline drove the Turks away from Africa. As highlighted in the second section, with the birth of the Republic (1923), the rise of the Kemalist establishment oriented solely to the world and Western civilization led to the closure of relations with the African continent. The process of state- and nation-building promoted by Mustafa Kemal sanctioned the removal of the imperial past and with it the long history of contact with the African people. The Cold War and the decolonization path of African states increased the distance with Turkey by making SSA a forgotten and neglected region in the eyes of Turkish policymakers and the public. The first signs of change were felt after the military coup d'état of 1980. During the following decade, which was dominated by the political figure of Turgut Özal, a combination of systemic, regional and domestic factors have led Turkey to the first bashful openings towards Africa. The latter are highlighted in the third part of the chapter.

In the new millennium, the determining factors leading Africa back to the centre of global interests were international security, in relation to the phenomenon of Islamic radicalism and the spread of piracy along the eastern coasts, and the growing search for raw materials and new markets by the rising powers. An innovative element compared to the past is the fact that this phenomenon (the scramble) is not limited only to the Western powers and large corporations but also involves the so-called latecomers' states. Nowadays, Africa is at the heart of the interests not only of the United States and European states but also of other major powers such as China and Russia, as well as a growing number of emerging middle powers (India, Brazil) engaged in a frenzied race to ensure access to its natural resources, new markets and political alliances. The emerging players also include the Middle Eastern States, primarily Gulf monarchies, which seek to diversify their investments in developing sectors complementary to that of oil and natural gas on which almost all their domestic products are based. The race for raw materials and, more generally, the growing interest in Africa reflect many of the transformations caused by the change in the global balances.[1] Rather, it should be emphasized that the growing importance of the BRICS and, in general, of the emerging players in the African context has had profound repercussions on relations between African countries and the traditional Western powers. The growing presence of new extra-regional players has given new impetus to the traditional powers which, instead of leaving the African context, have redesigned their relationship with the continent by renewing their commitment through the promotion of new development and growth programmes.

2.1 The Ottoman period: The internalization of the idea of the 'divided continent'

As noted in the introduction, although more recent studies have highlighted the Ottoman projection towards the heart of the African continent, research remains very limited due to a general lack of interest on the part of Turkish historiography. Studies of the Hobsbawm 'Age of Empire' have, until recently, rested on overwhelmingly Eurocentric foundations. Thankfully, a recent shift in perspective has transcended 'the West and the rest' approach of late-nineteenth-century studies and provided us with a more nuanced lens through which to view the period. The new historiographic trend and the opening of the Ottoman archives have allowed us to shed light on imperial policies in Africa. Until

---

[1]   Desai, Radhika. 2013. *Geopolitical Economy: After US Hegemony, Globalization and Empire*. London: Pluto Press.

Napoleon's troops conquered the Syrian province (1798–1801), North Africa, and in particular Egypt, constituted an essential region of the imperial domains. For nearly four centuries, the Sahara marked the boundary of what was considered to be the empire's granary, as it was in the Roman times. During that time, the desert was a physical and mental barrier that the Ottomans rarely crossed. The Ottoman geopolitics was structured along three axes: the eastern one, characterized by the political and religious rivalry with the Safavid Empire; the northern one, divided between the Balkans and the Black Sea, distinguished by clashes with the other two great traditional empires (Habsburg and Russian); and, finally, the Mediterranean, where the historical competition with Venice has progressively given way to the rise of new powers, above all, Great Britain and France. North Africa, with Egypt at its core, was considered an integral part of this last geopolitical axis. For this reason, it is understandable that the Ottoman orientation considered the southern Saharan lands as an area of low political and economic relevance. The only exception was the Horn of Africa (HOA), where the Ottomans arrived in the mid-sixteenth century via the Red Sea by establishing the imperial province of Habeş. There, the main rivalry was with Portugal, at the time a great maritime and colonial power, against which the Ottoman fleet also clashed in the Indian Ocean.

Already several centuries before the Ottoman age, other dynasties of Turkic origin or Turkic components controlled and dominated parts of Africa, among which was the Tulunid (868–905 AD). However, the real Turkish presence in Africa was established with the conquest by Sultan Selim I of Egypt, at that time a Mamluk domain. The sultan's military campaign, which ended with the battle of Aleppo (1516), opened to Selim I not only the gates of North Africa (1517) but also of the entire Arabian Peninsula, which was part of the Mamluk territory. The multidirectional character of the Ottoman expansion led to the annexation of the provinces and many small realms distributed from Egypt to the west coast of Morocco. Since the beginning, imperial control over these lands proved to be very hard, and in many of them direct control of the Sublime Porte was never established[2] – a condition that worsened with the beginning of a slow but steady decline that according to the traditional historiography began with the death of Sultan Süleyman I (1566). Consequently, in the domains of North Africa, as well as in the other peripheries of the empire, there was a shift in power from almost direct control of the Porte to the formation of a number of tributary or vassal states, led by a bey. However, the sultan's army had to intervene several

[2] Hess, Andrew C. 2011. *The Forgotten Frontier: A History of the Sixteenth-Century Ibero-African Frontier*. Chicago, London: University of Chicago Press.

times, both to mediate disputes between different tribal groups and family clans and to ensure the defence of the territories from external attacks. The sultan was responsible for the protection of not only his own domains but also of the land of Islam. Indeed, with his conquests, Selim I became the master of the Hejaz, that is, Mecca and Medina, the cradle of Islam, and as such the sultan had to shoulder the responsibility of resisting the invaders. In other words, by taking over the Mamluk domains in 1517, the Ottomans had inherited the role of defenders of the holiest places in Islam.

Selim's conquest also gave to the Ottomans easy access to the Red Sea.[3] The Red Sea was vital for the protection of the Holy Cities, and an important hinterland of the imperial domains. During those same years, a new threat was emerging in the area: the Portuguese. Indeed, as a result of the oceanic revolution ushered in by Vasco da Gama's circumnavigation of Africa, the Portuguese viceroy Afonso de Albuquerque took control of the Kamarān island (1513) in the Red Sea. Since then, the Portuguese ships became a real threat to the Muslim ships, generating concern in Selim himself, who was well aware of the weakness of the Mamluk army. According to some scholars,[4] Selim I was pushed to intervene in the area in order to protect the entire region from the Portuguese advance. Already his predecessor Bayezid had sent personnel and materials several times to support the Mamluks' defence in the Red Sea and also in the Indian Ocean.[5] Therefore, the Ottoman strategy did not imply an intention to expand the Ottoman territory in the region beyond Egypt and the Hijaz, but, rather, reflected a defensive posture to keep the empire free from threats. This interpretation helps us to understand why the Ottomans never went south of the Sahara Desert and the Red Sea shoreline, trying, rather, to maintain their positions by countering any threats. As a matter of fact, from 1517 the Ottomans prevented the Portuguese advance by constructing fleets at Suez using Cilician timber, engaging artisans who had gained experience in the dockyards of Istanbul, and employing commanders battle-tested in the Mediterranean, among whom the most outstanding was captain Selman Reis.[6]

---

[3]   Hess, Andrew C. 1973. 'The Ottoman Conquest of Egypt (1517) and the Beginning of the Sixteenth-Century World War'. *International Journal of Middle East Studies* 4 (1): 55–76; Aksan, Virginia H. 2007. *Ottoman Wars: An Empire Besieged*. Abingdon: Routledge; Minawi, Mostafa. 2016. *The Ottoman Scramble for Africa: Empire and Diplomacy in the Sahara and the Hijaz*. Stanford: Stanford University Press.

[4]   See, for example, Emiralioglu, Pinar. 2014. *Geographical Knowledge and Imperial Culture in the Early Modern Ottoman Empire*. Abingdon: Ashgate.

[5]   Brummett, Palmira Johnson. 1994. *Ottoman Seapower and Levantine Diplomacy in the Age of Discovery*. Albany: State University of New York Press (SUNY); Casale, Giancarlo. 2010. *The Ottoman Age of Exploration*. Oxford, New York: Oxford University Press.

[6]   Inalcık, Halil and Donald Quataert. 1994. *An Economic and Social History of the Ottoman Empire, 1300-1914*. Cambridge: Cambridge University Press.

Among the Mamluks' outposts was also the island of Suakin. The island, which gained renewed importance for Turkey in 2017 – see Chapter 6 – had withstood the Portuguese siege of 1513. A different fate, however, came in 1541 when the Portuguese troops, led by the viceroy of India Estêvão da Gama, took control of the island.[7] Although the Portuguese presence in Suakin was short-lived, the middle of the sixteenth century was characterized by rivalry with the Porte. In other words, in northern SSA, the Ottomans were part of the balance of the power system, having alliances and conflicts with local kingdoms. The most heated conflict involved the Christian Ethiopia supported by the Portuguese crown. In 1541 the successor of Selim I, Süleyman (known as Süleyman the Magnificent in the West and Kanuni in his realm) was persuaded by the former governor of Yemen, Özdemir Pasha, to lead a jihad against Ethiopia by supporting the Muslim ally Aḥmad ibn Ibrāhīm al-Ghāzī, the leader of the Somali Sultanate of Adal (Awdal).[8] To support the operations, the Ottomans established a massive presence in Suakin that would become a military base camp. It was in this context that after a few years (1555), to ensure greater control of the region, the Ottoman government founded the province (*eyalet*) of Habeş, with its capital at Suakin and Özdemir Pasha as its first governor (*Beylerbeyi*).[9] The Ottoman Empire expanded to encompass parts of the modern Sudan, Eritrea and the Ethiopian borderlands, and fought with the Funj sultanate of Sinnar for control of the Nile valley, where Ottoman territories briefly extended south as far as the Third Cataract.[10] On the eve of the seventeenth century, the Ottoman Empire reached its zenith and achieved the maximum extension of its dominions in Africa. During that period, there is much evidence of agreements of a defensive and commercial nature between the Sublime Porte and some local potentates, mainly with the Muslim regions of west Africa. Among these was the powerful empire of Kanem-Borno, [11]which lay around the shores of Lake Chad, with which the Ottomans formed an alliance in 1575.[12] The agreement, signed by Sultan Murad III, set out the sending of military equipment and trainers to the region. Another demonstration of the Turkish presence in the power dynamics of the region was the intervention of

---

[7] Peacock, A. C. S. 2012. 'Suakin: A Northeast African Port in the Ottoman Empire'. *Northeast African Studies* 12 (1): 29–50.

[8] Lewis, Ioan M. 2002. *A Modern History of the Somali: Nation and State in the Horn of Africa*, 26. Athens: Ohio University Press.

[9] Orhonlu, Cengiz. 1974. *Osmanli Imparatorlugu 'nun Güney Siyaseti: Habes Eyaleti*. Istanbul: Istanbul Üniversitesi Edebiyat Fakültesi Matbaasi; Peacock, A. C. S. 2018. 'The Ottomans in Northeast Africa'. *African History*. doi: 10.1093/acrefore/9780190277734.013.190.

[10] Peacock, A. C. S. 2012a. 'The Ottomans and the Funj Sultanate in the Sixteenth and Seventeenth Centuries'. *Bulletin of the School of Oriental and African Studies* 75 (12): 87–111.

[11] Borno is the name of a state in the northeast of today's Nigeria southwest of Lake Chad.

[12] Davidson, Basil. 1968. *History in Africa*, 79–81. London: The Macmillan Company.

the imperial flotilla, led by Seydi Ali Reis (1498–1563), in defence of the island of Zanzibar.[13] Despite a small presence, the Ottoman influence was felt much more broadly in northeast Africa in places as distant as Mogadishu, at least nominally recognized as under Ottoman suzerainty.[14] Direct Ottoman control was limited to the Red Sea coast and some commercial emporiums.[15] Highly relevant, commercially and strategically, were the ports of Massawa and Suakin, which remained loosely under Ottoman rule until 1811, at which point they were transferred to Egypt, nominally an Ottoman vassal (*Khedive*) but effectively independent. Outposts like Suakin along the Red Sea coasts guaranteed the transit of goods, in particular coffee, which from the end of the sixteenth century rapidly increased its diffusion and popularity in Europe. The rapid increase in coffee consumption in the main European cities made the product one of the primary sources of income for the Ottoman treasury.[16] A further reason for the Ottomans to strengthen their relations with certain parts of Africa, even south of Sahel, was the discovery of rich gold and diamond mines.

The almost three centuries between the formation of the Habeş province and the passage under the control of the Khedive Muhammad Ali testified to the split between the northern and southern areas. Whereas Egypt, like the Libyan provinces was an area of great Ottoman influence and presence, relations in the other African domains were exclusively commercial and, in many cases, linked only to forms of Islamic proselytism. In the northern region of SSA, the Sublime Porte established a 'soft' occupation, advancing sporadically to the areas of the western Sahel region.[17] The way the empire related to the region south of the Sahara Desert was different from that of the Maghreb. This is witnessed by the fact that only in 1894, the sultan, Abdülhamit II, conferred the title of *bey* – probably the appointment was as a member of the Order of Medjidie – on a leader of a sub-Saharan community.[18] Mohammad Shitta (1824–95) was invested in Lagos. The decision was part of the wider pan-Islamic policy promoted during that period by the sultan. Although the religious dimension had always played a role in the Ottomans' relations with Africa, only following Abdülhamit II's choice

---

[13] Casale, *The Ottoman Age of Exploration*, 99–102.

[14] Peacock, 'Suakin: A Northeast African'.

[15] Tedeschi, Salvatore. 1973. 'Note Storiche Sulle Isole Dahlak'. In *Proceedings of the Third International Conference of Ethiopian Studies*, Addis Ababa.

[16] Ogot, Bethwell Allan ed. 1999. *Africa from the Sixteenth to the Eighteenth Century, UNESCO General History of Africa* (Book 5), 75. Berkeley: California University Press.

[17] Holt, Peter Malcolm. 1961. *A History of the Sudan: From the Coming of Islam to the Present Day*. London: Weidenfeld and Nicolson.

[18] Deringil, Selim. 2000. 'Les Ottomans et le partage de l'Afrique, 1880–1900'. In *The Ottomans, the Turks and World Power Politics*, edited by Selim Deringil, 101–30. Istanbul: Gorgias Press & The Isis Press.

to welcome the title of caliph – the head of the Muslim community (*ummah*) – Islam became an asset, aiming to strengthen ties with Muslim communities. As had happened in the Balkans and Anatolia during the early stages of expansion, the empire sent some imams to SSA. Among them was Abu Bakr Effendi who in 1863 reached the Cape of Good Hope, now in South Africa, but at the time under the administration of the UK. His arrival paved the way for the establishment of strong ties between the local Muslim community and the Sublime Porte[19] – a relationship attested by the significant participation of South African Muslims in the fundraising campaign for the construction of the Hejaz railway.[20] Later, some members of Effendi's family took an active part in South African social and political life. Nowadays, the Effendi surname is still known and respected within the South African Muslim community.[21] But the Sublime Porte's imams were not the only brokers in the spread of Islam and Ottoman religious culture. Together with the official imams, the other important channel of diffusion was the Sufi confraternities' (*tariqat*) expression of the unofficial Turkish heterodox Islam. The Sufi lodges (*tekke*) became a place, mostly clandestine, of social cohesion and meeting, turning out to become a destabilizing element for the colonial administrations, such as the British one in Sudan.[22]

The Ottoman presence in Africa was also internationally recognized with the signing of the Treaty of Carlowitz (1699) between the empire and the Holy League. One of the conditions imposed on Porte was the obligation to ensure the control of trade routes along the Maghreb coast. The European monarchies were worried about the continuing pirate attacks on their merchant vessels. The repression of piracy had a 'boomerang' effect, with consequences for the economy of the African provinces of the empire. Indeed, the loot was an important source of income for the economic sustenance of the Ottoman vassal kingdoms.[23]

During the Ottoman era, the Turkish cognitive map of Africa as a broken continent had been shaped – a geographical perception that remained unchanged even after the fall of the empire and the constitution of the Republic. Samples of the cognitive, political and geographical map of the Ottoman Empire can be found in various European cartographic examples. Among these, two are particularly significant in order to understand the Ottoman perception of Africa

[19] Özkan, 'What Drives Turkey's Involvement in Africa?' 534.
[20] Özyüksel, Murat. 2014. *The Hejaz Railway and the Ottoman Empire: Modernity, Industrialisation and Ottoman Decline*. London: I.B. Tauris.
[21] Argun, Selim. 2000. 'The Life and Contribution of the Osmanli Scholar, Abu Bakr Effendi: Towards Islamic thought and Culture in South Africa'. MA Thesis, Johannesburg University.
[22] O'Fahey, Rex S. 1996. 'Islam and Ethnicity in the Sudan'. *Journal of Religion in Africa* 3 (3): 258–67.
[23] Quataert, Donald. 2005. *The Ottoman Empire, 1700–1922*. Vol. 34, 118–19. Cambridge: Cambridge University Press.

as a divided continent. The first is a map by an anonymous author dated 1652, in which only the northern and western coastal areas of the continent are depicted. The second sample is a map (1680) by the European cartographer Frederik de Witt (1629/1630–1706) who included in his '*Atlas Maior*' a representation of the Ottoman lands. The section concerning the Ottoman Empire, entitled '*Tvrcicvm Imperivm*', borders the territories to the north of the Sahara Desert, while ignoring the southern province.[24] Both illustrations show a Eurocentric projection of the Ottoman territories, ignoring the empire's ties with the HOA. Nevertheless, this projection was gradually internalized by the Ottomans during the long process of modernization and westernization that began in the seventeenth and eighteenth centuries. In the nineteenth century, before the second European colonization wave, the perception of a broken Africa was widespread among the Ottoman elite: the lands north of the Sahara Desert, at the time still peripheries of the empire, and the regions beyond which were considered lands characterized by pitfalls, threats and backwardness – a perception that would have remained unaltered also at the collapse of the empire.

2.2 The Republican period: The lowest point of the relationship

The geographical perception of Africa built and partly internalized during the Ottoman period was embraced by Republican Turkey. In the conception and imagination of the Turkish public, North Africa was never considered a distant region. This was due to its historical proximity, derived from the common Ottoman past and from religious affinities. This led Turkey to consider, for almost a century, the North African region as part of its immediate neighbourhood, while SSA was considered as a distant destination, rife with problems such as disease, hunger, famine and civil war. These ideas have shaped Turkish geopolitical projection of the early Republican period. Africa and, specifically, the countries south of the Sahara, were for decades almost irrelevant to Ankara's agenda. A variety of factors contributed to these developments, many of which can be traced back to the reform process undertaken by an emerging elite at the beginning of the century. Already in the last imperial decade, with the rise to power of the Young Turks, the Turkish ethnic nationalism and the

---

[24] Manners, Ian. 2007. *European Cartographers and the Ottoman World, 1500–1750: Maps from the Collection of O. J. Sopranos*, 39, 105. Chicago: Oriental Institute Publications of the University of Chicago.

positivist ideas promoted by the new regime had split the identity link with many populations of African dominions. In particular, the downsizing of the religious dimension of the national identity had, in fact, severed one of the main affinities with many African communities. The First World War did the rest. The former historic Ottoman dominions that included the territories of several modern states such as Egypt, Libya, Tunisia, Morocco, Algeria and Ethiopia were divided by the European powers. Their control passed under the rule of the UK, France and Italy. With the birth of the Republic (1923), relations with Africa progressively diminished, reducing to their lowest levels. Already in this period, it is possible to observe the relationship of steady interaction between domestic policy choices and foreign policy behaviours. At that time, the Republic, and the elites that led it, was struggling with a laborious process of state- and nation-building: Turkey and the Turks had to be created. Accordingly, Turkish policy towards Africa was also shaped by a combination of factors which belong to both the domestic and the international sphere – the first being that of the new international configuration, with the spread of European mandates and protectors over many countries in the Middle East and Africa. Between the two world wars, the scramble or race for Africa among the colonial powers, which began in the previous century, reached its peak.[25] After the establishment of the Republic, the priorities of Turkish foreign policy and relations were to resolve outstanding issues in the immediate neighbourhood, and establishing good relations with neighbouring countries. These priorities resulted in the opening of embassies in several European and Middle Eastern countries, but none were opened in Africa.[26] A further key factor was the radical change promoted in a top-down manner in Turkey by Mustafa Kemal Paşa (Atatürk), the founder of the Turkish Republic, after the empire collapsed. During the first decade of the Republic's life, among the aims of the reforms promoted by Mustafa Kemal was a tenacious willingness to include Turkey in the mainstream of Western political and cultural civilization. According to the founder of modern Turkey, this process would be the only way to reach the level of developed states. To this end, it was also extremely necessary to sever Turkey's ties with its imperial past – a determination that matched well with the process of secularization within the country and the adoption of a wary and Western-oriented foreign policy. Turkey's foreign policy attitude, before and after the death of Mustafa Kemal, was shaped by the Kemalist tradition in which more emphasis was centred on non-

---

[25] Although there are many studies on the period, for clarity and completeness of analysis, see Chamberlain, M. E. 2010. *The Scramble for Africa*. Third edn. London, New York: Routledge.
[26] Wheeler, 'Ankara to Africa', 44.

intervention, vigilance towards national sovereignty and a Western orientation. Turkey was very sceptical about being part of any conflict, preferring, rather, to be neutral in its foreign affairs so as to protect its territorial integrity[27] – an approach well summarized by the famous Mustafa Kemal's motto 'peace at home, peace abroad', that distinguished Turkish passive foreign policy until the 1980s.[28] Although recent studies have shown that the interregional relations in the early post-Ottoman period were more complex and multifaceted,[29] there is no doubt that the outlook of the early Republican Turkey was far from Africa.

From the Kemalist perspective, the foreign policy and the international role of Turkey had to be functional to domestic policy and to the radical transformation process that Mustafa Kemal had launched in 1923. Therefore, in addition to adopting a cautious international approach and maintaining cordial relations with the European powers, a further decisive element in understanding the closure to Africa was the identity process. An integral part of the westernization path was the adoption by the Kemalist elite of ideas related to social Darwinism that have their origins in the thoughts of the Young Turks.[30] These ideas, together with the blood-based definition of the Turkish nation and the idea of Turkish purity, or Turkishness, fuelled a xenophobic conception of ethnicity and race (*soy*) – a notion that generated an intolerant nationalism, which created a gap with the people of the so-called Global South. Echoes of this discriminatory approach towards Africans and Arabs are still perceptible in parts of Turkish society. Psychologically the process of alienation from the areas and populations previously part of the Ottoman domains was also facilitated by the fresh memory of the decision of the Arab people, including those of North Africa, to rebel against the Porte. Their decision to take the side of the powers that were against the empire was felt to be a betrayal by the Turks. Moreover, the acquisition of Western modernity and culture also entailed an orientalist approach to everything that was not part of that culture.

In this unfavourable context, the only sign of openness was the establishment of the first diplomatic representation on the continent, in Ethiopia (1926).

[27] Hale, *Turkish Foreign*; Gözen Ercan, Pınar, ed. 2017. *Turkish Foreign Policy: International Relations, Legality and Global Reach*. Cham: Palgrave Macmillan.

[28] For an in-depth analysis of the influence of Mustafa Kemal and his ideas on Turkish foreign policy after his death, see Uzer, Umut. 2011. *Identity and Turkish Foreign Policy: The Kemalist Influence in Cyprus and the Caucasus*. London: I.B. Tauris.

[29] See, for example, Bein, Amit. 2017. *Kemalist Turkey and the Middle East*. Cambridge: Cambridge University Press.

[30] See, for example, Zürcher, Erik J. 2010. *The Young Turk Legacy and Nation Building: From the Ottoman Empire to Atatürk's Turkey*. London, New York: I.B. Tauris; Üngör, Ugur Ümit. 2011. *The Making of Modern Turkey: Nation and State in Eastern Anatolia, 1913-1950*. Oxford: Oxford University Press.

Actually, an Ottoman mission under the *chargé d'affaires* present in Addis Ababa, one of the rare independent states of the time, turned into an embassy.[31]

These factors constrained Turkey's attitude towards Africa, especially during the decolonization phase. After the death of Mustafa Kemal (1938) and in the face of the new winds of war, Turkey opted to strengthen its policy of neutrality and isolationism, considered the best choice to guarantee the country's sovereignty and territorial integrity. This stalemate persisted almost unaltered until the end of the Second World War. While domestic policy, especially the identity process promoted by Kemalist reforms, had resulted in a break with the old Ottoman domains, including African countries, the post-Second World War global balances prevented the Ankara government from playing a primary role among the countries either newly constituted or in search of full independence. The new international bipolarism forced Turkey to take a clear stand, putting an end to the neutrality that had characterized the Republic during the previous decades. As an immediate neighbour of the Soviet Union, Turkey's perception of insecurity grew. Thus, Turkey approached the Atlantic bloc, for which it served as the south-eastern flank. The assistance received within the framework of the aid provided by the Marshall Plan and the Truman doctrine, and the deployment of 4,500 soldiers and officers in Korea to join the United Nations Command were all steps towards the Atlantic bloc, ratified in 1952 with the accession to NATO and confirmed with the signing of the Balkan Pact (1954) and the Baghdad Pact (1955). The decision to join the Western bloc was conditioned by adherence to its democratic and liberal principles. As a result, Turkey, still governed by a single-party regime, was called upon to promote the democratization of state structures, institutions and practices.[32] The introduction of a multiparty system allowed for the opening of a new phase of Turkish politics, led by the figure of Adnan Menderes and his Democratic Party. The decade under the Menderes leadership coincided with the decolonization period and the first declarations of independence by the African countries. Faced with these rapid developments, the Menderes government was more interested in strengthening its special relationship with the United States and the Western alliance system in order to ensure its own security.[33] Therefore, the African issues were not considered of great relevance to Turkish interests. Even the policy of recognition of the new

---

[31] Ipek, 'Turkey's Foreign Policy towards Sub-Saharan Africa'.
[32] VanderLippe, John M. 2005. *The Politics of Turkish Democracy: Ismet Inonu and the Formation of the Multi-Party System, 1938-1950*. Albany: State University of New York Press.
[33] Pelt, Mogens. 2014. *Military Intervention and a Crisis Democracy in Turkey: The Menderes Era and Its Demise*. London: I.B. Tauris.

independent African states was only another opportunity to prove its alignment with US positions.

Indeed, Turkey merely recognized, de jure and de facto, those countries that had already shown their intention to reject Soviet influence and move closer to the Atlantic bloc. Also in those cases, the Turkish initiative stopped at simple recognition, without ever establishing permanent bilateral relations. Furthermore, whenever an African issue concerning a country or the whole continent was brought to the attention of the United Nations General Assembly, Turkey kept a detached attitude, either by not taking a stand or by taking a stand alongside the Western powers. This was the case, for example, of the demands for independence claimed by Tunisia and Algeria. In both cases, Turkey stressed that the problem was an 'internal' issue to be solved solely by France.[34] Turkey's choice was always to follow the preference of the US vote. This was an attitude for which Turkey had to pay in terms of losing popularity and the confidence of the African states. Turkey, which during the Menderes government depended on the Atlantic bloc economically as well as in terms of security, did not miss any opportunity to demonstrate its loyalty to Washington and its European allies. During the Suez crisis (1956) and Nasser's decision to nationalize the channel, Ankara sided with France and the UK. A year earlier, at the Bandung Conference (1955), Turkey had adopted a position that would condition relations with African states and more, in general, with the Global South for many years.

The historic Asian–African conference was organized with the aim of creating a cohesion among countries of the Global South. That was the first time in world politics that the free states of Asia and Africa congregated to discuss common problems and to establish a united approach particularly in terms of anti-colonialism and Afro–Asian solidarity. The conference aimed to materialize a new group in world politics, which made the United States uneasy. Turkey attended the Bandung Conference via American encouragement. The conference was a persuasive platform for Turkey to show how staunchly committed it was to protect Western interests and to champion the Western ideals. Yet, during the conference, the Turkish delegate Fatin Rüştü Zorlu tried to persuade the participant countries that membership in collective defence organizations such as NATO would make more sense, emphasizing that it was not possible for the impartiality to be successful under the circumstances. Zorlu's efforts were not very successful and, moreover, alienated the sympathies of many acceding

---

[34] Tepeciklioğlu, Eiem Eyrice. 2012. 'Afrika Kıtasının Dünya Politikasında Artan Önemi ve Türkiye-Afrika İlişkileri'. *Ankara Üniversitesi Afrika Çalışmaları Dergisi* 1 (2): 67.

countries including African states. Indeed, Turkey received strong criticism from Zhou Enlai and Jawaharlal Nehru because of its pro-NATO position. Turkey did not take part in the 'third world' network organizations such as the Non-Aligned Movement (NAM) and the G77 which emerged after the conference and which would appear as an effective bloc within the United Nations. These failed initial movements towards these alternative blocs provoked a sense of distance and mistrust with the non-aligned countries.[35]

In the subsequent period, Turkey strengthened its Western-oriented foreign policy and maintained a general lack of interest in Africa, African problems and African demands. This attitude was still determined by some factors due to the nexus between foreign and domestic policy. The key factor was the vision of the Kemalist elite in power, whose perception of Africa was still significantly influenced by the collective memory and the mental maps of the beginning of the century. In the Turkish policymaker's outlook, the idea of a broken continent was still strong; Turkey's attention was focused only on the Maghreb countries, in particular Nasser's Egypt, belonging at that time to the Soviet bloc. Turkey's policy coordination with the West during the Suez crisis played an important role in the negative progress in relations with Africa. Notably, the Turkish decision not to attend the conference held in London (August 1956) to which many countries adhered, including all the states of the NAM, caused a further loss of sympathy among African and Asian countries. On the contrary, the conference was attended by Greece, which used the opportunity to create a network of relationships and friendships that would be useful a few years later in the Cyprus issue.[36]

In the early 1960s, after the Menderes era, Turkey had necessarily to turn to African countries to seek diplomatic support in the Cyprus dispute. The growing tensions between Turks and Greeks in Cyprus led to Bloody Christmas (1963). The situation in Turkey worsened rapidly, leading to the collapse of the power-sharing government. Turkey began to turn to the African continent in order to establish relations with its nations in its quest for diplomatic support in the UN over the Cyprus issue. However, Turkey had a negative image in the eyes of many developing countries in the third world, mainly due to its special alliance with the United States, whereas President Makarios of the Republic of Cyprus was an important figure in the NAM.[37] It was thus not surprising that the NAM

---

[35] Arıboğan, Deniz Ülke. 2004. 'Opening the Closed Window to the East: Turkey's Relations with East Asian Countries'. In *Turkish Foreign Policy in the Post-Cold War Era*, edited by Idris Bal, 401–20. Boca Raton: Brown Walker Press.

[36] Tepeciklioğlu, 'Afrika Kıtasının', 71.

[37] Moran, Michael. 2001. 'Cyprus and the 1960 Accords: Nationalism and Internationalism'. *Perceptions: Journal of International Affairs* 6 (2): 1–9.

conference in Cairo in 1964 ended with a declaration condemning Turkey's Cyprus policy.[38] The final declaration supported the Makarios government's policy of regarding the Turkish Cypriots as a minority, not a partner. Two months later, the same points stressed in the Cairo final declaration were included in the UN Resolution thanks to the solid position of the NAM.[39] The extreme attempt to send seven 'goodwill delegations' to countries in Asia, Latin America and Africa was in vain.[40] These efforts did not achieve the intended results, and the African countries voted against Turkey. The growth of the countries that had gained independence had reshuffled the balances within the international fora, particularly in the UN. The detached and cold attitude of Ankara during the season of decolonization and self-determination of the African people was paid for dearly by Turkey in the Cyprus issue. On the one hand, it was a foreign policy failure for Turkey, and on the other hand, it demonstrated the African countries' role in proving their legitimacy in the UN. It was a very important lesson for Turkey.

In 1965 the Justice Party came to power and immediately set itself the goal of revising the isolationist policies of Menderes, especially with regard to the Arab world and the countries of the Global South. During this period, Turkey undertook a series of initiatives to erase its negative image in the eyes of these countries, as well as the first concrete measures to establish and improve relations with Asian and African countries. Once again, however, the focus was on the Maghreb, in particular Tunisia and Egypt, with which Turkey had signed trade agreements. Despite these small and few attempts, Turkey still did not have a coherent and comprehensive African agenda in the 1960s. Aside from the search for votes and support within international organizations, Turkish policymakers still had a general disinterest in Africa and African issues. This attitude inevitably resulted in a lack of knowledge of the African continent and, consequently, further trouble in relating to it.

During the 1970s, the situation did not change significantly. Turkey established a recognition and a warm bilateral relationship with some sub-Saharan countries such as Cameroon, Ghana, Niger, Togo and Zaire. However, what was striking was Turkey's attitude towards countries seeking self-determination: the Turkish Government never took a position, abstaining during the votes of the General

[38] Kösebalaban, Hasan. 2011. *Turkish Foreign Policy: Islam, Nationalism, and Globalization, Middle East Today*, 96. New York: Palgrave Macmillan.
[39] Dodd, Clement. 2010. *The History and Politics of the Cyprus Conflict*. London: Palgrave Macmillan.
[40] Fırat, Melek. 1997. *1960–71 Arası Türk Dış Politikası ve Kıbrıs Sorunu*, 191–2. Ankara: Siyasal Kitabevi.

Assembly. Moreover, there was never any pronouncement by the Turkish authorities against the European colonial experience. Such an inclination was evident in the case of Portugal, one of the countries most reluctant to give up its colonies in Africa. Turkey repeatedly expressed its reservations about the removal of the country from the UN's specialized agencies and the implementation of embargoes and sanctions against it.[41] Declarations of support for the independence of Mozambique – although never mentioning Portugal – and Eritrea were signed. Turkey also allocated aid to these two countries. However, the amount of aid provided to these countries in the 1970s was meaningless and a serious relationship could not be established. Furthermore, the positions taken in favour of the Eritrean independence movement created problems with Ethiopia, alienating the sympathies of one of the main regional powers.[42] As Özkan pointed out,

> although the lack of action in regards to establishing stronger relations with Africa could be seen partly as a result of other issues persisting on the Turkish agenda of the time, the main reason was lack of Turkey's interest, knowledge and strategy about what to do in Africa.[43]

2.3 From Özal to Cem: The basis of Turkish policy towards Africa (1980–2002)

During this phase, relations with Africa remained very limited. However, it is possible to draw a picture of the main events and political figures that favoured an initial change of mentality and perception towards regions that had long been ignored, such as Africa. The period that began with the election of Özal (1983) and ended with the appointment of Cem at the foreign ministry (1997–2002) created the conditions for the implementation of JDP's proactive foreign policy. The collapse of the Soviet bloc created a new international environment around Turkey, providing new opportunities as well as creating uncertainties and threats that prompted a new round of debate on Turkey's international role.[44]

---

[41] Tepeciklioğlu, 'Afrika Kıtasının', 75.
[42] Fırat, Melek, and Ömer Kürkçüoğlu. 2002. 'Ortadoğu'yla İlişkiler'. In *Türk Dış Politikası (1919 - 1980)*, edited by Oran Baskın, 785–9. İstanbul: İletişim Yayınları.
[43] Özkan, Mehmet. 2010a. 'Turkey's Rising Role in Africa'. *Turkish Policy Quarterly* 9 (4):97.
[44] Öniş, Ziya. 1995. 'Turkey in the Post-Cold War Era: In Search of Identity'. *Middle East Journal* 49 (1): 48–68.

This systemic-level change coincided with the diversification of the societal and political sources that affected the Turkish foreign policymaking process.[45]

By the end of the 1970s, Turkey had recognized all the new African states that had gained independence in the previous decades, establishing formal relations with them by opening a number of consular offices. The way of relating to Africa was still presented by a different approach depending on the geographical area of the country of interest. Relations with North African countries had been strengthened to a limited extent through economic and political tie-ups. However, relations with sub-Saharan countries remained very limited.[46] The willingness to establish relations was not completely lacking among the Turkish policymakers. Indeed, in the mid-1970s for the first time a plan for opening up to Africa had been drawn up with the aim of expanding political, economic and commercial relations. However, its implementation was made impracticable by the domestic and international contingencies and constraints. The Cyprus issue, social violence towards far-right and far-left movements, the emergence of the PKK terrorist threat, the instability of coalition governments, the lack of adequate economic resources and the absence of a proactive vision of foreign policy were all factors that prevented Turkey from developing an effective agenda for Africa. As a result, still in the early 1990s, Africa occupied a marginal position in Turkish foreign policy. It was not a coincidence that the first signs of opening up to the continent were determined by a multiplicity of changes across the country between 1980 and 1997. This season of deep change involved several levels: domestic, regional and systemic.

Domestically, the instability and violence of the 1970s led the military to a new intervention – in the political life of the country. The coup d'état of 1980, the third since the death of Mustafa Kemal, was a turning point in the history of modern Turkey. The power was concentrated in the hands of the army, which two years later drew up the new constitution (1982). During that period, the military junta intended not only to put an end to the situation of anarchy and widespread violence but also to implement radical and in-depth reforms in the entire sociopolitical structure of the country. The military's decisions were also determined by the recent regional developments – the Iranian revolution and the Soviet invasion of Afghanistan (1979) – that imposed a new and complex phase of cultural identity transition, for which it was necessary to reorganize

---

[45] Sayari, Sabri. 2000. 'Turkish foreign policy in the post-cold war era: The challenges of multi-regionalism.' *Journal of International Affairs* 54 (1): 169–182; Robins, Philip. 2003. *Suits and Uniforms: Turkish Foreign Policy Since the Cold War*. London: Hurst & Co.

[46] Ozkan, 'Turkiye'nin Afrika'da Artan Rolü', 21.

and re-elaborate the very foundations of Turkish society and identity. The core aspect of this process was the rehabilitation of the religious component. The two regional events persuaded the United States, which despite the tensions remained the main sponsor of the Turkish military, of the importance and at the same time of the risks associated with the political use of Islam. For Washington, Islam could be a weapon to be used against the Marxist-Leninist ideology; however, the Iranian case had shown how the loss of control or excessive oppression of religion by the authorities could turn against American interests. Against this backdrop, the United States decided to support radical Jihadist groups, which were destined to hinder the Soviet advance in Afghanistan and, at the same time, pressure the Middle Eastern allies, old (Turkey) and more recent (Egypt), to lead from above a gradual reintegration of Islam into public life.[47] The idea was that this would prevent the emergence of a new 'Khomeini' in the region. This is even more complicated to implement in a country like Turkey, where for decades the fear of Islamic *irtica* (reaction) had represented, in the eyes of the secular components, one of the main reasons for the power attributed to the military itself. In other words, the foundations had been laid for the development of a new idea of nation no longer defined exclusively by the Turkish character but, rather, by the strong sense of belonging to a common culture, the genesis of which dates back to centuries before the birth of the Republic.

The core of this process was the introduction by the military of the Turkish-Islamic Synthesis as an integral part of the official state ideology. In this context, the first elections of the Third Republic saw the success of Turgut Özal and his Motherland Party (ANAP). Among the factors that determined Özal's success there was also the foreign policy and in particular the international isolation of Turkey due to the worsening of the Cypriot crisis (1974). The cooling of relations with the United States and Europe further aggravated the already fragile economy of the country. A few months before the military intervention, inflation had reached a record rate of 90 per cent.[48] Özal's personality and background were also decisive. He was a businessman, a fervent admirer of the United States and economic liberalism, with a conservative cultural background and political experience within the Islamic party.[49] In other words, he would have been the right man to lead the country through a phase of deep

---

[47] Kepel, Gilles. 2000. *Jihad: expansion et déclin de l'islamisme*, 87–105. Paris: Gallimard.
[48] Terzioglu, Aysecan, Cenk Ozbay, Maral Erol and Z. Umut Turem, eds. 2016. *The Making of Neoliberal Turkey*. London: Ashgate.
[49] Taspinar, Omer. 2005. *Kurdish Nationalism and Political Islam in Turkey: Kemalist Identity in Transition*. New York: Routledge.

transformation starting with the economic structures. Until then, Turkey had adopted a statist industrialization policy, considered the best way to move from a backward, rural peasant economy to a modern industrial country. Once he took over the government as the prime minister, Özal liberalized the state-dominated and heavily protected economy with policies designed to rationalize the tax system and encourage exports. These structural changes set off Turkey from the stagnating economy and encouraged foreign investments, including many from the Gulf monarchies. Özal opened up the Turkish economy to private enterprises and created an environment for economic growth that, in less than twenty years, has projected Turkey among the twenty world economic powers.[50]

Özal's policies and the influx of new foreign capital benefited rural and conservative entrepreneurship, which in a few years gave rise to industrial districts in the main centres of Anatolia, such as Konya and Kayseri. The so-called Anatolian Tigers, the real driving force behind the country's economic growth, were less dependent on the state and more embedded in Turko-Islamic culture. The private capital stockpiling by this new Anatolian bourgeoisie was partly reinvested in business activities and partly donated to Islamic communities for redistribution through charitable activities and charity foundations.[51] These, taking advantage of the post-coup openings and enjoying huge resources, were able to quickly spread and take root. The Islamic communities became real, informal and heterogeneous networks able to quickly consolidate their social and material bases. This process allowed the affirmation of a wealthy Muslim bourgeoisie and the consequent development of a modern civil society willing to play an active role in the public and political life of the country.[52] The birth and rise of a new proactive civil society was a determining factor in both the JDP's subsequent political success and in Turkey's prompt opening up to the world.

The political and commercial isolation convinced Özal to diversify the country's bilateral relations and open up Turkey to the global economy.[53] Özal's

---

[50] Turkey has been a member of the G20 since its creation in 1999.

[51] The Islamic finance provides that a percentage of the profits be allocated to the community, as *zakat* (charity). See Warde, Ibrahim. 2000. *Islamic Finance in the Global Economy*, 187–8. Edinburgh: Edinburgh University Press. Regarding the dynamics of the development of Anatolian entrepreneurship and its characteristics see, Yavuz, Hakan M. 2003. *Islamic Political Identity in Turkey*. Oxford, New York: Oxford University Press; Vali, Nasr. 2009. *Forces of Fortune: The Rise of the New Muslim Middle Class and What It Will Mean for Our World*. New York, London: Free Press; Çağaptay, Soner. 2014. *The Rise of Turkey: The Twenty-First Century's First Muslim Power*. Lincoln: Potomac Books.

[52] Özgur, Dönmez Rasim and Enneli Pinar. 2011. *Societal Peace and Ideal Citizenship for Turkey*. Plymouth: Lexington Books.

[53] Eligür, Banu. 2014. *The Mobilization of Political Islam in Turkey*. Cambridge, New York: Cambridge University Press.

world view promoted Turkey's neighbourhood as a new hinterland for the state. Therefore, several steps were taken in order to enhance Turkey's relations with neighbouring countries regardless of religion, sect or race. While in the previous decades international relations were based solely on strategic and securitarian logic, under Özal's leadership they began to be interest-oriented. Özal's foreign policy agenda became increasingly functional to the promotion and protection of Turkish economic interests in the world. Turkey expanded commercial and economic relations with the Balkans, the Black Sea and the Middle East. In order to restore Turkish relations with the Arab world, Özal leveraged himself as a neoliberal conservative politician and pious believer close to the world of the Sufi guilds. Even though Özal often relied on religious connections in order to open doors in international business and politics, his approach was pragmatic. Turkey would appear to serve Western capitalism and Islam at the same time. Özal was fully aware that the rehabilitation of the Muslim identity in foreign policy would also allow Turkey to be considered by the United States as an indispensable ally.

These dynamics received a further stimulus with the candidacy to join the European Union (1987) and the reshuffling of the international balances caused by the end of the Cold War, at the end of which Turkish political relations became multidirectional without any neglected regions. After the collapse of the Soviet Union, Ankara tried to take advantage of the many changes in regional and global geopolitical structures. Concerned about the loss of geostrategic prominence for its US ally as a bulwark against the Soviet Union, Turkey tried to carve out its own space for autonomous manoeuvring in the newly independent states of Central Asia. The Russian territorial downsizing and the birth of five 'Turkic' republics[54] had provoked so much euphoric reaction among the Turkish public that Özal himself greeted the event by declaring the birth of a new 'Turkic century'. Turkey, encouraged by the United States, which feared Iranian influence, invested heavily in the region, supporting the paths of state-building and economic development. Although the attempt to promote a feasible model of government and development for the 'Turkic sisters' led to poor results, it became a model of intervention for the involvement in Africa.[55] In a few years,

---

[54] Kazakhstan, Kyrgyzstan, Tajikistan, Turkmenistan, and Uzbekistan.

[55] On the topic, see Balci, Bayram and Buchwalter, Bertrand. 2001. *La Turquie en Asie centrale: la conversion au réalisme: 1991-2000*. Istanbul: Institut Français d'études Anatoliennes Georges Dumézil; Aras, Bülent, Kenan Dağcı and M. Efe Çaman. 2009. 'Turkey's New Activism in Asia'. *Alternatives: Turkish Journal of International Relations* 8 (2): 24–39; Cinar, Kursat. 2013. 'Turkey and Turkic Nations: A Post-Cold War Analysis of Relations'. *Turkish Studies* 14 (2): 256–71; Bilgin, Pinar and Ali Bilgic. 2011. 'Turkey's "new" Foreign Policy toward Eurasia'. *Eurasian Geography and Economics* 52 (2): 13–195; Bal, Idris. 2018. *Turkey's Relations with the West and the Turkic Republics: The Rise and Fall of the Turkish Model*. Abingdon: Routledge.

Turkey also established relations with the states of North Africa and undertook a slow thawing with the Arab world, starting the process of repositioning on the regional and global stage. The foreign policy introduced by Özal and known as Ozalism was, for some scholars, a form of *ante litteram* 'Neo-Ottomanism',[56] for others a kind of 'Westernist Eurasianism',[57] oriented to the Turkish-speaking populations. Regardless of the definition, what matters is that from this moment on the 'mental map' or geographical perception of Turkish policymakers and society had begun to change. While these changes in the short period did not have a direct impact on Turkish policy towards Africa, they created the right conditions for the breakthrough at the beginning of the new millennium. Indeed, in a few years, the struggle to redefine a world view focused on the economy and a more inclusive identity paved the way for the definition of a new 'national role' and a different orientation of foreign policy.[58]

It was during Özal's term as prime minister that an initial rapprochement with Africa took place. Turkey was seeking a partner for the development of an industrial zone on the Mediterranean. It needed a supply of thirty million tonnes of low ash coal a year to deal with the air pollution caused by Turkey's own low-quality brown coal. Özal was therefore receptive to apartheid South Africa's covert proposal to meet his country's requirements but the agreement never came into force because of the South African regime change in 1992.[59] Turkey also contributed multilaterally to UNOSOM II, the second attempt by the UN to deal with the instability and violence in Somalia (1993–5), and between April 1993 and January 1994, Turkish lieutenant-general Çevik Bir was the force commander of the UN mission.[60] During the final years of Özal's government, Turkish society began to develop the perception that it could play an active role in the sociopolitical development of the country.[61] The emergence of a public sphere beyond state control was the outcome of the emancipation process of civil society as well as the beginning of the gradual downsizing of the old Kemalist establishment. Until then, in fact, there was a widespread belief that the first and only agent of social renewal was the state, understood in a paternalistic way as

[56] Laçiner, Sedat. 2009. 'Turgut Özal Period in Turkish Foreign Policy: Özalism'. *USAK Yearbook of International Politics and Law* 2:153–205.

[57] Tüfekçi, Özgür. 2017. *The Foreign Policy of Modern Turkey: Power and the Ideology of Eurasianism*. London: I.B. Tauris.

[58] Özkan, 'What Drives Turkey's Involvement in Africa?' 117.

[59] Wheeler, 'Ankara to Africa', 45.

[60] Ibid.

[61] Kuzmanovic, Daniella. 2012. *Refractions of Civil Society in Turkey*. New York: Palgrave Macmillan.

devlet baba.[62] The change was profound even on a psychological level. The Islamist movements benefited from the new public space and the sociocultural mood. In a short period of time, many associations and activities were born, independent from the state and characterized by Islamic grassroots: charitable foundations (*vakiflar*), Islamic associations (*derneks*), educational institutions, NGOs and new media (radio, newspapers, TV).[63] All of them were operating within the country, but a few slowly began to promote projects abroad, including in Africa. Also among them were two private non-state actors who would play a primary role in the subsequent policy of opening up towards the African continent: the Gülen movement and the Humanitarian Relief Foundation (IHH).

In addition to the obvious material constraints, the attitude of the policymakers contributed to hindering Turkey from developing stable economic and political relations with African countries. Despite Özal's first half-hearted attempts at openness, the suspicious attitude towards SSA permeated Turkish diplomacy, blocking any initiative in its infancy. Exemplifying the nature of Turkey's relations with Africa until 1998 was the experience of a Turkish diplomat who served in Africa in the 1960s and 1990s:

> Just before I left Ankara to take up my duty to Nigeria in 1990, the first meeting of Joint Economic Commission was held in Ankara. The second meeting had to be held in Nigeria. But, it was not possible to organize this meeting during 5 years I served there. There was a standing invitation to our Foreign Minister to visit Lagos. I tried to do my best for the realization of this visit. I was not able to make it possible too. Among the decisions of 1st Joint Economic Commission there was cooperation on energy matters and possible import by Turkey of Nigerian oil and liquefied natural gas. I tried to get the view of the Government on this matter – Surprisingly I had a reply. It was as follows; 'Turkey is in negotiation with neighbouring countries and was not interested in Nigerian oil and gas'.[64]

Two years after Özal's death (1993), for the first time in Republican history an Islamic party leader, Necmettin Erbakan, was appointed as the prime minister (1995). Although his experience at the helm of the country was very brief, interrupted by a new military intervention (1997), the executive led by Erbakan marked a further relevant step in the changing of Turkish foreign policy. The objective of Erbakan's international agenda was to reorient Turkish geopolitical

[62] Göle, Nilufer. 1997. 'Secularism and Islamism in Turkey: The Making of Elites and Counter-Elites'. *The Middle East Journal* 51 (1): 46–58.

[63] Atalay, 'Civil Society as Soft Power', 167.

[64] Karaca, Salih Z. 2000. 'Turkish Foreign Policy in the Year 2000 and Beyond: Her Opening Up Policy to Africa'. *Dis Politika* 25 (3–4): 118.

projection towards the Muslim countries of which Turkey should have been the leader. As evidence of this new orientation, Erbakan visited the Islamic Republic of Iran on his first foreign trip in office. The bilateral meeting was the beginning of his attempts to signal a more balanced foreign policy, which would take relations with the Islamic world more seriously than in the past. The decisions began, inevitably, to worry the military who, despite the Özal decade, still held primary control over foreign policy.[65] Among the journeys that aroused the anger of the Turkish military officials was the one to Libya, when Erbakan was hosted by Muammar Gaddafi. During the meeting, the latter harshly attacked the Turkish policy against the Kurds, which caused domestic political problems for Erbakan. Despite several attempts to control the government's policy, the generals alarmed by the anti-Western rhetoric of the prime minister, issued a strong public statement condemning Erbakan. Threatening to intervene directly in the country's political life, the military forced the resignation of the prime minister in February 1997. It was the so-called 'postmodern' coup d'état. As well noted by Çelik, even though 'Erbakan did succeed in shifting Turkey's foreign policy behaviour during the time that he was prime minister, he was not able to alter the country's foreign policy orientation'.[66] Erbakan's brief experience, however, highlighted two elements of high continuity with the previous period. The first was the multi-oriented foreign policy introduced by Özal. The second was that the secular and pro-Western military apparatus still had the last word on foreign policy choices. However, while for the latter, the opening up of a multiplicity of regions was intended to be functional to the economic and security interests with the West, for Erbakan it was an alternative option. In other words, they acted as a constraint to a proactive policy. Domestic political events, economic instability and the border crisis with Syria (1998) diverted Turkish attention from other foreign policy objectives.

After the forced resignation of Erbakan's government, Mesut Yılmaz became prime minister. At the Ministry of Foreign Affairs was appointed İsmail Cem, who played a decisive role in the international revival of Turkey.[67] Cem was able to promote its vision and implement it by giving a significant boost to Turkish international relations. Although a strongly secular pro-European social democrat, Cem was very concerned about Turkey's alienation from its own cultural and historical roots. In an international environment in which identity

---

[65] Robins, *Suits and Uniforms*, 262–3.
[66] Çelik, Yasemin. 1999. *Contemporary Turkish Foreign Policy*, 160. Westport, London: Praeger.
[67] Although he served as a minister on behalf of a minority government (1997–9) and then a coalition of three parties, İsmail Cem was able to achieve the strength and confidence needed to fill the office effectively.

was acquiring greater value, he was convinced that the Ottoman past should be rehabilitated because it would become a tool for restoring ties and acquiring influence.[68] Like Davutoğlu after him, Cem was persuaded that Turkey should take advantage of the new regional balances to play a more assertive role. His vision had a twofold objective: one to consolidate its relationship with Europe to which Turkey belonged, historically, geographically and economically,[69] and two, to remember some of Özal's insights, Cem aspired to transform Turkey as a pivotal state. He was convinced that Turkey had the right credentials for such a role, as a diversified industrial base, with a deep-rooted democracy and a well-trained and -equipped army.[70] To this end, although its primary focus remained the Eurasian region, Cem revitalized the need for a multi-oriented foreign policy through the preparation of development plans towards different regions. To this end, the ministry organized a series of meetings involving interested parties, including Turkish ambassadors in Africa, representatives of other ministries, non-governmental organizations (NGOs), the private sector and honorary consuls of African countries in Turkey in order to discuss to 'Opening a Gateway to Africa'.[71] As a result, in 1998, Cem promoted the drafting of a new plan for Africa entitled the 'Action Plan for Opening to Africa'.[72]

> The Africa Policy was made up of several areas, such as developing diplomatic relations, and political, economic, and cultural co-operation. In the diplomatic area, it was suggested that the level of diplomatic representation in Africa be upgraded. Under economic measures, it was proposed that Turkey should conclude trade agreements with African countries and encourage exchange visits by businesspeople between Turkey and African countries.[73]

The policy plan was based on the finding that the level of relations between Turkey and Africa was too low and too underdeveloped. Meanwhile, it provided policymakers with a fresh and conflict-free start given the disputes that had clouded other relations. Within this framework, Turkey hoped to further develop its political, economic and cultural ties with Africa. With regard to the diplomatic

---

[68] Cem, Ismail. 2001. *Turkey in the New Century*. Ankara: Rustem.
[69] Tuğtan, Mehmet Ali. 2016. 'Kulturel degiskenlerin dis politikadaki yeri: Ismail Cem ve Ahmet Davutoğlu'. *Uluslararasi Iliskiler* 13 (49): 3–24.
[70] Örmeci, Ozan. 2011. 'Ismail Cem's Foreign Policy (1997-2002)'. *SDU Faculty of Arts and Sciences Journal of Social Sciences* 23:223–45; Tüfekçi, *The Foreign Policy*.
[71] Wheeler, 'Ankara to Africa', 45–6.
[72] Afrika'ya Açılım Eylem Planı.
[73] Özkan, 'What Drives Turkey's Involvement in Africa', 534. For a comprehensive summary of the plan, see Hazar, Numan. 2000. 'The Future of Turkish-African Relations'. *Dış Politika* 25 (3–4): 111–13.

sphere, the plan suggested to raise the level of cooperation and bilateral relations with African countries through the opening of three new embassies, the accreditation of ambassadors directly from Ankara to some countries – where the opening of a resident embassy was not possible due to financial problems – and organizing a series of diplomatic missions to different continents' capitals.[74] On security-related issues, the plan aimed at improving the cooperation on military training, the Turkish contribution to UN peacekeeping activities and the invitation to African countries for military exercises in Turkey.[75] Besides the diplomatic, economic and military cooperation, the Action Plan also proposed several measures to improve cultural interaction within the educational field. The invitation of African scholars to various international seminars and conferences was suggested, as was the establishment of an Institute of African Studies, in order to enlighten the Turkish public and to better understand Africa and its problems.[76] It was recognized that in Turkey there was a lack of basic knowledge of Africa, its history and the many cultures that inhabited it.

Everything seemed ready for the start of an era of fresh relations between Turkey and Africa, but resources were still lacking, as well as a radical change in the perception of the African continent towards which widespread distrust remained. For the majority of Turkish policymakers, Africa, especially SSA, was still unknown. Therefore, the lack of logistics and knowledge, as well as the domestic instability, followed by the severe economic recession between 1999 and 2001 prevented Turkey from implementing its Africa Action Plan. The efforts made by Cem and by the general director for Africa and the Middle East, Ambassador Numan Hazar, proved to be fruitless due to the country's structural constraints.[77] However, the document is a milestone in Turkish foreign policy regarding Africa.

---

[74] Ipek, Volkan and Gonca Biltekin. 2013. 'Turkey's Foreign Policy Implementation in Sub-Saharan Africa: A Post-international Approach'. *New Perspective on Turkey* 49:139–40.

[75] Özkan, Mehmet and Birol Akgün. 2010. 'Turkey's Opening to Africa'. The Journal of Modern African Studies 48 (4), p. 527.

[76] Hazar, 'The Future of Turkish-African Relations', 113.

[77] In August 1999 Turkey was hit by a number of destructive earthquakes (commonly known as the Marmara earthquake) that left an estimated 20,000 people dead. Besides the physical destruction, the political consequences were significant, leading to Turkey review its position in the world and changing the attitude of the Turkish people towards the governance of their country. See Kubicek, Paul. 2002. 'The Earthquake, Civil Society, and Political Change in Turkey: Assessment and Comparison with Eastern Europe'. *Political Studies* 50 (4): 761–78. Moreover, the country's economic and financial situation was very precarious, partly because of political instability and partly due to an inflation as high as 100 per cent per annum. Called in to rescue the country financially towards the end of 1999, the International Monetary Fund concluded a standby agreement with Turkey that required major financial reforms and adherence to fiscal discipline over the next two years. See Öniş, Ziya and Barry M. Rubin, eds. 2003. *The Turkish Economy in Crisis: Critical Perspectives on the 2000-1 Crises*. London, Portland: Frank Cass.

3

Turkish rapprochement with sub-Saharan Africa (2002–11)

At the beginning of the millennium, despite some modest signals of openness, Turkey's relations with Africa were poor and limited to the North African countries. While, like other emerging powers, the permissive international environment, analysed in the first chapter, has created favourable conditions for the progressive involvement in Africa, it cannot be considered a sufficient condition. Another decisive variable has been the political, social and cultural transformation that has characterized Turkey in the past decades, favouring the emergence of a new political class. The beginning of the JDP era led to both a radical change of approach and strategy in foreign policy and the replacement of foreign policy executives or elites. The chapter, in addition to the analysis of the main stages of the Turkish policy of opening up to Africa, highlights the intertwining of domestic and international variables, thereby providing the decisive impulse for the launch of Turkish policy towards Africa. A decisive factor has been the different perceptions promoted by the FPEs of the Turkish role at the international arena and the formulation of a new national role conception: the idea of the central country.

3.1 A new place for Turkey in the world: A new role, different perceptions and a proactive foreign policy

During the last two decades, Turkey's foreign policy has undergone considerable changes in terms of both its regional scope and strategic priorities. Its active role in international relations is paralleled by its economic growth as well as by some profound sociopolitical changes promoted by the JDP since its coming to power in 2003. JDP's victory election in November 2002 was a turning point in the political life of modern Turkey. The rise of a single-party government with Islamic grassroots launched a thorough process of reform and change which involved Turkish society and institutions. Within a few years, thanks to the significant economic growth, the government led by Erdoğan developed an agenda aimed at rehabilitating its image and its concrete presence in the international arena. The simultaneous European Union accession process, witnessed in the adoption of the so-called Copenhagen packages, started the downsizing of the military's interference within the institutions. The path of rapid de-securitization was accompanied by the rise of a generation of young emerging officials who went on to occupy prominent positions within key ministries including that of the foreign ministry. Simultaneously, the EU's admission of Turkey to the path to European membership[1] refocused Turkish attention on Europe and its Western bent. These transformations were decisive for the start of a new course of foreign policy, aimed at expanding the country's political and economic relations, even in areas long considered distant and hostile. In addition to these policies, Africa was from 2005, designated by the JDP government as the 'Year of Africa', and became one of the regions in which Turkey was called on to concentrate its efforts.

Without any drastic breakdown, Turkey embarked on a more independent international course of action shortly after the JDP took power. In fact, Turkey first gave highest priority to EU membership without in any way denying its ties with NATO or its general role of supporting the United States in the Middle East. At the same time, JDP expressed its ambition to restore Turkey's centrality, in terms of influence and presence, outside its territorial borders – a move dictated both by material motivations, linked to economic development, and by cultural and psychopolitical reasons taking a principal form of a 'revived motivation to assert regional primacy in the spirit of but not the imperial manner, of its Ottoman glory days'.[2] As had happened during the Özal period, the changes that affected Turkish foreign policy during this phase were also the result of factors external and internal to the country.[3] The systemic changes at the end of the Cold War produced a new scenario which offered a possibility to empower Turkey's role beyond the general Atlantic alliance and NATO membership.

[1] In December 1999, the EU reversed its decision taken in Luxembourg (1997) and accepted Turkey as a candidate. See, for example, Hughes, Edel. 2011. *Turkey's Accession to the European Union: The Politics of Exclusion?* London, New York: Routledge.
[2] Falk, Richard. 2018. 'Through a Glass Darkly: The Past, Present, and Future of Turkish Foreign Policy'. In *Middle Powers in Global Governance*, edited by Emel Parlar Dal, 35–51, 39. Abingdon: Palgrave Macmillan.
[3] Hermann, Charles F. 1990. 'Changing Course: When Governments Choose to Redirect Foreign Policy'. *International Studies Quarterly* 34 (1): 3–22.

Another decisive driver of change came from the reshuffling of the balances within the black box with the rise of a new generation of foreign policy executives. As shown earlier, in the previous decade the greater openness to the Turkish political sphere had allowed the rise of religious and nationalistic groups with different preferences and priorities of Turkish foreign policy. Moreover, the civil wars and ethnic conflicts in the post-Cold War era, together with the spread of theories such as the 'clash of civilizations',[4] contributed to the emergence of an identity consciousness among these peripheral groups that have constantly exerted pressure on governments to act more independently of the West.[5] With the rise of the JDP, the most dynamic groups in civil society became more relevant and showed greater interest in developing links with the countries of the Middle East, Eurasia, the Balkans and Africa. After the JDP's electoral victory in 2002, this elite has found political space within the new establishment. The rise of a new leadership with a completely different background and identity from the previous ones and the reforms promoted in the framework of the EU accession process favoured the reshuffling of the country's bureaucratic cadres and administrative apparatus. Specifically, the gradual downsizing of the military's role in the decision-making process led to the establishment of a new body of foreign policymakers that began to cautiously revitalize Turkey's role in the international sphere.[6] Indeed, the shift – from status quo to proactive orientation – was also conditioned by profound changes within the foreign policy executive. From the JDP's first mandate, leading government figures began recruiting a separate group of advisers in the realm of foreign affairs. The identity of this rising cadre marked a break with the past. Indeed, the shift of decision-making power away from the secular military-bureaucratic elite had brought up new leaders with completely different backgrounds and identities. In the course of a few years, foreign policy became more and more the subject of a civil bureaucracy with strong Islamic grassroots, culturally and ideologically distant from the previous secular establishment. With the change of the elites, the preferences and perceptions of the surrounding international context also inevitably changed. Furthermore, the decline of the political power of the military had allowed the civil government to adopt a less securitized and more autonomous approach to foreign policy. Yet, the opening of a space for a political

---

[4] Huntington, 'The Clash of Civilizations'.
[5] Akgün and Özkan, 'Turkey's Opening', 527.
[6] Yilmaz, 'Conceptual Framework of Turkish Foreign Policy in the AK Party Era', 68–73; Göksel, Oğhuzan. 2016. 'The End of Military Tutelage in Turkey and the Re-Making of Turkish Foreign Policy under the AKP'. In *Democratic Peace across the Middle East: Islam and Political Modernization*, edited by Yakub Halabi, 46–73. London, New York: I.B. Tauris.

solution to the Kurdish issue created a new domestic environment characterized by a high level of state formation and social inclusion. As a consequence, since then foreign policy has gone through a phase of reform.

The first JDP government was characterized by a strong Europeanization of foreign policy, understood as the adoption of the rules and instruments typical of European countries. In a broader way, this period coincided with a general de-securitization of both foreign and domestic policy, due to the EU accession process. The improvement of relations with the EU continued until 2007 when, after the JDP's election for the second term, the government's approach towards the EU membership process gradually began to change. Thanks to these reforms, the decision-making process of foreign policy changed both in structure – from a bureaucratic model to a 'groupthink' model – and in the identity of the political decision makers. The foreign policy agenda was dictated by figures no longer coming from the military environment but mostly from the academic one. Among these, the most influential and studied figure was Ahmet Davutoğlu, at the time the prime minister's foreign policy adviser. The presence of a new foreign policy executive allowed for the change, more easily, of both the conception of security – from hard to soft security – and the perceptions of insecurity, modifying, consequently, the international agenda. In particular, the regional policy towards the Middle East underwent a drastic change. The latter was modelled around the idea, inspired by Europe, of building a 'ring of friends' through the consolidation of political and economic ties. The new approach towards neighbouring countries highlighted a radical change in the geographical perception of foreign policy executives and, more generally, in the conception of a new national role. This role included the policymakers' own definitions of the general kinds of decisions, commitments, rules and actions suitable to their state and of the functions, if any, the state should perform on a continuing basis in the international system or in subordinate regional systems.[7] Within the IR studies, the role theory holds that national role conceptions are in part derived from domestic values and cultural heritage.[8] As Krotz and Sperling underline:

---

[7] Holsti, Kal J. 1970. 'National Role Conceptions in the Study of Foreign Policy'. *International Studies Quarterly* 14 (3): 245–6.

[8] For a better analysis of the role theory, see Wendt, Alexander. 1999. *Social Theory of International Politics*. Cambridge: Cambridge University Press. For the use of national role conception in the foreign policy study, see Holsti, Kal J. 1970. 'National Role Conceptions in the Study of Foreign Policy'. *International Studies Quarterly* 14 (3): 233–309; Walker, Stephen G., ed. 1987. *Role Theory and Foreign Policy Analysis*. Durham: Duke University Press. For the conceptualization of the national role conception to the study of the foreign policy of the Middle Eastern states, see Korany, Bahgat

National role concepts result from national historical experiences and memories and from the dominant interpretation of what these remembered experiences mean or imply [and thus it] cannot be reduced to the interests or ideologies of dominant groups, parties, or individuals in power, nor organizational features of state and society.[9]

The Turkish foreign policy approach, introduced by the JDP, has been based on a different conception of the Turkish role in the international system. Following the idea theorized by Davutoğlu, Turkey should no longer conceive of itself as a 'border' country, and not just as a 'bridge' state between the West and the East, but, rather, it should become aware of its historical and geopolitical status as a central country (*merkez ülke*).[10] Like Cem before him, Davutoğlu rejected the bridge narrative as 'passive' but at the same time he also rejected Cem's idea of a crossroad country. For Davutoğlu, Turkey must consider itself not as a frontier country that sits at the edge of the Middle East and the West but, rather, as a pivotal state. In other words, he rejected the geographical representation of Turkey as a peripheral country – an idea that had deeply limited Turkish activism in previous decades. Ideally, placing the country at the centre of a macro-regional system favoured the change in Turkish geographical perception or spatial consciousness of distance from the surrounding regions. The idea of being equidistant from other regions soon became a rationale for the launch of a multidirectional policy, which has become a peculiarity of JDP foreign policy. Moreover, Turkey's status as a central country gave it the responsibility to open relations with all the neighbouring areas. According to Davutoğlu's geographical imagination,[11] Turkey was called on to emerge as a leading and inspiring country

and Hillal Dessouki, eds. 2008. *The Foreign Policies of Arab States: The Challenge of Globalization.* Cairo: American University in Cairo Press.

[9] Ulrich, Krotz and James Sperling. 2011. 'Discord and Collaboration in Franco-American Relations: What Can Role Theory Tell Us?' In *Role Theory in International Relations: Approaches and Analyses*, edited by Sebastian Harnisch, Cornelia Frank and Hanns W. Maull, 213–33, 213. Abingdon, New York: Routledge.

[10] Davutoğlu, Ahmet. 2008. 'Turkey's New Foreign Policy Vision: An Assessment of 2007'. *Insight Turkey* 10 (1): 77–96. See also Aras, Bülent. 2009. 'The Davutoğlu Era in Turkish Foreign Policy'. *Insight Turkey* 11 (3): 127–42; Kara, Mehtap and Ahmet Sözen. 2016. 'Change and Continuity in Turkish Foreign Policy: Evaluating Pre-AKP and AKP Periods' National Role Conceptions'. *Uluslararası İlişkiler* 13 (52): 47–66.

[11] Davutoğlu's idea of geographical imagination has interdisciplinary roots that can be traced back, on the one hand, to the geographical revolution carried out in the 1970s by the Anglo-Saxon current known as Behaviourism and, on the other hand, to the historical tradition of the Ottoman past. The trend of behavioural geography, also known as 'geography of perception', develops a new form of geographical investigation in which the subjective components of the analysis, especially the individual's 'mental maps', assume greater interest for the geographer. See Downs, Roger M. and David Stea, eds. 1973. *Image and Environment: Cognitive Mapping and Spatial Behavior.* Chicago: Aldine.

for the surrounding regions at the confluence of 'Afro-Eurasia',[12] a definition that broadly reflected the contours of the former *Pax Ottomanica*,[13] by adopting a new foreign policy strategy based on three pillars: a greater depth (strategic), a multifaceted orientation (multidirectionality) and the inclusion of non-state actors in the conduct of foreign policy (total performance) considered decisive for the consolidation of interdependence. Kardaş argues that while the 'zero problems' policy has drawn wide scholarly attention and media coverage, the 'central country' concept is more important to understand Turkey's foreign policy before and after the Arab turmoil of 2011.[14] These theories completely overturned the previous paradigm and geopolitical representation of Turkey's 'cuspness', namely of a country on the periphery of international politics.[15] Although the influence of Turgut Özal and Ismail Cem in diversifying Turkish foreign policy should not be underestimated, it was in the JDP era that Turkish foreign policy came to be truly multidimensional.[16]

Another domestic factor for Turkey's diversified foreign policy was the definitive affirmation of the Muslim middle class, whose growth had begun during the Özal period. The opening of political space made Turkish policymakers more responsive to public opinion and civil society.[17] Traditionally, the role of civil society in Turkish foreign policy was marginal and was limited to playing a passive role of complementarity with the state. The civil society's organizations soon became active players both in the decision-making process and in the practices of foreign policy, by actively promoting policies backed by the state.[18] Undoubtedly, various powerful business groups and NGOs in Turkey pursue different political agendas; but their investments and their humanitarian and educational activities abroad have been critical in shaping Turkey's new foreign policy vision, as well as in strengthening its soft power instruments in various regions of the world. As a consequence, issues such as economics, development, cooperation and humanitarian aid have become increasingly relevant, and a

---

[12] Davutoğlu, Ahmet. 2001. *Stratejik Derinlik. Türkiye'nin Uluslararası Konumu*, 195, 331. İstanbul: Küre.

[13] Erşen, Emre and Seçkin Köstem, eds. 2019. *Turkey's Pivot to Eurasia: Geopolitics and Foreign Policy in a Changing World Order*. Abingdon: Routledge.

[14] Kardaş, Şaban. 2012. 'From Zero Problems to Leading the Change: Making Sense of Transformation in Turkey's Regional Policy'. *TEPAV-ILPI Turkey Policy Brief Series* 5 (1): 1–8.

[15] Altunışık, Meliha B. 2014. 'Geopolitical Representation of Turkey's Cuspness: Discourse and Practice'. In *The Role, Position and Agency of Cusp States in International Relations*, edited by Marc Herzog and Philip Robins, 25–40. London: Routledge.

[16] Akgün and Özkan, 'Turkey's Opening', 528.

[17] Kubicek, Paul. 2005. 'The European Union and Grassroots Democratization in Turkey'. *Turkish Studies* 6 (3): 361–77.

[18] Akgün and Özkan, 'Turkey's Opening', 539.

broader agenda has emerged in the international context, characterized by the reduction of the value of military power and territorial defence. Simultaneously, the overemphasis on the security factors has slowly changed towards a more trade-oriented foreign policy in both the regional and global arena. Turkey's foreign and security policy has moved towards a more Kantian approach, with emphasis on being active, cooperative and constructive. The interlocking tripod of power, wealth and status has helped to frame the Turkish foreign economic policy.[19] In this tripod, the quest for wealth and status has required additional efforts in order to increase the engagement of new actors and non-traditional regions, extending beyond the regional limits of Turkey's foreign policy. Thus, Turkey has moved from its traditional 'threat assessment approach' towards an 'active engagement in regional political systems'.[20] As part of this new agenda, Turkey has expanded its diplomatic, economic and humanitarian networks towards different regions, including SSA, adopting a multidirectional approach. Turkey's approach is defined by the ability to project her influence and interests in different directions, while being open to all regions around the Turkish cornerstone.[21] These developments reflect a new stance towards the Global South – especially towards the Least Developed Countries (LDC) – after years of disinterest, opening a new window for channelling Turkey's interests in the global political economy. As such, during the last two decades, Turkey has developed a unique ability to talk to both the West and the Rest.[22]

The change in geopolitical representation was a direct consequence of the systemic and regional upheavals which followed the fall of the Berlin Wall. According to Davutoğlu, the brief American hegemony and the beginning of a multipolar or nonpolar era was providing a significant range of opportunities for Turkey to improve its international status. However, in order to exploit the many external incentives, the country was called upon to conduct a wide-ranging review of its identity and its role in the international context. In other words, Turkey had to change its national role conception in order to improve its foreign policy behaviour. Turkey had to stop thinking only about itself as a passive ally of the West and promote its own autonomous strategy that drew on

[19] Katzenstein, Peter J., ed. 1978. *Between Power and Plenty: Foreign Economic Policies of Advanced Industrial States*. Madison: University of Wisconsin Press.
[20] Kardaş, Şaban. 2010. 'Turkey: Redrawing the Middle East Map or Building Sandcastles?' *Middle East Policy* 17 (1): 115–36.
[21] Davutoğlu, 'Turkey's New Foreign Policy Vision', 77–96; Danforth, Nicholas. 2008. 'Ideology and Pragmatism in Turkish Foreign Policy: from Ataturk to the AKP.' *Turkish Policy Quarterly* 7 (3): 83–95; Sözen, 'A Paradigm Shift in Turkish Foreign Policy', 103–23.
[22] Donelli, Federico and Ariel S. González Levaggi. 2016. 'Becoming Global Actor: The Turkish agenda for the Global South.' *Rising Power Quarterly* 1 (2): 93–115.

the historical, geographical and cultural past. It was also the others' perception about Turkey that had to change. This would be possible through new foreign policy behaviour, characterized by increased public diplomacy, positioning itself to enhance stability in the region by seeking innovative mechanisms and channels to resolve conflicts, by encouraging positive change and by building cross-cultural bridges of dialogue and understanding.[23] In line with the broader opportunities in the international political system and Davutoğlu theories, Turkey has redefined its international identity from being a passive to a constructive and more independent global actor. In this sense, its role in world politics has been shaped by ruptures, alliances, tensions and realignments that can be interpreted in relation to its geographical location and the multiple geopolitical identities.[24] Simultaneously, Turkey started to replace its traditional foreign policy. The JDP government rejected the former wary attitude towards any region other than the West and it adopted a proactive foreign policy aimed at creating a 'strategic depth' by expanding Turkey's zone of influence in different regions, drawing on the opportunities based on geography, economic power and the imperial past to reconnect the country with its historical hinterland.[25] Emblematic of the de-securitization of foreign policy promoted by JDP was the development of a medium power conception, with the consequent change in the tools used in international relations. Specifically, in post-2003, a firm incentive from the system for Turkey's rising role in regional politics came from the endorsement and support of the United States. According to the Bush administration Turkey appeared as the Sunni's 'light green' power perfect to counterbalance the rising Shia's green wave of the Islamic Republic of Iran. As such, Turkish foreign policymakers adopted a more regionally oriented foreign policy. The Turkish soft power quickly gained credibility not only in the Middle East but also in the West. In a period of history distinguished by the worsening of the complex relationship between the West and the Islamic world, the international fame of

---

[23] Wheeler, 'Ankara to Africa', 47.

[24] Turkey's alternative geopolitical identities have been defined, according to Şener Aktürk, in four senses – Pan-Islamism, Pan-Turkism, Western-ism, and Eurasianism – which reflect alternative interpretations about Turkey's national interests in the contemporary world. See Aktürk, Şener. 2015. 'The Fourth Style of Politics: Eurasianism as a Pro-Russian Rethinking of Turkey's Geopolitical Identity'. *Turkish Studies* 16 (1): 54–5.

[25] For a comprehensive discussion on the new course of Turkish foreign policy under the JDP rule, see Öniş, Ziya and Şuhnaz Yılmaz. 2009. 'Between Europeanization and Euro-Asianism: Foreign Policy Activism in Turkey during the AKP Era'. *Turkish Studies* 10 (1): 7–24; Saraçoğlu, Cenk and Özhan Demirkol. 2015. 'Nationalism and Foreign Policy Discourse in Turkey Under the AKP Rule: Geography, History and National Identity'. *British Journal of Middle Eastern Studies* 42 (3): 301–19; Stein, Aron. 2015. *The Rise and Fall of the AKP's Foreign Policy: In Pursuit of a New Regional Order*. London: Routledge; Özcanab, Mesut, Talha Köseb and Ekrem Karakoç. 2015. 'Assessments of Turkish Foreign Policy in the Middle East During the Arab Uprisings'. *Turkish Studies* 16 (2): 1–24.

Turkey, as a Muslim state, popularized the idea of a Turkish model suitable to be applied to other regional countries. In the eyes of the Western observers, the Turkish peculiarity lay in the ability to harmonize Islam (cultural rather than political and ideological), democracy (mature by the standards of the region) and secularism (the logic of the state prevails over that of religion). A key element of the renewed Turkish regional activism was the rehabilitation of the imperial past and the recovery of the Ottoman cultural heritage. The strategic depth, cultural more than geographical, in the neighbouring regions was supported by a neo-Ottoman rhetoric tailored to the specific context, including an African one. Furthermore – as will be discussed in Chapter 6 – the reshuffling of the Middle East's geopolitical balances following the US invasion of Iraq gave new impetus to the race for regional leadership. The first decade of the new millennium, in particular, was marked by the growth of Iranian influence, the so-called Shiite Crescent. As a result, the Sunni powers, including Turkey, developed containment and counteraction strategies. These were the first stages of what was dubbed the new Middle East Cold War.[26] Among the regional complexes in which Iran had acquired important positions, there was also SSA and, in particular, the HOA. For this reason, behind the decision to adopt an assertive and multidirectional foreign policy there was also the conviction that the Middle East arena had expanded beyond the traditional borders.

The new Turkish autonomous and multidirectional approach set the stage for a debate on Turkey's 'shift of axis', that is, the erosion of Turkey's predominantly Western orientation.[27] Even though the Turkish FPE firmly denied arguments to that effect, Turkish foreign policy undoubtedly took an autonomous course, that diverged from or converged with Western partners from time to time.[28] Such a shift proved one of the classic realism principles: that states with greater power resources – wealth, population, size, social and historical coherence – are more likely to have a proactive foreign policy.[29] Part of this growing assertiveness

[26] Gause, Gregory F. 2014. *Beyond Sectarianism: The New Middle East Cold War*. Doha: Brookings Institute Center; Santini, Ruth Hanau. 2017. 'A New Regional Cold War in the Middle East and North Africa: Regional Security Complex Theory Revisited'. *The International Spectator* 52 (4): 93–111.

[27] Zalewski, Piotr. 2010. 'The Self-appointed Superpower: Turkey Goes It Alone'. *World Policy Journal* 27 (4): 97–102; Kiniklioglu, Suat. 2010. 'Turkey's Neighbourhood and Beyond: Tectonic Transformation at Work?' *The International Spectator* 45 (4): 93–100; Bagdonas, Özlem Demirtaş. 2012. 'A Shift of Axis in Turkish Foreign Policy or A Marketing Strategy?'. Turkey's Uses of Its "Uniqueness" vis-à-vis the West/Europe'. *Turkish Journal of Politics* 3 (2): 111–32.

[28] Yorulmazlar, Emirhan and Ebru Turhan. 2015. 'Turkish Foreign Policy towards the Arab Spring: Between Western Orientation and Regional Disorder'. *Journal of Balkan and Near Eastern Studies* 17 (3): 337–52.

[29] Walt, Stephen M. 1987. *The Origins of Alliance*. Ithaca: Cornell University Press.

has been an increasingly active emphasis on Africa. In other words, Turkey's growing relationship with Africa was the result of the interweaving of domestic and systemic – regional and international – transformations.

3.2 The open policy towards sub-Saharan Africa (2003–10)

The new foreign policy course followed by JDP-led governments fostered a gradual rapprochement with SSA. The open policy towards SSA (2003–11) should therefore be included in the wide scenario of change in the Turkish strategic approach, aimed at gaining greater depth through a vision-oriented, flexible, proactive and constructive approach that would expand the number of its international partners. Indeed, following the new approach to the external environment – systemic and sub-systemic – and the aim of increasing its international status as a global actor, Turkey improved its ties beyond the traditional links with North Africa and SSA, and these are probably the regions in which Turkey has decided to invest most and, as the former ambassador Hazar pointed out, the Africa initiative is likely to become a lasting element of Turkey's foreign policy.[30] In order to encourage these developments, a shift was necessary in the Turkish geographical imagination of both its own country (*national role conception*), nowadays conceived as an Afro-Eurasian state,[31] and of SSA, which was no longer considered as a poor and backward place but as a fecund ground full of opportunities. Even at the beginning of the new millennium, the geographical representation of the continent prevalent among policymakers and the Turkish public was very confused. Egypt was grouped with the Middle East rather than being considered as an African country. The other Muslim countries on the Mediterranean coast made up a separate area, a sort of periphery of the old empire and an appendix to the Middle East. Sub-Saharan countries, instead, including countries on the Red Sea that had once had links with the empire, were considered part of a 'remainder', unknown to most. Modern Turkey had paid little attention to SSA, known to the Turkish public only by way of TV

---

[30] Hazar, Numan. 2015. 'Turkey's Policy of Outreach to Africa: An Assessment'. *Journal of Business Economics and Political Science* 4 (7): 3–11.

[31] The new orientation of Turkish policymakers was also confirmed by official statements. The same website of the Ministry of Foreign Affairs in the section related to Africa underlined that 'Turkey, essentially positioned as an Afro-Eurasian country, in 1998 instigated an Action Plan for Opening to Africa in the frame of its multilateral foreign policy, in order to accelerate its political, military and economic relations with Africa'. http://www.mfa.gov.tr/turkey-africa-relations.en.mfa. See also, Aras, Bülent. 2007. 'Turkey and the Middle East: Frontiers of the New Geographic Imagination'. *Australian Journal of International Affairs* 61 (4): 471–88.

images of famine, poverty, AIDS and other negative aspects. For this reason, simultaneously with the opening of official relations, the approach to SSA was marked by a significant psychological path directed towards the internalization of a new awareness of the southern lands of the Sahara Desert. Despite all the efforts made, Turkey's perception of Africa is still of a divided continent. North Africa is still considered an adjunct of the Middle East, to the extent that it is treated together by the same ministry's department or desk. Unlike in the past, however, SSA is not neglected or downgraded as an area of low relevance but has acquired a central place on Turkey's foreign policy agenda as a land full of opportunities and prosperity.

Turkey initially operated in SSA similarly to other non-traditional extra-regional actors, focusing on economic development, diplomatic relations and humanitarian aid without concern for political issues. Recalling some of the guidelines drawn by Cem's document 'Opening up to Africa Policy' (1998), the JDP government decided to set up an opening strategy after it assumed power. The new government's intentions were made public with the approval of the Development of the Economic Relations with African Countries strategy prepared by the undersecretary of foreign trade in 2003. As prescribed by the previous plan drawn up by Cem, Turkey, in order to increase its involvement in Africa, had to exploit all the tools of its soft power such as political contact, image-building, cultural contacts, scholarships and technical assistance. Soft power was considered the easiest way to break the mutual distrust. Turkey's political activities in Africa were immediately distinguished by a simultaneous involvement of Turkish social forces and close cooperation with their African counterparts. Since 2004, Turkey has pursued concrete policies towards Africa, gradually increasing the budget for aid – humanitarian and development – directly or through international organizations, through economic and trade agreements, bilateral projects of development and emergency aid. However, the real turning point came in 2005, designated in Turkey as the 'Year of Africa'. As Siradağ has underlined, such designation represented unmistakable proof of Turkey's commitment to building stronger relations with Africa.[32] It was also the beginning of Turkey's involvement through a greater diplomatic activism both bilaterally and multilaterally, and it marked a period of diversification of relations across a range of areas. Turkey enhanced its relations at the institutional level with Africa, and it has multiplied its diplomatic representations. In 2004 there

---

[32] Siradağ, Abdurrahim. 2013. 'The Making of the New Turkish Foreign and Security Policy towards Africa'. *Africa Insight* 43 (1): 15–31.

were only twelve Turkish embassies in Africa. Over the last fifteen years, efforts in this direction have favoured the rapid spread of Turkish diplomatic representations on the continent. A decade later, the number had risen to thirty-four embassies (2013), and then it grew again to the current number of forty-one (2019). Increasing its diplomatic representation corps also paved the way for more frequent visits between representatives of Turkey and those of the African states. In turn, new embassies from sub-Saharan African countries have also been opening in Ankara.[33] The large-scale Turkish diplomatic effort is unparalleled and differs from that of other emerging extra-regional players. The results of these efforts started to bear fruit in 2005 when Turkey obtained observer status with the AU. More precisely, on 5 May 2005, the Turkish Embassy in Addis Ababa was recognized as the most important African regional organization. The decisive factor for the recognition was the trip made two months earlier by Prime Minister Recep Tayyip Erdoğan, who visited Ethiopia and South Africa as a tangible sign of the renewed Turkish propensity towards SSA. The trip also had significant value for the Turkish bureaucracy and public opinion, since it was the first time that a Turkish prime minister officially visited a country south of the equator. In the following months, Turkey's visibility in SSA increased thanks to bilateral initiatives and to Turkey's multilateral commitments. Ankara significantly increased its humanitarian assistance and contributions to UN missions on the continent.[34] As a clear implementation stage of its wider African policy, Turkey provided personnel to five UN peacekeeping operations in Africa. Turkey also contributed financially towards UN peacekeeping missions and is reported to have contributed US$7 million to the costs.[35]

Turkey's political activities in SSA were immediately distinguished by both the involvement of Turkish social forces and close cooperation with their African counterparts. Alongside the institutional commitment promoted by the state, Turkish civil society launched a series of autonomous initiatives. As mentioned earlier, the different state–society relationship promoted by the JDP government had opened foreign policy to the involvement of non-state actors. Moreover, the

---

[33] In 1997 the only sub-Saharan country to be represented in Ankara was South Africa. Nigeria reopened its embassy shortly thereafter, but most other African countries now represented responded to Turkey's new policy only after 2005. Further embassies were opened in Côte d'Ivoire and Tanzania in 2009, and in Angola, Cameroon, Ghana, Madagascar, Mali and Uganda in 2010, adding to its existing missions in the DRC, Ethiopia, Kenya, Senegal and Sudan.

[34] These were UNMIS, Sudan (police and military personnel), MINURCAT, Chad/Central African Republic (police), MONUC/MONUSCO, DRC (police), UNOCI, Côte d'Ivoire (police), and UNMIL, Liberia (police).

[35] Özerdem, Alpaslan. 2019. 'Turkey as an Emerging Global Humanitarian and Peacebuilding Actor'. In *The Routledge Handbook of Turkish Politics*, edited by Alpaslan Özerdem and Matthew Whiting, 470–80. London, New York: Routledge.

diversification of the actors involved in foreign policy decision-making processes reflected the new concept of total performance introduced by Davutoğlu that aimed to include non-state actors, including NGOs, businesses, charities, think tanks and the public, among others, in the process of policymaking.[36] As Akpınar has argued, under the direction of Davutoğlu, Turkish foreign policy shifted from a single-track diplomacy, in which the state (official and military bureaucracy) was the only primary actor, to a multitrack diplomacy, in which a growing number of actors became influential.[37]

The opening agenda towards SSA became a perfect laboratory for this new approach. Civil society organizations have contributed to the growth of Turkey–Africa relations in a private-led approach similar to that championed by the United States and the EU. The business-related sector began to promote bilateral investment and trade with Africa through various associations[38] such as the Union of Chambers and Commodity Exchanges of Turkey and its affiliate the Foreign Economic Relations Board,[39] the Independent Industrialists' and Businessmen's Association,[40] and the Turkish Confederation of Businessmen and Industrialists.[41]

Among the civil society's organizations, the Gülen movement had a special place in the formulation and practical implementation of Turkey's opening up to SSA, above all in the education sector through the spreading of schools. These schools were well known for their educational and humanitarian efforts, which are in line with the UN Sustainable Development Agenda.[42] Therefore, Gülenist schools had become the leading implementers of Turkey's public diplomacy in Africa and the first of its kind as a Turkish non-governmental engagement with the continent. Meanwhile, in order to increase the knowledge of the Turkish public and arouse their interest in Africa, a series of meetings, conferences

[36] Aras, Bülent. 2012. 'Turkey's Mediation and Friends of Mediation Initiative'. *Turkey Policy Brief Series (TEPAV)* 5:1–2.

[37] Akpınar, 'Turkey's Peacebuilding in Somalia', 735–57.

[38] Kanat, Kilic, Ahmet Tekelioglu and Kadir Ustun, eds. 2015. *Politics and Foreign Policy in Turkey: Historical and Contemporary Perspectives*, 49–56. Ankara: SETA; Mason, Robert. 2015. 'Patterns and Consequences of Economic Engagement across Sub-Saharan Africa: A Comparative Analysis of Chinese, British and Turkish Policies'. In *Working Paper Centre for International Studies (CIS)*. London: London School of Economics; Han, Aslan Davut and Selcuk Bahadir. 2016. 'Africa In Turkey's Foreign Policy Agenda: Trade, Economic and Military Cooperation'. *Kwartalnik Naukowy Uczelni Vistula* 4 (50): 139–48.

[39] At that time, this association represented major industrial and financial concerns which are generally considered to adhere to the secular approach to Turkish politics and lifestyle.

[40] An organization of small and medium businesspeople, often family-owned and known as the 'Anatolian Tigers'.

[41] Association that represents the companies affiliated to the Gülen Movement.

[42] Shinn, David. 2015. *Hizmet in Africa: The Activities and Significance of the Gülen Movement*. Los Angeles: Tsehai Publishers.

and discussions were organized by some of the first Turkish think tanks. For example, since 2005, TASAM[43] has hosted a Turkey–Africa Congress to which academics from both Turkey and African countries have been invited.[44] These seminars have had the merit of raising Turkish analysts' and scholars' awareness of African issues, opening the way to an increasing number of publications. Despite the fact that among the most active non-state actors there were two faith-based subjects – the Gülen movement and the IHH – during the period of opening up to Africa, the religious dimension was toned down. Turkey's approach was essentially pragmatic and interest-oriented. In this sense sectarian affinity was exploited in contexts where it could have facilitated relationships. It was the case, for example, in Cameroon, where Turkish entrepreneurs sought to establish alliances with local Muslim businesses in order to gain advantage over their Italian competitors.[45] Conversely, in countries where religion could have created problems, that is, Nigeria where religious conflicts are common between the Muslim and Christian populations, Turkey displayed its secular democracy and aspired to take credit for it.[46] In this initial phase, however, the involvement of non-state actors was not coordinated by the state. Although these always operated under government patronage, their actions were completely independent – an approach that provided several advantages but also led to many limitations; in particular, in some sectors such as the economic sector or epistemic communities, there was a clear overlap with a consequent waste of resources.

During these years, the relations with SSA made more progress than the Turkish authorities had initially predicted. Turkish policy began to pay back in economic and political terms. In 2000, Turkey's trade with sub-Saharan African countries was worth $742 million; by 2008 it had increased to $5.7 billion.[47] Turkey was able to capitalize on its efforts and the growing trust in 2008 when the AU summit, held in Addis Ababa, declared Turkey as a strategic partner – a recognition that until that moment only a few other extra-regional powers had received. A few months later, in May 2008, Turkey became the twenty-fifth non-regional member of the African Development Bank. Association with the bank was seen as a method of providing finance to Turkish construction companies

---

[43] Turkish Asian Center for Strategic Studies.

[44] Uchehara, Kieran E. 2008. 'Continuity and Change in Turkish Foreign Policy Toward Africa'. *Akademik Bakış* 2 (3): 43–64.

[45] At that time, Italians were the largest trade partners of Cameroon. 'Turkey and Africa: Ottoman Dreaming'. *Economist*, 27 March 2010.

[46] Korkut, Umut and Ilke Civelekoglu. 2013. 'Becoming a Regional Power While Pursuing Material Gains: The Case of Turkish Interest in Africa'. *International Journal* 68 (1): 196.

[47] Ministry of Foreign Affairs Website, http://www.mfa.gov.tr/turkiye-afrika-iliskileri.tr.mfa.

engaged in many contracts in African countries, while demonstrating Turkish goodwill in a practical way.[48] Turkey gained representation in other African regional organizations, such as the Economic Community of West African States in 2005 and the East African Community in 2010. During the same year, Turkey organized the First Turkey–Africa Cooperation Summit on the theme of 'Solidarity and partnership for a common future' in Istanbul under the auspices of the Turkish president Abdullah Gül. The summit, which had been preceded by two other fora – the Turkey–Africa Civil Society Organization Forum and the Turkish–Africa Business Forum – was considered to be the beginning of a steady and sustainable cooperation process. It was a meeting of high-level officials from Turkey and the African countries, with more than fifty African Union members, akin to the Forum on China–Africa Cooperation (FOCAC).[49] While FOCAC is mainly a ministerial conference, the Turkey–Africa Summit distinguished itself by including Turkish civil society representatives who contributed to assessing the opportunities and needs of the African continent.[50] Representatives of eighty civil society organizations from across Africa were invited. The African organizations were matched by eighty Turkish civil society organizations.

These initiatives constituted an important icebreaker in relations with African countries. To make up for lost time and accelerate relations between Turkey and Africa, the summit provided the diplomatic framework to increase bilateral contacts and search for new ways of developing relations.[51] At the same time, it highlighted the value of the role that non-governmental organizations could play in supporting and supplementing official activities to strengthen relations with African countries. Furthermore, and most importantly, Turkey had short- and long-term political expectations from the summit. In the short run, Turkey sought the support of African countries for the non-permanent seat at the UN Security Council in October 2008. Turkey secured the support of African countries, as it was elected to the Council with a vote of 151.[52] Another important Turkish action was the formation of the Africa Strategic Coordination Committee and this should not be ignored. The Committee was

---

[48] Wheeler, 'Ankara to Africa'.

[49] FOCAC was established in 2006 and Beijing committed to double aid to Africa up to 2009. This was designed to demonstrate the growing importance of Africa among Chinese decision makers. For details, see Taylor, Ian. 2006. 'China's Oil Diplomacy in Africa'. *International Affairs* 82 (5): 937–59; Li, Anshan and April Funeka Yazini. 2013. *Forum on China-Africa Cooperation: The Politics of Human Resource Development*. Oxford: Africa Institute of South Africa.

[50] Bilgic, Ali and Daniela Nascimento. 2014. 'Turkey's New Focus on Africa: Causes and Challenges'. NOREF Policy Brief.

[51] Özkan, 'What Drives Turkey's Involvement in Africa?', 535.

[52] Akgün and Özkan, 'Turkey's Opening', 536.

formed in 2010 and the Turkish Ministry of Foreign Affairs was assigned as the coordinating institution, arguably lending weight and credence to its mission.

The importance – symbolic and political – of these initiatives should not be ignored as they also assisted in changing perceptions in both Turkey and Africa. The election as a non-permanent member of the UN Security Council for 2009–10 was a great success for the Turkish government. By taking advantage of its election to the UN Security Council, Turkey increased its involvement in the activities of the main institutions of global governance, playing the role of a constructive global actor. At the same time, the Turkish agenda was characterized by the progressive transnationalization of agents in the field (multi-stakeholders) through the involvement of civil society organizations – NGOs, trade associations, charitable foundations – mostly engaged in humanitarian, educational and development aid. These Turkish non-state actors have common religious backgrounds and more or less direct links with the ruling JDP party. Thanks to this twin-track policy, cooperation within multilateral fora and the presence of an active and internationally recognized civil society, Turkish credibility increased. As pointed out by several scholars, international credibility is a determining variable for emerging states that want to contribute actively to the global governance and to solve international issues.[53] As a consequence, Turkey's international role was recognized and the policy pursued in those years in Africa proved successful. At the same time, Turkish policymakers became more confident that they could play a more important role in regional contexts, including in SSA. A second turning point came in 2011, after the one in 2005, with their growing involvement in the humanitarian crisis that devastated Somalia.

3.3 The main factors that drive Turkey's engagement

In the early years, the Turkish opening towards sub-Saharan countries produced political and economic results, increasing the total trade volume and raising Turkey's visibility throughout the whole continent. During the same period, through both its membership in international organizations and its own bilateral activism, Turkey received increasing recognition from the African people, as shown by the 2009 UN Security Council election. There is a complex set of

---

[53] Wang, Hongying and Erik French. 2013. 'Middle Range Powers in Global Governance'. *Third World Quarterly* 34 (6): 985–99.

factors explaining why the Turkish policy towards SSA has gained momentum over the past two decades. Among these, the nascent role of middle and great emerging powers in the global political economy, alongside the increasing presence of non-Western actors such as China, India, South Korea and Brazil in Africa, provides some clues to the state-to-system linkages. Ten years after the beginning of the new millennium, a new power dynamic is taking shape within the global political economy that marks the end of American hegemony. This dynamic is marked by the rapid shift of the centres of economic power away from the West.[54] At the same time, the political economy has been changing towards a more open and profit-oriented one, naturally inclined to search out new markets beyond the traditional ones.[55] Turkey, like other emerging powers, depends on a growing engagement with external markets to sustain its economic growth. Since 2005, Turkey has pursued material gains, such as increasing trade opportunities and investments, by convincing African states of their shared values and goals with Turkey. This has been the case in Turkey's growing economic relations with countries such as Zimbabwe, Mozambique and Angola, where the Ankara government has seen great potential – mostly in the textile, agricultural and construction sectors.[56]

The motives behind Turkey's opening up towards SSA can be categorized in three interrelated dimensions: changes in the international and regional environment (external factors), economic interests, and foreign policy considerations (strategy, national role identity). More specifically, the following seven reasons play an essential role in an explanatory framework:

first, Turkey's difficulties in the EU accession process – like Cem, Davutoğlu also believed that good relations with any other region, distinct from the EU, would be beneficial for Turkey's candidacy for EU membership; the difficulties of such a path were also evident since the beginning. In 2004, the negotiation progress began to slow down due to the admission of the old Turkish rival, the Republic of Cyprus, and the opposition from France, Germany and Austria. As a result, the diversification of political and economic relations became an increasingly urgent necessity.

[54] Shaw, Timothy M., Andrew F. Cooper and Gregory T. Chin. 2009. 'Emerging Powers and Africa: Implications for/from Global Governance?' *Politikon: South African Journal of Political Studies* 36 (1): 27–44.
[55] Özdemir, Elvan and Zehra Vildan Serin. 2016. 'Trading State and Reflections of Foreign Policy: Evidence from Turkish Foreign Policy'. *Procedia Economics and Finance* 38:468–75.
[56] Mason, 'Patterns and Consequences'.

second, to pursue material gains – as argued by Korkut and Civelekoglu, Turkey's presence in Africa is part of an attempt to involve African states in Turkey's pursuit of material gains by convincing those states of their shared values and goals with Turkey.[57] Material gains consist broadly of economic advantages, such as increased trade opportunities and investments, as well as political visibility in global affairs. In addition, the opening up to Africa was also determined by Turkey's need to diversify its economic relations in a new global political economy[58] and to search for new markets for Turkish products.[59] It should be noted that the export-oriented Anatolian entrepreneurs, the core of the JDP constituency, pushed the government to open new markets in which they could increase their business – an approach that can be seen in the early years of the JDP that led to the rise of a 'trading-state', which, according to some scholars,[60] was behind the Turkish foreign policy agenda, that is, it was a policy of economic interdependence aimed at earning material benefits.[61]

third, looking for greater operating autonomy from traditional Western allies in order to display Turkey's new proactive strategy – under JDP power, Turkey embarked upon an increasingly self-centred autonomous approach in international politics. The cornerstone of this new approach, as expressed by then Foreign Minister Davutoğlu (later, the prime minister), was to 'determine our vision, set our objectives […] We might succeed or fail in our initiatives, but the crucial point is that we implement our own policies'.[62] Even more than the Middle East, Africa was a perfect laboratory in which Turkey could pursue a policy

---

[57] Korkut and Civelekoglu, 'Becoming a Regional Power', 188.
[58] Özkan, Mehmet. 2012. 'A New Actor or Passer-By? The Political Economy of Turkey's Engagement with Africa'. *Journal of Balkan and Near Eastern Studies* 14 (1): 113.
[59] Eyrice Tepeciklioğlu, Elem. 2015. 'What Is Turkey Doing in Africa? African Opening in Turkish Foreign Policy'. *Centre for Policy and Research on Turkey (ResearchTurkey)* 4 (4): 95–106.
[60] Kirişci, Kemal. 2009. 'The Transformation of Turkish Foreign Policy: The Rise of the Trading State'. *New Perspectives on Turkey* 40:29–57; Özdemir and Serin, 'Trading State and Reflections of Foreign Policy', 468–75.
[61] The concept of trading-state, contextualized by Kirişci, was introduced by Rosecrance to describe the rising of a new trading world in which interdependence is replacing the use of the military in world politics. See Rosecrance, Richard. 1986. *The Rise of the Trading State: Commerce and Conquest in the Modern World*. New York: Basic Books.
[62] Davutoğlu, Ahmet. 2012. 'Principles of Turkish Foreign Policy and Regional Political Structuring'. *Turkey Policy Brief Series: TEPAV-ILPI* 3:6. A sign of this more independent approach was the vote in the Turkish Parliament on 1 March 2003 refusing permission to the Bush administration to use Turkish territory for the movements of US troops to the northern border of Iraq to open a second front against Saddam Hussein's government. Since that point, it has become clear that Turkey could strike out in a new, independent foreign policy path in the region and beyond.

independent of its traditional Western allies without incurring excessive costs.[63] Indeed, Africa represents a non-Western sphere in which Ankara can consolidate its economic and political interests with less constraints.

fourth, gaining political visibility and support for Turkey in international and regional fora – as shown in the previous chapter, Turkey has had first-hand experience of its low political weight in key international organizations. To prevent this from happening again, the JDP government adopted the idea of rhythmic diplomacy. This concept, which is considered as one of the crucial dimensions of the JDP's foreign policy paradigm, refers to Turkey's active involvement in international organizations and in international initiatives.[64] According to Turkish foreign policy makers, this approach allows the expansion of the network of relationships and, simultaneously, increases the position and international popularity of the country.

fifth, religious charitable duties – inspired by the Ottoman model of spreading cultural, political and religious influences abroad, Turkey's policy towards Africa and, more generally, towards the Global South also has some religious motives.[65] Even though religious ties are an important element in rapprochement with SSA, especially in a legitimizing way, it should not be overestimated. Religion appears to be a tool rather than the driving force. Religious motivation was fundamental especially for the involvement of Turkish civil society through NGOs and foundations that operate in Africa in various fields including humanitarian aid. Most of the activities carried out by these private non-state actors are promoted as Islamic duties.[66]

sixth, serving as an area of Turkish foreign policy that has produced a general domestic consensus and virtually no disagreement between the state, civil society and the business sector – the growing presence in Africa has gone hand in hand with the involvement of civil society, especially in the implementation policy on the ground. Indeed, when Turkey launched its policy of openness towards Africa, the relationship

---

[63] Donelli, Federico. 2015. 'Turkey's Presence in Somalia: a Humanitarian Approach'. In *The Depth of Turkish Geopolitics in the AKP's Foreign Policy: From Europe to an Extended Neighbourhood*, edited by Alessia Chiriatti, Emidio Diodato, Salih Dogan, Federico Donelli and Bahri Yilmaz, 35–51. Perugia: Università per Stranieri Perugia.

[64] Sözen, Ahmet. 2011. 'A Paradigm Shift in Turkish Foreign Policy: Transition and Challenges'. In *Islamization of Turkey under the AKP Rule*, edited by Birol Yesilada and Barry M. Rubin, 101–21, 116. Abingdon: Routledge.

[65] Wheeler, 'Ankara to Africa', 43.

[66] Özkan, 'Turkey's Religious and Socio-Political Depth in Africa', 48.

between the state and society had changed, moving from an attitude
of mutual hostility to constructive cooperation capable of promoting
joint actions, even abroad, while preserving mutual autonomy.[67] As will
be discussed in Chapter 5, this dynamic resulted in the adoption of a
multitrack approach. The multitrack concept asserts that the individual
efforts of a variety of actors can complement each other and combine
to form a larger framework of action. Turkey has chosen to use this
approach in an unconventional way by creating a state-controlled
interagency coordination.[68]

seventh, fostering sustainable economic development by exporting Turkey's
managerial skills and technological know-how – building on its previous
experience in Central Asia, Turkey has chosen to operate in Africa
with the belief of being able to export its model of institutional policy
development and economic growth. Turkey has attempted to promote
a middle way, or a third way, through the implementation of a win-win
policy in Africa which includes peacebuilding efforts and a policy of
mutual empowerment.

---

[67] For a comprehensive discussion on the changing relations between state and society under the JDP power, see Keyman, E. Fuat and Ahmet İçduygu. 2003. 'Globalization, Civil Society and Citizenship in Turkey: Actors, Boundaries and Discourses'. *Citizenship Studies* 7 (2): 219–34; Solberg, Anne R. 2007. 'The Role of Turkish Islamic Networks in the Western Balkans'. *Southeast Europe Journal of Politics and Society* 55 (4): 429–62; Özbudun, Ergun. 2012. 'Turkey-Plural Society and Monolithic State'. In *Democracy, Islam, & Secularism in Turkey*, edited by Ahmet Kuru and Alfred Stepan, 61–94. New York: Columbia University Press.

[68] Genc, Savas and Oguzhan Tekin. 2014. 'Turkey's Increased Engagement in Africa: The Potential, Limits and Future Perspective of Relations'. *European Journal of Economic and Political Studies* 7 (1): 87–115.

4

The Somali crisis and the emergence of Turkey's humanitarian-oriented policy

While the early years served the JDP government in launching a foreign policy strategy towards Africa almost from scratch, Turkey then chose to refine its agenda and target specific areas in which to increase its presence, such as the HOA. The real highlight of Turkey's African policy was the decision to intervene in the Somali crisis in 2011. Since then, Turkish involvement in the continent has changed rapidly to promote in the HOA and beyond the image of a reliable partner committed to the crisis resolution and the development of the continent. The cornerstone of the updated African agenda was the enhancement of humanitarian diplomacy. Somalia, at the time isolated internationally, provided an opportunity for the Turkish state to operate freely and test its humanitarian and post-crisis capacities. The change was also driven by regional developments and Turkey's desire to be a model and a source of inspiration for its neighbours, which had to cope with instability, regime change and domestic crises. Turkey's humanitarian commitment has allowed it to take a prominent role at the global level and to become one of the most committed countries in this area of niche diplomacy. These developments were particularly relevant because, on the one hand, they increased Turkish involvement in the HOA's issues, including political ones, and began to transform its initial approach and, on the other hand, they highlighted some of the peculiarities of Turkish intervention which, as discussed in the next chapter, will be expressed in Turkey's way for development and the idea of the Ankara consensus.

4.1 The HOA and the (long-ignored) Somali crisis

Following the 2008 summit, as pointed out by Özkan and Orakçı, after a first phase that was mainly formative in nature, relations between Turkey and Africa reached a new height in their complexities and, at the same time, evolved into a more mature political relationship.[1] The decision to play a leading role in the humanitarian and political crisis in Somalia was a landmark turning point in Turkey's African policy. When in 2011 the Turkish state chose to invest resources and part of the international credibility built up in the previous decade, Somalia was a country brought to its knees by a long civil war. Before the Turkish efforts, Somalia had witnessed the failure of twelve mediation attempts between 1991 and 2009, which were promoted by external actors (Ethiopia, Egypt, Djibouti, Kenya) and international organizations (UN, the Arab League, the Intergovernmental Agency on Development). Therefore, Turkey's engagement with Somalia began during a time of deep chaos for the African country and it represented a political gamble for the JDP government. At the same time, however, the harsh environment was particularly suitable for an emerging power eager to test new tools and its growing capabilities to consolidate its international role. The Turkish bet proved to be partly successful, making the country and its leaders popular throughout the continent. Besides, the role assumed by Turkey in Somalia pointed to a shift in its focus towards the political aspects of SSA's problems, opening a new phase in the Turkish African agenda.

The initial Turkish approach to SSA was spread evenly across all the regions, aimed at opening as many channels and relationships as possible. Since 2008, Turkish action has focused more on specific areas of the continent. The main Turkish focus in Africa became the HOA sub-region, which represents an important crossroad of interests and clashes. The HOA was still the core of the 'arc of instability' that was once defined by political observers in the 1970s as stretching from Afghanistan to the Middle East and West Africa via Yemen and Nigeria. Poverty, underdevelopment, anarchy, political instability, corruption and the suppression of human and civil rights in general are the characteristic features of the sub-region.[2] In this highly complex context, Turkey has increased its efforts to promote a new regional scenario in order to guarantee peace and stability which are considered necessary conditions for any other development. The decision to commit to solving the dramatic humanitarian and political crisis that had been afflicting Somalia over two decades changed the nature of Turkish involvement in sub-Saharan Africa. Indeed, Somalia holds a special place in Turkey's sub-Saharan engagement; it sets an example for understanding Turkey's

[1] Özkan, Mehmet and Serhat Orakçı. 2015. 'Viewpoint: Turkey as a "political" Actor in Africa – An Assessment of Turkish Involvement in Somalia'. *Journal of Eastern African Studies* 9 (2): 343–52.
[2] Bereketeab, Redie. 2013. *The Horn of Africa: Intra-State and Inter-State Conflicts and Security.* London: Pluto Press.

engagement with regions beyond its immediate neighbourhood. Turkey's efforts in relation to Somalia have marked a real turning point in the Turkish approach to the continent and specifically to the sub-region of the HOA. This shift in approach was part of a new phase in the Turkish agenda of opening up to the continent. To this end, Turkey increased the use of new policy tools such as mediation and peacekeeping. These political instruments offered Turkey a legitimate ground for its activities in a region from which it had been distant for many decades.[3] Thanks to them, the Turkish state was able to acquire greater regional and international visibility and increased influence over the whole continent. Furthermore, interventions aimed at improving dialogue between local actors helped to legitimize activities beyond national borders in the eyes of Turkish society. This trend helped to raise the Turkish public's awareness of African issues and problems, laying the groundwork for the emergence of the idea of the Ankara consensus.

The HOA is not only considered a gateway to the whole continent for the sale of Turkish goods but, from the new conservative elite's outlook, it is also part of the Greater Middle East or the New Middle East.[4] From this perspective, the HOA includes the dynamics, tensions and rivalries of Middle East geopolitics. Therefore, one can presume that Turkey aims to achieve two main goals: first, as an emerging middle power, Turkey seeks to expand its political influence to the detriment of regional rivals such as Saudi Arabia, Egypt and Iran; second, Turkey aspires to spread its interpretation of Islam in order to acquire a leading role within the Sunni world. Following these main objectives, since 2008 Turkey has increased its efforts to promote a new regional scenario in order to guarantee peace and stability, considered to be necessary conditions for any further development. In order to increase the involvement in the HOA, the Ankara government acted to consolidate existing bilateral ties with local actors. The first of these was Ethiopia. As seen earlier, diplomatic relations with Ethiopia started in 1896 during the reign of Sultan Abdülhamid II, and Ethiopia

---

3   Akpınar, 'Turkey's Peacebuilding in Somalia', 735–57.
4   While the term 'the Broader Middle East' has been officially accepted by NATO during the summit held in Istanbul on 28 and 29 June 2004, the term 'the Greater Middle East' has more commonly been used in the scientific literature and public opinion. For the birth of the idea of the 'Greater' Middle East during the Cold War, see Barrett, Roby Carol. 2007. 'Greater Middle East and the Cold War and the US Foreign Policy Under Eisenhower and Kennedy'. London: I.B. Tauris; about the current position in global politics, see Amineh, Mehdi Parvizi. 2007. *The Greater Middle East in Global Politics: Social Science Perspectives on the Changing Geography of the World Politics*. Leiden: Brill; about the effects of a new geographic imagination in Middle Eastern politics, see Harkavy, Robert. 2001. 'Strategic Geography and the Greater Middle East'. *Naval War College Review* 54 (4): 36–53; Rubin, Lawrence. 2014. *Islam in the Balance: Ideational Threats in Arab Politics*. Stanford: Stanford Security Studies.

still represents Turkey's first trading partner in the sub-region.[5] But Ethiopia is also the main power in the Horn. Its regional influence, its role in Africa's international relations and its place in the African Union make it one of the main critical players in regional diplomacy and security as well as a sort of failed hegemon in the Horn.[6] Therefore, Ethiopia is a country with which all extra-regional actors must interface if they wish to operate in the area. The agenda used by Turkey to establish and to strengthen relations with Ethiopia by opening a variety of channels in different fields became a sort of *roadmap* to be used with the other countries of the Horn. In the HOA, Turkey's engagement has been multifaceted: it has built major infrastructure projects, provided humanitarian assistance, financed scholarships, offered military training, facilitated political dialogue, supported institutional capacity building and given budgetary aid. In order to tighten links with sub-Saharan countries, Turkey has followed an agenda in which non-state actors prevail by (1) providing basic services in different fields (education, health, religion) through NGOs and other citizen-based organizations; (2) including businesspeople and other representatives of civil society in diplomatic delegations; (3) establishing an office of the Turkish Cooperation and Coordination Agency (TİKA); (4) starting scheduled flights by Turkish Airlines; and (5) opening an embassy and consulates. Through the coordinated actions of state institutions and civil society organizations, this strategy and programme has been replicated several times in different countries in the wide HOA, such as Djibouti, Uganda, Sudan, Kenya and Eritrea.

Turkey's greater diplomatic presence in the sub-region has brought it material gains and political visibility, but Somalia had been ignored by Turkey, as well as by other powers, until 2011. As previously seen, ties with the HOA date back to the golden age of the Ottoman era. Despite this, the historical engagement with Somalia was mostly peripheral and occasional. The Ottomans were briefly allied with the Muslim Sultanate of Adal, providing weapons and support in its wars against Ethiopia and in attempts to repel Portuguese invaders in the sixteenth century. During that period, the Porte was involved in the de facto independent state of Somaliland because the Sultanate's original capital was located in northern Somalia near what is now Djibouti, at Zeila (*Zayla*), prior to moving to Harar, which is currently located in Ethiopia.[7] During the Cold War, Turkey's relations with Somalia were almost negated. Turkey's engagement with Somalia

---

5   Turkey's trade volume with Ethiopia jumped from $40 million in 2003 to some $4 billion in 2013.
6   Verhoeven, Harry. 2015. 'Africa's Next Hegemon: Behind Ethiopia's Power Plays'. *Foreign Affairs*.
7   Cannon, Brendon J. 2016. 'Deconstructing Turkey's Efforts in Somalia'. *Bildhaan: An International Journal of Somali Studies* 16 (14): 105.

began during a time of deep chaos for the African country. Since the collapse of the Siad Barre regime in 1991, Somalia has been descended into civil war and has become the most renowned 'failed state'[8] in the world.[9] The general power vacuum led Somalia to anarchy with clashes between the centre and periphery over resources and power control. This resulted in two decades of clan conflicts, warlords, slaughter along sectarian and ethnic lines, famine crises, piracy along the coasts, extreme poverty and religious fundamentalism.[10] The effects of the conflict on the Somali population prompted the international community to promote three separate attempts to mediate and provide humanitarian aid.[11] The Somali civil war erupted at a time of profound change in the global order, and Somalia became a laboratory for a new form of international engagement through humanitarian and military intervention on an unprecedented scale.[12] The United Nations-sanctioned multinational force Unified Task Force (UNITAF) also included members of the Turkish army. Turkish troops not only took an active role in the operations during the UNOSOM II, but also took command of the operations under the orders of Lieutenant-General Çvik Bir. These UN-led peace operations attempted to support a state-building process and provide security for aid workers. These missions, however, quickly became

---

[8] The failed states are those in which the central government is no longer in operation, and the state has essentially imploded. According to the commonly accepted definition, the failed state is a state in which the basic functions of the state are no longer performed, and which is manifested in the inability to impose order within it. Failed states are tense, deeply conflicted, dangerous and contested bitterly by warring factions. In most failed states, government troops battle armed revolts led by one or more rivals. Occasionally, official authorities in a failed state face two or more insurgencies, varieties of civil unrest, different degrees of communal discontent and a plethora of dissent directed at the state and at groups within the state. Some scholars such as Helman and Ratner base the definition of failed state primarily on the government structure, while Rotberg classifies states under five progressive categories according to their capacity to deliver the most important political goods effectively. Others such as Krasner, starting from Weber's definition of the State, consider that a state fails when it is no longer able to maintain the monopoly of force within its territory. See Helman, Gerald B. and Steven R. Ratner. 1992–3. 'Saving Failed States'. *Foreign Policy* (89): 3–20; Krasner, Stephen D. 2001. *Problematic Sovereignty: Contested Rules and Political Possibilities*. New York: Columbia University Press; Rotberg, Robert I., ed. 2003. *State Failure and State Weakness in a Time of Terror*. Washington: Brookings Inst. Press.

[9] According to the annual ranking by Foreign Policy and the Global Fund for Peace, at http://ffp .statesindex.org.

[10] For a synthesis of the conflict's dynamics following the eruption of the civil war, see Bradbury, Mark and Sally Healy. 2010. *Endless War: A Brief History of the Somali Conflict*. London: Conciliation Resources; Kapteijns, Lidwien. 2013. *Clan Cleansing in Somalia: The Ruinous Legacy of 1991*. Philadelphia: University of Pennsylvania Press.

[11] There were three operations between 1992 and 1995: the United Nations operation called United Nations Operation in Somalia (UNOSOM-I) in 1992; the joint UN–US mission known as Operation Restore Hope (1993); and finally, the second UN operation, UNOSOM II (1993–5). See Koops, Joachim A., Norrie MacQueen, Thierry Tardy and Paul D. Williams, eds. 2015. *The Oxford Handbook of United Nations Peacekeeping Operations*, 408–15, 429–41. Oxford: Oxford University Press.

[12] Clarke, Walter S. and Jeffrey I. Herbst. 1997. *Learning from Somalia: The Lessons of Armed Humanitarian Intervention*. Oxford: Westview Press.

mired in the politicization of aid and became targets of the worsening inter-clan and warlord infighting.[13] Following the battle of Mogadishu in 1993, there was a gradual withdrawal of the multinational forces and a long period of international isolation of Somalia began.[14]

Throughout the second half of the 1990s, the void created by the sudden loss of interest in Somalia on the part of the international community was in part filled by several Islamic NGOs, linked to different Muslim states and Islamist movements, which took over responsibility for reactivating the fundamental social services involving Somali professionals and civil society.[15] Since 1996, among the faith-based NGOs there was also the Humanitarian Relief Foundation (IHH), one of Turkey's most important humanitarian organizations. Even though until then the IHH had operated in Somalia with small and localized projects, its activities were fundamental to establishing early contacts between components of Turkish civil society and the Somali population.

During the first decade of the new millennium, thanks to the internal developments ushered by the rise to power of the Islamic Courts Union (ICU),[16] the international isolation of Somalia increased. As the movement coalesced and seized control of Mogadishu, the ICU became an alternative to the internationally recognized, yet internally disputed, Transitional Federal Government (TFG).[17] The ICU enjoyed great support in the country but soon lost control of the most extreme fringes of the Islamic movement, including Harakat al-Shabaab (the Youth Movement). At the end of 2006, these developments gave Ethiopia the opportunity to intervene with US support in the framework of the fight against terror. The country fell again into chaos.

Despite Somalia being recognized as a single unitary state by the international community, the reality presents a fractured state, an agglomerate of thirteen

[13] Harper, Mary. 2012. *Getting Somalia Wrong: Faith, War and Hope in a Shattered State*. Chicago: Zed Press.

[14] Lewis, *A Modern History of the Somali*.

[15] Among the most active countries was Saudi Arabia, which, exploiting the presence of a large Somali diaspora on its soil, developed a humanitarian intervention network. See Abdulleh, Jabril I. 2008. 'Civil Society in the Absence of a Somali State'. In *Somalia – Current Conflicts and New Chances for State Building*, edited by Heinrich Böll Foundation, 70–87. Berlin: Heinrich Böll Stiftung; Saggiomo, Valeria. 2014. 'Rebuilding the State from Below: NGO Networks and the Politics of Civil Society in Somalia'. In *Informal Power in the Greater Middle East: Hidden Geographies*, edited by Luca Anceschi, Gennaro Gervasio and Andrea Teti, 129–42. Abingdon: Routledge.

[16] In 2006, a variety of Islamist organizations, centred on a long-standing network of local Islamic or sharia courts in Mogadishu, had come together under an umbrella organization, popularly known in the Western media as the Islamic Courts Union. See Marchal, Roland. 2004. 'Islamic Political Dynamics in the Somali Civil War'. In *Islamism and Its Enemies in the Horn of Africa*, edited by Alexander De Waal, 114–45. London: Hurst.

[17] Barnes, Cedric and Harun Hassan. 2007. 'The Rise and Fall of Mogadishu's Islamic Courts'. *Journal of Eastern African Studies* 1 (2): 151–60.

self-governing federal states[18] and three separate state entities each with its own population and national idea.

- Mogadishu and southern Somalia are formally placed under the control of the Somali Federal Government (SFG) which is internationally recognized as Somalia's official central authority. However, a widespread anarchy and lawlessness remains, together with the threat of the Islamic group al-Shabaab that still controls the southern districts.[19] Currently there is a peacekeeping mission (AMISOM)[20] operated by the AU with UN approval in support of the SFG.

- Puntland is a form of 'ethno-state' founded on the unity of the Harti clan. It includes the northern region of the country where an informal semi-autonomous state, legally and politically similar to Iraqi Kurdistan,[21] was established in August 1998. After the withdrawal of the international peacekeeping forces (1995), Puntland sadly became known as the den of the warlords and Somali piracy. As a non-secessionist state, Puntland embodies a building block for a future federal Somali state.[22]

- Somaliland declared independence in 1991 as a Republic and it includes the semi-desert territory in the northwest area on the coast of the Gulf of Aden. Though not internationally recognized, Somaliland has a working political system, government institutions and its own currency. After twenty-three years of independence, Somaliland has all the attributes of a sovereign state, but it is still struggling to gain diplomatic recognition as an independent state.[23]

---

[18] Currently there are many self-governing regions in Somalia, such as Ximan, Xeeb, Galmudug and Ahlu Sunna Waljama'a.

[19] Al-Shabaab has also shifted part of its resource base northwards into the mountainous areas in the Puntland-Ethiopia-Somaliland border region, which is important for maintaining connections to supplies and finances flowing along the long-established smuggling routes from Yemen. See Marchal, Roland. 2009. 'A Tentative Assessment of the Somali Harakat Al-Shabaab'. *Journal of Eastern African Studies* 3 (3): 381–404; Vidino, Lorenzo, Raffaello Pantucci and Evan Kohlmann. 2010. 'Bringing Global Jihad to the Horn of Africa: al Shabaab, Western Fighters, and the Sacralization of the Somali Conflict'. *African Security* 3 (4): 216–38; Hansen, Stig Jarle. 2012. *Al-Shabaab in Somalia: The History and Ideology of a Militant Islamist Group 2005-2012*. Oxford: Oxford University Press.

[20] The African Union Mission in Somalia is the Regional Peacekeeping Mission created by the African Union's Peace and Security Council, with the Approval of the United Nations. See, AMISOM website http://amisom-au.org/. For a comprehensive analysis of the regional peacekeeping mission, see Williams, Paul D. 2018. *Fighting for Peace in Somalia: A History and Analysis of the African Union Mission (AMISOM), 2007-2017*. Oxford: Oxford University Press.

[21] Gullo, Matthew T. 2012. *Turkey's Somalia Adventure: the Quest for Soft Power and Regional Recognition*. London: Research Turkey.

[22] Höhne, Markus V. 2006. 'Political Identity, Emerging State Structures and Conflict in Northern Somalia'. *Journal of Modern African Studies* 44 (3): 397–414; Murphy, Martin N. 2011. *Somalia: The New Barbary?: Piracy and Islam in the Horn of Africa*. New York: Columbia University Press.

[23] Bradbury, Mark, Adan Yusuf Abokor and Haroon Ahmed Yusuf. 2003. 'Somaliland: Choosing Politics over Violence'. *Review of African Political Economy* 30 (97): 455–78; Bulhan, Hussein A. 2004. 'Somaliland in Ruin and Renewal: The Story of Somaliland'. In *Conflict Analysis Regional Report*. Hargeysa: Centre for Creative Solutions; Bradbury, Mark. 2008. *Becoming Somaliland*. London:

The Turkish state's relations with the Somali authorities remained almost non-existent until the visit of President Sheikh Sharif of the TFG in 2009. The meeting was very important because it broke the ice between the two countries and it is quite likely that since then the Turkish authorities started to be interested in Somalia and to evaluate a possible involvement.

4.2 Turkey's engagement in the Somali crisis as a mediating actor (2011)

In this extremely complex and sensitive context, Turkey decided to intervene in a decisive and concrete manner. Turkey's rapprochement with Somalia formally began with the Istanbul Conference on Somalia on 21–23 May 2010 as part of the Djibouti Agreement.[24] The conference set up a roadmap for peacebuilding and development in Somalia thanks to many bilateral agreements signed by Turkey and the Mogadishu government in the fields of the military, education, and technical and scientific cooperation.[25] Between February and March 2011, several representatives from Somali civil society, who have collaborated with İHH, requested aid to face the growing famine and the spread of diseases.[26] After the efforts of İHH and other NGOs, the Turkish government also took steps towards recognizing the unfolding tragedy in Somalia and opened a privileged channel offering humanitarian aid to the Somali people.

The Turkish commitment to Somalia became manifest with two important events that brought the drama of the Somali people to the attention of international public opinion: the fourth UN Conference on the Least Developed Countries (LDCs) and the official visit of Prime Minister Erdoğan to Mogadishu. In May 2011, Turkey hosted the fourth UN conference on LDCs. This was

---

Progressio; Walls, Michael and Steve Kibble. 2010. 'Beyond Polarity: Negotiating a Hybrid State in Somaliland'. *Africa Spectrum* 45 (1): 31–56.

[24] The Djibouti Agreement was signed by representatives of Somalia's Transitional Federal Government and the Alliance for the Re-liberation of Somalia at the end of the peace conference held in Djibouti between 31 May and 9 June 2008 with the mediation of the United Nations Special Envoy to Somalia, Ahmedou Ould-Abdallah. See Williams, *Fighting for Peace*, 64–8.

[25] According to the then foreign minister Ahmet Davutoğlu, the conference was concluded with a strong message for Somalia built on three major dimensions. The first highlighted the future of Somalia, focusing on peace, political reform, security and economic development in the country. The second was about regional ownership, and called on Somalia's neighbours to give their full support for peace in the country. Finally, the third concerned international ownership, and called on the international community to support peace in Somalia. Ahmet Davutoğlu, 'Press Conference Proceedings, Istanbul Conference on Somalia', 22 May 2010.

[26] Interview with Serhat Orakçi, Africa Desk Director, IHH Humanitarian Relief Foundation, 29 May 2014.

organized in a similar way to the Turkey–Africa summit format and it brought together various representatives from governments, business circles, NGOs and media from the LDCs. In other words, it gave full prominence to civil society and its contribution. For the first time in the history of the UN LDC Conference, an Intellectuals Forum was held bringing together internationally renowned scholars working on various issues concerning the LDCs.[27] Among these issues a special place was given to the problems of Africa and in particular to the dramatic conditions of the Somali population who, in addition to the outcomes of the civil war, were suffering from famine.

After a few weeks, Erdoğan decided to visit Somalia personally at a time when other leaders refrained from visiting the country on the pretext of poor security measures. Erdoğan was the first non-African leader to visit Somalia in nearly two decades. The trip, occurring during the Muslim holy month of Ramadan, was the real turning point in Turkish commitment towards Somalia. Erdoğan's visit coincided with the opening of a privileged channel of humanitarian aid towards the Somali people hard hit by the long famine. During the visit, Erdoğan not only promised to provide immediate aid to address the humanitarian emergency through governmental and non-governmental agencies but also made a long-term commitment to Somalia. The Turkish prime minister undertook to support the peace process and mediation between the parties to the conflict, as well as to assist in the state-building process.[28] He brought his family and an entourage, consisting of various cabinet members, while visiting Mogadishu,[29] the refugee camps and hospitals to witness the devastation caused by the severe drought. Pictures of the Turkish prime minister and his wife Emine carrying a starving child soon went viral. Erdoğan's visit had a highly political significance because it brought the Somali situation onto the international agenda and paved the way for rapprochements with intergovernmental organizations. Following his trip to Mogadishu, Erdoğan wrote a passionate article 'The Tears of Somalia' that was published by Foreign Policy in which he underlined the culpability of the international community in the face of the Somali crisis.[30] The trip also had an important symbolic meaning because it showed to the Turkish people Somalia's human tragedy, hitherto unknown, and showed to Somalia, where the feeling of being completely isolated from the international community was widespread,

---

[27] Davutoğlu, Ahmet. 2012. 'A New Vision for Least Developed Countries (LCDs)'. In *Vision Papers*, 4–5. Ankara: Center for Strategic Research.

[28] Cannon, 'Deconstructing Turkey's Efforts in Somalia', 108.

[29] At that time, the city had been categorized, even by UN agencies, as no-go-zone since the beginning of the civil conflict.

[30] Erdoğan, Recep Tayyip. 2011. 'The Tears of Somalia'. *Foreign Policy*.

that they were not alone. At the domestic level, the trip aroused both media attention and Turkish feelings; as a result, Turkey's public got involved through financial donations and a social media campaign. A huge public awareness campaign was run by Turkish NGOs and celebrities, showing images of emaciated women and children. With the aim of giving more media visibility to the Somali issue, Erdoğan introduced a practice that would become recurrent in the Turkish authorities' visits to Africa: the presence of celebrities from the show business. In his first visit to Somalia, Erdoğan was accompanied by music artists Ajda Pekkan, Nihat Dogan, Sertab Erener and Muazzez Ersoy. This interaction has given greater exposure to African problems among the Turkish public, prompting the artists themselves to take independent initiatives. For example, both Erener and Pekkan held concerts, the proceeds of which were donated to Somalia, while Dogan declared that he would donate half the income he earned from his subsequent album to the Somali people.[31]

Within a few weeks, a widespread campaign in Turkey, led by NGOs such as İHH, Kimse Yok Mu (KYM), Deniz Feneri Derneği and Cansuyu Charity, made a considerable contribution in finding substantial resources for relief efforts, raising over $365 million in humanitarian aid.[32] The impact of this campaign was decisive in mobilizing the Turkish public on the plight in Somalia.[33] This wide participation of Turkish people has made the intervention in Somalia somewhat of a 'domestic' issue which has, in turn, driven the government's actions.[34] In addition, at the outbreak of the famine in 2011, the NGOs played a leading role, lobbying the Turkish government indirectly to intervene with greater commitment.

As a demonstration of Turkey's commitment to the present and future stability of Somalia was the reopening of the Turkish Embassy in Mogadishu in November 2011, which had been closed since the collapse of the Siad Barre regime. Significantly, Ankara appointed Cemalettin Kani Torun, a member of Doctors Worldwide, as Turkey's ambassador in Somalia. The consolidation of diplomatic presence was very important, and included the Turkish Airlines opening a Istanbul–Khartoum–Mogadishu route in March 2012. The diplomatic office and infrastructure connections symbolized the Somali reconnection to the world community and a great step forward in the normalization process.

[31] Ipek and Biltekin, 'Turkey's Foreign Policy Implementation', 139–40.
[32] ICG. 2012. 'Assessing Turkey's Role in Somalia'. In *ICG Africa Briefing*. International Crisis Group.
[33] Sazak, Onur and Auveen Elizabeth Woods. 2017. 'Thinking Outside the Compound: Turkey's Approach to Peacebuilding in Somalia'. In *Rising Powers and Peacebuilding*, edited by Charles T. Call and Cedric de Coning, 167–89, 171. London: Palgrave Macmillan.
[34] Özkan, *Turkey's Involvement in Somalia*.

After facing the humanitarian emergency, Turkey decided to mediate between the conflicting parties. Despite the fact that the determination to build a role for Turkey as a regional mediator was introduced during the coalition government under Bülent Ecevit's leadership, it was with the JDP's rise to power that it materialized.[35] Indeed, the idea of making Turkey a reliable and credible international mediator became part of the new foreign policy course and inherent in the national role conception as a 'central country'. According to this idea, Turkey, thanks to its geographical and historical centrality, would have the chance to maintain good and solid relations with a multiplicity of actors belonging to different geopolitical areas or complexes. Exploiting this nature would allow the country to become an international mediation centre – an idea widely developed by the new foreign policymaking elites and expressed clearly in an official statement released by the Ministry of Foreign Affairs:

> Pursuing a more dynamic foreign policy in recent years and exerting great efforts to place cooperation and dialogue on solid foundation in Afro-Eurasian Turkey attaches special importance to preventive diplomacy, pioneers a great deal of mediation attempts in a wide geography and endeavors actively for the peaceful settlement of disputes.[36]

Before intervening in Somalia, Turkey had already realized its mediation capabilities in the Balkans (Bosnia-Herzegovina), the Israeli–Palestinian conflict, Iraq, Afghanistan, the Iranian nuclear issue and several others. In addition to carrying out mediation services in areas of ongoing crises, Turkey also pursued an ambitious project entitled 'Friends of Mediation'.[37] In coordination with the UN and through support from Finland, two resolutions were passed in the General Assembly, and a UN guide for effective mediation was prepared. Following the guidelines prescribed by Ahmet Davutoğlu, the architect of Turkish foreign policy and the major designer of the involvement in Somalia, the JDP government has embarked on a difficult path of reconciliation and stabilization of the country. In the Somali crisis, the Turkish mediation strategy has stressed as its first goal the study of conflict, to understand its causes and also the reasons for the failure of previous mediation attempts. The previous failed mediation attempts, at least twelve of them, had brought about a general lack of confidence among the Somali parties involved in the conflict. From the

[35] Gürkaynak, Esra Çuhadar. 2007. 'Turkey as a Third Party in Israeli-Palestinian Conflict'. *Perceptions* 7 (1): 89–108.

[36] Ministry of Foreign Affairs. 2011. *Resolution of Conflicts and Mediation*. URL: http://www.mfa.gov.tr/resolution-of-conflicts-and-mediation.en.mfa

[37] Aras, 'Turkey's Mediation and Friends of Mediation Initiative'.

Somali perspective, there are a number of views as to why these attempts failed. Somali people often blame different external actors for having their own agendas and interests (Ethiopia), lacking enough will for peacebuilding (United States), arriving too late (UN) and lack of sufficient insight among the mediators into the on-ground realities. The external interventions and their unwillingness to create a dialogue with all the conflicting parties has increased Somali dissent and distrust towards the international community.[38] Turkey has understood the need to overcome this obstacle by working actively at the ground level, and it has structured its intervention in the framework of soft power and confidence-building strategies. Turkey's principled approach helped to create an atmosphere of mutual confidence between the Somalis and the Turkish people as a whole. As Davutoğlu argued, mediators cannot achieve success without mutual trust because the psychological dynamics of a dispute cannot be understood without empathy.[39] As Aras underlined, 'the uniqueness of Turkish mediators in the Somali context comes from a combination of their broad perspective and material capabilities which are the result of experience and access to a wide cultural and civilizational outreach'.[40]

In 2012, for the first time in its history, Turkey was trying to act as a peacemaker.[41] The Ankara government brought the issue to the UN General Assembly meeting and called on the international community to undertake a continued approach to find a long-lasting solution. As part of its diplomatic efforts, Turkey hosted the second Istanbul Conference on Somalia between 31 May and 1 June 2012. Unlike the preceding London Conference on Somalia's future (February 2012), the Istanbul one adopted an inclusive approach. The conference was attended by a large number of international and regional actors and all Somali parties, including representatives of the Somali diaspora and 135 clan elders involved in the civil conflict.[42] The clan dimension was crucial for understanding the causes of the civil conflict and the many mutual claims.[43] The

---

[38] Menkhaus, Ken. 2004. *Somalia: State Collapse and the Threat of Terrorism*. New York: Routledge; Menkhause, Ken, Hassan Sheik, Ali Joqombe and Pat Johnson. 2009. *A History of Mediation in Somalia since 1988*. Nairobi: Interpeace; Elmi, Afyare Abdi. 2010. *Understanding the Somalia Conflagration: Identity, Islam and Peacebuilding*. London: Pluto Press.

[39] From Davutoğlu's perspective, a successful mediation effort has four dimensions: psychological, intellectual, ethical and methodological. Davutoğlu, Ahmet. 2013. 'Turkey's Mediation: Critical Reflections from the Field'. *Middle East Policy* 20 (1): 83–90.

[40] Aras, 'Turkey's Mediation and Friends', 4.

[41] Özkan, *Turkey's Involvement in Somalia*, 13.

[42] Hassan M. Abukar, 'The Istanbul Gathering of the Somali Civil Society'. Ward-heernews.com, 6 June 2012, at:www.wardheernews.com/Articles_12/June/Abukar/ 06_The_Istanbul_Gathering_of _the_Somali_Civil_Society.html.

[43] The current structure of the Federal Government is still based on the exclusionary 4.5 formula. This distributes seats equally among the four major Somali clans (the Darod, Dir, Hawiye and the

controversial inclusion of almost 300 civil society associations in the conference notwithstanding, the Turkish state's commitment is an illustration of fostering national unity through engagement and dialogue. It also demonstrates how Turkish mediation efforts take into account the different 'voices' of common Somali people in spite of the reluctance of the international community.[44] At the heart of this was one of the key principles of Turkey's mediation approach, namely, that national stability and cohesion require the strengthening of the public and private sectors. Even though the event was not instrumental in radically changing the future of Somalia, it was hugely successful for Turkey's image. Regardless of the long-term results of its involvement in Somalia, Turkey was elevated to the position of being a 'new humanitarian aid power' in Africa.[45] Yet, the engagement has arguably made Turkey indispensable in Mogadishu to many Somalis.[46] The problem was that, as highlighted by Özkan, these developments

> pose a threat of evolving into a 'Somali fatigue' – the gradual decline in Turkey's effectiveness in aiding Somalia – due to the lack of local expertise and the perception of Turkey as an idealized super country.[47]

Since its high-profile intervention during the height of the famine in 2011, Turkey has elevated its level of engagement with Somalia. In contrast to widespread international disinterest and the many failed attempts to find a solution to the Somali crisis, Turkey has approached the crisis in Somalia on a delivery basis, rather than promises and plans like other donors, and made significant inroads that were not seen before.[48] Indeed, as Cannon underlined, 'Turkey's actions were different because it has actually attempted to assuage rather than solve Somalia's long-standing problems outright'.[49] The Turkish will was to create a condition fit for the establishment and consolidation of basic state institutions.

Digil and Mirifle). The minority clans, who are sometimes referred to as the Fifth Clan, are together allotted just half the number of seats of one whole clan receiving 0.5 per cent representation. This is a deeply unequal system that sidelines all minority class, regardless of their population size. Harper, *Getting Somalia Wrong*.

[44] Editorial, 'Assessing Turkey's Role in Somalia'. Policy Briefing: Africa Briefing, No. 92, October 2012, at: www.crisisgroup.org/~/media/Files/africa/horn-of-africa/somalia/ b092-assessing-turkeys-role -in-somalia.pdf; Ladan Affi, 'Somali Civil Society Discusses Somalia's Future'. *Insight on Conflict*, June 2012, at: www.insightonconflict.org/2012/07/istanbul-conference-somalia-civil-society/.

[45] Abdirahman, 'Turkey's Foray into Africa'.

[46] Haşimi, Cemalettin. 2014. 'Turkey's Humanitarian Diplomacy and Development Cooperation'. *Insight Turkey* 16 (1): 127–8.

[47] Özkan, *Turkey's Involvement in Somalia*, 10.

[48] Aynte, Abdihakim. 2012. *Turkey's Increasing Role in Somalia: An Emerging Donor?* Doha: Al Jazeera Centre for Studies.

[49] Cannon, Brendon J. 2017. *Turkey in Africa: Lessons from Somalia*. Rising Powers in Global Governance Project.

Turkey accepted responsibility for furthering the state-building process under very volatile security conditions. After its experiences with the non-recognized Turkish Republic of Northern Cyprus, it was the second time that Turkey had embarked on a project of this magnitude. This helps to understand how much the first decade of JDP leadership has radically changed the perspective of Turkish leaders: from a wait-and-see approach to regional and international events to a proactive one. It also shows how the good results achieved in those years had increased Davutoğlu and Erdoğan's self-confidence, both of whom had at the same time nurtured the dream of taking the lead in the post-Arab Spring Middle East. The Turkish stabilization efforts were facilitated by the election in 2012 of a new SFG, with more power and much more international prestige than the previous body: the Somali Transitional Government. With the election of the SFG, Turkey was blessed with willing partners who had a mandate to rule and distribute resources until well into 2016.

At the political and intrastate level, Turkey supports national reconciliation and the preservation of the territorial integrity of the whole of Somalia.[50] For this reason, Turkey promoted the strengthening of the SFG institutions, concurrently seeking involvement of other political entities through dialogue and bilateral meetings.[51] In this regard, many speculations have been advanced about relations between Turkey and al-Shabaab. As a matter of fact, Turkey had made more than one attempt to involve al-Shabaab in the talks by establishing some type of line of communication between the Islamic group and SFG. Although these attempts have been widely criticized by other actors, local and external, they demonstrate how the Turkish mediation approach is inclusive of all the parties in the conflict. Initially, some Somalis criticized Ankara's policy, considering that it was too focused on Mogadishu and uncritically supportive of the SFG. However, over time, Turkey has expanded its activities into other areas, including Puntland and Somaliland, thus reducing its Mogadishu-centric reputation. Today, even though Turkey's position is to support the central government and the territorial

---

[50] Kadayifci-Orellana, Ayse S. 2016. 'Turkish Mediation in Somalia for Peace and Stability'. In *Turkey as a Mediator: Stories of Success and Failure*, edited by Doga Ulas Eralp, 99–124. Lanham: Lexington Books.

[51] Turkey encouraged mediation talks and promoted a set of indirect talks between the SFG and the Islamic group al-Shabaab and direct talks between the central government and the representatives of institutions of Somaliland. In April 2013, Turkey arranged a meeting for the Somali president Hassan Sheikh Mohamud and the Somaliland president Ahmed Silanyo in Ankara, which concluded with the signature of the 'Ankara Communiqué'. In March 2015, Turkey hosted the eighth round of talks between the governments of Somalia and Somaliland as they sought to reach agreement on issues such as security, piracy and illegal fishing. Again, in the spring of 2019, under the aegis of the previous ambassador to Somalia, Olgan Bekar, Turkey tried to strengthen relations with Somaliland as a necessary step for the stability of the whole of Somalia.

integrity of the country, Ankara has very good relations with all the entities including Somaliland and Puntland.

But why did Turkey choose to become involved in Somalia rather than another African state? First of all, because the umpteenth famine that afflicted the Somali people came at the right time for Turkey. In particular, if one looks from the perspective of multilevel analysis – international, regional and domestic – it is clear that 2011 was a critical moment in the new course of JDP foreign policy. The United States was orienting its international efforts towards the Yellow Sea by encouraging a shift of geopolitical axes eastwards. In doing so, it inevitably had to reduce its presence and engagement in some areas such as Africa and the Middle East. This, understood as 'the Greater Middle East' underwent a revolutionary wave, the so-called Arab Spring, which led to a reshuffling of regional balances and the rise of more stable powers such as Turkey. Furthermore, from the geostrategic point of view, Somalia is a key country not only for the balance of the HOA but also for the control of the Red Sea, the Gulf of Aden and the Arabian Peninsula. In other words, in the reconfiguration of Middle Eastern power relations, Turkish influence in Somalia would be an important card for Ankara. Finally, in the domestic sphere, the ruling JDP party had consolidated its political power and control over institutions, particularly the military-bureaucratic elite, and was able to launch interventionist policies across the borders. Therefore, Turkish policymakers chose to involve the country in a highly unstable and dangerous situation, like Somalia, because they had nothing to lose and could test the extent of their new role as a middle power. However, it was a controlled and reasoned risk. Indeed, Turkish leaders were aware that the country's capabilities, such as soft power and the ability to start from scratch, could be more effective in a context of instability, violence and a history of failed international attempts to bring peace and stability.

In other words, any Turkish success in Somalia would have been oversized, given the difficulty of an environment suffering from a violent clan policy, a terrorist insurgency and a crumbling or destroyed infrastructure typical of failed states. Thus, Prime Minister Erdoğan and his close government ministers, particularly Davutoğlu, chose Somalia, despite the significant risks, because of the potential payout in terms of international recognition, increased diplomatic profile and profit.[52] In terms of material gains, intrepid Turkish businesses found willing partners in Somalia. Though a bit clichéd, trade and entrepreneurship are considered by many to be the lifeblood of the Somali people, and they

---

[52] Çağaptay, Soner. 2014. 'The New Davutoğlu'. *Foreign Affairs*.

have flourished in many areas during the last decade in spite of the instability, terrorism and lack of infrastructure. Moreover, Erdoğan's government and the Turkish civil society's links to the rising Muslim middle class understood that by gambling in volatile Mogadishu they would automatically be viewed as intrepid and visionary as well as humanitarian. Although some scholars have focused on the relevance of the sectarian motives behind Turkey's efforts in Somalia, it should not be overestimated. Indeed, as Cannon argued,

> This involvement came about not because of Turkey's and Somalia's common Sunni Muslim heritage, or its Muslim Brotherhood ties, or because of some greater appeal to charity and development – though these clearly were motivating factors. Rather, Turkey's main aim in engaging Somalia is the political and diplomatic capital it receives outside of Somalia and the region. This comes in the form of commendations and applause for Turkey's diplomatic and humanitarian efforts in a volatile corner of the world.[53]

In other words, direct involvement in Somalia has enabled Turkey to give a boost to its real aim: to gain political and diplomatic capital outside Somalia.[54] Along with its self-interested goals such as prestige, Turkey was convinced that it would be able to further develop its business interests. Behind the Turkish choice of a greater involvement in Somalia there was also the support of Turkish businesspeople, who were constantly pursuing new markets and wealthy orders linked, in the case of Somalia, to the reconstruction of the main infrastructures. In addition to the businessmen's interest, other evaluations were also crucial in the domestic sphere. One of these was the Turkish government's awareness that the engagement in Somalia would strengthen the image of the ruling JDP party and its leader Erdoğan, especially affecting the conservative and religious electorate.[55]

4.3 Humanitarian-oriented policy: The change in Turkey's assertive foreign policy

In order to facilitate a mediation that would prove to be more effective than the previous international and regional attempts, Turkey was aware that it had

---

[53] Cannon, 'Deconstructing Turkey's Efforts in Somalia', 103.

[54] Ülgen, Sinan. 2010. 'A Place in the Sun or Fifteen Minutes of Fame?: Understanding Turkey's New Foreign Policy'. Carnegie Endowment for International Peace, Carnegie Europe.

[55] Gizem, Sucuoglu and Jason Stearns. 2016. 'Turkey in Somalia: Shifting Paradigms of Aid'. In *Research Report*. South African Institute of International Affairs.

first and foremost to win the trust of the disputing parties. To do this, Turkey developed its own method of intervention in a post-conflict scenario based on two main elements: humanitarian assistance and the multitrack approach. As will be discussed later, humanitarian assistance in the Somali context proved to be the most suitable trust-building tool as well as the most distinctive element of the Turkish presence in the political and humanitarian crisis. Already during the consolidation of soft power instruments launched in 2003, the Turkish government had chosen to strengthen specific niche fields. Among these, primary attention, especially following the Arab upheavals of 2011, was given to humanitarian diplomacy. 'Humanitarian diplomacy' is an emerging and deeply contested term. Its definition does not match completely with that of conventional diplomacy, whose objective is to manage the international relations of states through negotiation. Instead, humanitarian diplomacy focuses on maximizing support for operations and programmes and building the partnerships necessary if humanitarian objectives are to be achieved. Some organizations and scholars use other terms that are very similar, such as 'intervention diplomacy',[56] 'disaster diplomacy',[57] or 'human rights diplomacy'.[58] Humanitarian diplomacy is not yet a solidly established concept generally recognized by the international community;[59] one of the most accepted definitions conceptualizes humanitarian diplomacy as

> The activities carried out by humanitarian organizations to obtain the space from political and military authorities within which to function with integrity. These activities comprise such efforts as arranging for the presence of humanitarian organizations in a given country, negotiating access to civilian populations in need of assistance and protection, monitoring assistance programs, promoting respect for international law and norms, supporting indigenous individuals and institutions, and engaging in advocacy at a variety of levels in support of humanitarian objectives.[60]

---

[56] Ware, Glenn T. 1997. 'The Emerging Norm of Humanitarian Intervention and Presidential Decision Directive'. *Naval Law Review* 44:1–58.

[57] Kelman, Ilan. 2011. *Disaster Diplomacy: How Disasters Affect Peace and Conflict.* London: Routledge.

[58] Pease, Kelly-Kate. 2016. *Human Rights and Humanitarian Diplomacy.* Manchester: Manchester University Press.

[59] In 2009, in an attempt to define the strategic concept of humanitarian diplomacy, the International Federation of Red Cross and Red Crescent Societies (IFRC) found that there were eighty-nine different definitions among the relevant agencies and in the grey and scientific literature. See IFRC. 2009. IFRC Annual Report 2009. Nairobi: International Federation of Red Cross and Red Crescent Societies.

[60] Minear, Larry and Hazel Smith, eds. 2007. *Humanitarian Diplomacy: Practitioners and Their Craft,* 1. New York: United Nations University Press.

Even though such expression has since been used with growing frequency by a number of state and non-state actors that operate in the humanitarian field, several others interpret the concept differently.[61] Among these actors Turkey also has progressively made it a strong point of its global activism. Indeed, the environment of post-Arab uprisings has partly invalidated Turkey's ambitious policy, forcing Ankara to review and adapt its assertive approach. Following the 2011 events, Turkish foreign policy has been modified in its content, instruments and mechanism but the 'central country' doctrine remains the main framework. Turkey's agenda has assumed a more liberal, value-based approach due to a new space of opportunity to get in direct contact with people. As a result, there has been an increase in Turkey's civilian capacity through the involvement of non-state actors in the policymaking process and in its use of new soft power tools in cultural, public and humanitarian diplomacy. At the same time, the growing number of non-state actors' activities beyond the border has led Turkey's policymakers to attach greater importance to the humanitarian discourse in some crisis countries such as Afghanistan, Myanmar and Somalia. Thus, foreign policy has adopted the approach of humanitarian diplomacy to tackle both regional crises and issues, and challenges in the wider framework. In other words, as Akpinar has highlighted, Turkish discourse on humanitarian diplomacy emerged as 'a result of an ongoing recalibration process of its own foreign policy agenda.'[62]

The aftermath of this shift towards a more 'humanitarian' oriented foreign policy has been seen clearly in the growth of Turkey's official development assistance (ODA)[63] since 2011. Turkey, a founding member of the Organization for Economic Cooperation and Development (OECD), is also an observer of the Development Assistance Committee (DAC). However, when compared to the twenty-eight OECD–DAC donor countries, Turkey has provided more assistance than traditional donors such as Italy. The Global Humanitarian Assistance report 2017 highlighted that Turkey's expenditure on humanitarian aid in 2016 comes second after that of the United States, which spent $6.3

---

[61] For a broader analysis of humanitarian diplomacy, see Régnier, Philippe. 2011. 'The Emerging Concept of Humanitarian Diplomacy: Identification of a Community of Practice and Prospects for International Recognition'. *International Review of the Red Cross* 93 (884): 1211–37; Harroff-Tavel, Marion. 2005. 'La diplomatie humanitaire du comité international de la Croix-Rouge'. *Relations internationales* 121 (Spring): 73–89.

[62] Akpınar, 'Turkey's Peacebuilding', 739.

[63] The book assumes the definition of Official Development Assistance provided by the OECD as 'all contributions of concessional public resources to developing countries (or multilateral institutions) with the main objective of promoting economic development and welfare'. http://www.oecd.org/dac /financing-sustainable-development/index-terms.htm#ODA.

Table 1 Turkey's Official Development Assistance and International Humanitarian Aid

	2016	2015	2014	2013	2012	2011
Net ODA	6.1bn [1]	3.9bn	3.5bn	3.3bn	2.6bn	1.3bn
ODA/GNI[2] (%)	0.79	0.50	0.45	0.40	0.32	0.16
IHA[3]	4.2bn	2.7bn	2bn	1.3bn	0.8bn	0.2bn
Bilateral share (%)	98	98	97.5	95.4	98	97.5

1. Billions of USD.

2. ODA as a percentage of GNI.

3. International Humanitarian Aid as a specific sector which includes Emergency Response, Disaster Prevention & Preparedness and Reconstruction Relief & Rehabilitation.

Source: Development Initiatives based on Organization for Economic Cooperation and Development (OECD), Development Assistance Committee (DAC), UN Office for the Coordination of Humanitarian Affairs (OCHA), Financial Tracking Service (FTS) and UN Central Emergency Response Fund (CERF) data. Data for 2016 OECD–DAC is preliminary.

billion.[64] Indeed, as illustrated in Table 1, Turkish ODA reached $6 billion in 2016, and in terms of the ratio of ODA to Gross National Income (GNI), Turkey emerged as the most generous donor with a figure of 0.75 per cent. Turkey provided the largest share of its bilateral development cooperation to Syria, Somalia, Kyrgyzstan, Albania and Afghanistan. Today, the main sectors for Turkey's bilateral development cooperation are humanitarian aid and refugee support, governance and civil society, and education, health and population. By using development cooperation as a way to convey a positive image of the country to the foreign public, Turkey aims to gain support for Turkish concerns in international fora and to foster the expansion of foreign trade.

It is remarkable that in 2013, for the first time in the Republican history, all sub-Saharan African states, with the exception of three island countries, received Turkish ODA.[65] Turkey is among one of the top donors to Somalia and is the only non-DAC member of this group. The top three donors of gross ODA for Somalia between 2014 and 2015 were the United States with $205.4 million, followed by the United Kingdom at $195 million and Turkey, which provided $194 million.[66] It should be stressed that there is still a significant gap between North Africa and SSA. As noted by Belder and Dipama,

[64] Global Humanitarian Assistance Report 2017. Available at http://devinit.org/post/global-humanitarian-assistance-2017/#.

[65] It is also important to note that of the US$191 million provided by Turkey to SSA, Somalia alone received US$116 million, making Turkey the fourth largest donor there. See Hausmann, Jeannine and Erik Lundsgaarde. 2015. *Turkey's Role in Development Cooperation.* Tokyo: United Nations University Centre for Policy Research.

[66] OECD. 2015. Aid Statistics, Recipients at a Glance. URL: http://www.oecd.org/countries/somalia/recipientcharts.htm.

despite Turkey's attempts to create a 'One Africa' image erasing all geographical, religious, and ethnic differences, ODA flows illustrate the selectiveness of Turkish foreign policy.[67]

In line with Turkish foreign policy, after 2011 the distribution of Turkish aid increased progressively towards SSA. The only exception was the biennium 2012–13, when Turkey's financial support to the Egyptian government of the Muslim Brotherhood led to the concentration of investment in Egypt.[68] As highlighted by the chart, after Mohamed Morsi's overthrow (July 2013), the allocation of Turkish regional ODAs has been concentrated on sub-Saharan areas. Most Turkish funds went to poorer and Muslim-majority countries, some with Ottoman-era connections such as Somalia and Sudan. In addition, most of these aid-recipient countries are located in the HOA, with the exception of Senegal, Niger and, to a certain extent, Mauritania.[69]

A key role in the definition of humanitarian-oriented policy was played, again, by Davutoğlu. A clarification is needed in this respect. Despite Davutoğlu's departure the politics in May 2016, after a brief period as prime minister, the impact of his ideas and his approach to the international politics on Turkish foreign policymakers' and academia's outlook was so disruptive that his influence has carried on in the following years. For this reason, even the post-Arab Spring shift in Turkish foreign policy's approach, its tools and norms has been supported by Davutoğlu's theoretical reflection and practical choices. The remarkable Turkish investment in a niche area such as humanitarian diplomacy, whose effects still persist, is also due to Davutoğlu's thought, which had the merit of introducing new concepts into the Turkish foreign policy agenda. A feature relevant to Turkish humanitarian diplomacy is the discourse and the use of highly popular – yet often misconstrued – concepts that impart meaning to its practical efforts. Indeed, in spite of there being no single definition of humanitarian diplomacy in the literature but many,[70] none of these are still completely suitable to the Turkish understanding. According to Davutoğlu,

[67] Belder, Ferit and Samiratou Dipama. 'A Comparative Analysis of China and Turkey's Development Aid Activities in Sub-Saharan Africa'. In *Middle Powers in Global Governance: The Rise of Turkey*, edited by Emel Parlar Dal, 231–53, 244. London: Palgrave Macmillan.

[68] The Turkish government signed a protocol with the Egyptian Ministry of Finance to provide a loan of up to US$1 billion to Egypt (as a result, the first portion of US$500 million of the loan given to this country in 2012 and the second portion of 500 million in 2013). Given the worsening of the relations between Turkey and the new Egyptian government following the coup d'etat fomented against Morsi, the implementation of this agreement has come to a halt. Belder and Dipama, 'A Comparative Analysis', 245.

[69] Belder and Dipama, 'A Comparative Analysis', 245.

[70] According to a research conducted by the International Federation of Red Cross and Red Crescent Societies, currently there are almost eighty-nine different definitions of humanitarian diplomacy.

Turkey's approach to humanitarian diplomacy emerges from its determination to become a regional and global actor within 'the rapid stream of history'.[71]

In the face of history's inflow, there are three positions that can be taken: resist change; float in this flux as far as possible; or take an active stance. Under the JDP government, Turkey's preference has been for the third position – moving as an actor who can change the course of history rather than being an ordinary and passive component of it. As evidence of these changes, humanitarian diplomacy was the main theme of the Fifth Annual Ambassadors' Conference held in Ankara and Izmir between 2 and 7 January 2013. Even if Turkey's humanitarian policy was designed before the Arab upheavals,[72] Davutoğlu posed a new notion of humanitarian diplomacy to explain and legitimize Ankara's involvement in different regions affected by crisis and political instability. As pointed out by Akpinar, the discourse on humanitarian diplomacy emerged as a result of Turkey's recalibration process, in particular to explain the widening of focus and scale of its foreign policy, which went beyond the immediate borders towards distant regions such as Africa, Latin America and East Asia.[73] Turkey's definition of humanitarian diplomacy resonates with Régnier's definition that the term [humanitarian diplomacy] is used not only by humanitarian organizations but also by national cooperation agencies and ministries (foreign affairs, defence, development, civil protection) comprising humanitarian aid departments to respond to domestic or international emergencies.[74] Indeed, Turkey has emphasized the role of the state as a humanitarian actor, highlighting a type of diplomacy that is multitrack in nature. In this perspective, Turkey's view underpinned the role of both the state and the non-state actors in humanitarian diplomacy. In Davutoğlu's perspective, humanitarian diplomacy or the rise of a human-oriented policy represented the beginning of a more enlightened foreign policy. Davutoğlu believed that a new international system requires an approach based on a 'critical equilibrium between conscience and power', and that Turkey was determined to be a leader in establishing such an understanding on a global scale.[75] Since then, the Turkish government has welcomed being

---

[71] Davutoğlu, Ahmet. 2013a. 'Turkey's Humanitarian Diplomacy: Objectives, Challenges and Prospects'. *Nationalities Papers: The Journal of Nationalism and Ethnicity* 41 (6): 865.

[72] Haşimi, 'Turkey's Humanitarian Diplomacy'.

[73] Akpinar, 'Turkey's Peacebuilding'.

[74] According to Régnier, humanitarian diplomacy is 'a multi-level process' because there are several levels of contact and intermediation: internationally, nationally, sub-nationally, locally and on the field. Régnier, 'The Emerging Concept', 1219–20.

[75] Davutoğlu, 'Turkey's Humanitarian Diplomacy', 866.

called an 'emerging donor'[76] because the status of being 'emerging' and thus increasingly significant and influential, plays a decisive role in Turkey's identity as a self-confident international actor.[77] Indeed, in a global context, Turkey's humanitarian-oriented approach is used as a way to live up to the expectations of international solidarity and problem-solving initiatives that come with the status of being a 'rising power'.[78]

In fractured Somali contexts, the main risk is that humanitarian aid and assistance can never appear as neutral resources but, rather, as part of a hidden agenda. For this reason, Turkey had worked to gain the confidence of all actors through the use of humanitarianism's creed of neutrality as a core principle.[79] These considerations convinced the Turkish policymakers that negotiation and dialogue were the primary means through which Turkish organizations, both state institutions and civil society, should conduct their aid programmes. This require the perception of impartial engagement with all actors. In order to break the mistrust of the Somali people, Turkey had adopted a dual strategy: implementing a *total performance policy* and fulfilling its operative actions of a humanitarian rhetoric. As stressed previously, total performance means a process of involving all the political and socio-economic groups, from universities to trade associations and NGOs, in foreign policymaking and actions.[80] In Turkey's vision, the role of NGOs can be central due to their ability to create links on the ground through micro-level visible assistance that touch people's lives directly and facilitate trust-building. The humanitarian purpose and its strong rhetoric have been used at the international level to legitimize Turkey's cross-border engagements.[81] At the same time, providing comprehensive humanitarian aid creates an umbrella on the ground under which Turkish assistance appears transparent, inclusive and neutral. This aid provided Turkey with legitimacy when developing its subsequent policies towards Somalia.[82] Turkey's choice to

---

[76] The OECD's DAC categorizes Turkey as an emerging donor – a country that has moved from being an aid recipient to providing increasing amounts of ODA and Other Official Flows (OOF).

[77] Binder, Andrea. 2014. 'The Shape and Sustainability of Turkey's Booming Humanitarian Assistance'. *Revue Internationale de Politique de Développement* 5 (2). doi: https://doi.org/10.4000/poldev.1741; Binder, Andrea, Claudia Meier and Julia Steets. 2010. 'Humanitarian Assistance: Truly Universal?: A Mapping Study of Non-Western Donors'. In *Global Public Policy Institute Research Paper*. Berlin: Global Public Policy Institute.

[78] Parlar Dal, Emel. 2014. 'On Turkey's Trail as a 'Rising Middle Power' in the Network of Global Governance: Preferences, Capabilities, and Strategies'. *Perceptions: Journal of International Affairs* 19 (4): 107–36.

[79] Murphy, Teri and Auveen Elizabeth Woods. 2014. *Turkey's International Development Framework Case Study: Somalia*. Istanbul: Istanbul Policy Center.

[80] Aras, 'Turkey's Mediation and Friends'; Kara and Sozen, 'Change and Continuity'.

[81] Tank, Pinar. 2013. *Turkey's New Humanitarian Approach in Somalia*. Oslo: Peace Research Institute Oslo.

[82] Özkan, *Turkey's Involvement in Somalia*, 22.

operate from Mogadishu, in the heart of the country, while all other donors have operated following a long-distance approach from their offices in Nairobi,[83] has improved its knowledge of local actors in Somali NGOs and civil society. Since then, Turkish development and humanitarian aid approach is guided by principles of impartiality and responsiveness to local needs, by involving a variety of governmental, non-governmental and private sector actors, and it is marked by its bilateral orientation.[84]

As a result, Turkey's humanitarian engagement has grown and its reputation as a 'humanitarian state' rings louder over all of Afro-Eurasia. The start of this path that brought recognition and popularity to Turkey was, in 2011, the choice to operate in a comprehensive and effective way in Somalia, a country in which no other external actor was willing to engage. Turkey has utilized its interventions in Somalia as 'showpieces' for its humanitarian clout throughout sub-Saharan Africa. They also underscored the material capabilities of Turkey as an emerging economy, tangibly demonstrated in terms of aid and trade assistance.[85] The intervention in Somalia also allowed Turkey to spread its idea of political and economic development based on its own experience – an idea that would be refined later and embodied in the formula of the Ankara consensus. It was not a coincidence that after the involvement in the Somali crisis, the Turkish agenda for Africa began to change and enter into a new stage in which humanitarian and development efforts were complemented by a growing interest in the political issues of the continent. By doing so, Turkey became a hybrid in the landscape of extra-regional actors. Furthermore, the former foreign minister believed that Turkey should be a compassionate (soft power) and powerful (hard power) state. According to him, one will be compassionate 'if one's conscience dictates where one should go and to whom one should reach' and, at the same time, one will need to have power, 'so that one has the ability to reach where needed'. This approach, which can help move beyond the hard-power versus soft power dichotomy, requires that NGOs and the state apparatus act in coordination as 'a combination of power and compassion' because 'if either of them is missing, the result will be either cruelty or weakness'. Davutoğlu's holistic meaning of humanitarianism is multifaceted and multichannelled. This idea has been

---

[83] Other international donors base themselves in Nairobi or in the heavily guarded AMISOM base in Mogadishu and rely on local but impersonal channels to send aid and provide assistance. The result of this approach meant that Somali recipients were burdened by a slow, bureaucratic aid system with little to no consultation with communities and the frequent diversion of aid into local war economies. See Sazak and Woods, 'Thinking Outside the Compound', 170.

[84] Binder, 'The Shape and Sustainability'.

[85] Langan, 'Virtuous Power Turkey', 1400.

operationalized by Turkey on the ground through an inter-agency coordinated policy useful in the management of crisis situations as well as in establishing and consolidating new relationships. This approach is in contrast to that of traditional donors in Somalia who are often accused of being overly bureaucratic, slow and isolated – either bunkered in the airport in Mogadishu or providing aid remotely from other neighbouring countries.[86]

Turkey's actions in Somalia have been viewed as largely positive, inside and outside Somalia. The ability of Turkish charities and government employees to work in areas of the Somali capital seen by Westerners as too dangerous, is greatly admired. While Turkey's engagement in Somalia has probably produced some positive results, Turkey needs to understand that this alone cannot solve the country's many challenges. Indeed, Turkey has demonstrated its ability to manage local tensions, but Somali politics, both internal and regional, is more complex. In order to ensure stability and national reconciliation Turkey will need to address the interests and needs of both internal and external actors by establishing joint projects with other Western and non-Western powers. Having said that, Ankara's partial success in Somalia has improved Turkey's image in the whole continent and demonstrated how Turkey has tried to become regionally and globally influential via soft power, mediation efforts, development assistance and humanitarian aid. All of these elements find a place in the ambitious idea of promoting its own way or formula of development and stability: the Ankara Consensus. Indeed, as stressed by President Erdoğan during the UN's High-Level Partnership Forum on Somalia (2016), one of the most successful aspects of Turkey's involvement in the Somali crisis has been that the Turkish model of aid has gained recognition in the literature and among the international community.[87]

---

[86] Wasuge, Mahad. 2016. *Turkey's Assistance Model in Somalia: Achieving Much With Little*. Mogadishu: Heritage Institute for Policy Studies.

[87] Presidency of the Turkish Republic. 2016. Somalia has become a Symbol of the Relations We Wish to Establish with Our Brothers in Africa. URL: http://www.tccb.gov.tr/en/news/542/39918/somalia-has-become-a-symbol-of-the-relations-we-wish-to-establish-with-our-brothers-in-africa.html.

5

Turkey's way for development

The Ankara Consensus

As discussed in the previous chapter, Turkey's growing involvement in the Somali crisis since 2011 has deepened its presence in SSA, thus changing the nature of Turkey's engagement with the continent, and paving the way to a new phase distinguished by a growing interest in high politics, that is, political matters and security issues. Since then, the nature of that engagement has been a combination of aid-oriented efforts and an achievement of political and economic goals. The restoration of a basic political order in Somalia, the confidence gained in the eyes of the different factions and the renewed international concern for the fate of the whole sub-region HOA have elevated Turkey to being a stakeholder whose opinions are widely appreciated. Over the years, a kind of 'Turkish model' of engagement has emerged, starting from the experience gained on the ground in Somalia. It is characterized by the quick delivery of assistance and programmes with Turkish personnel in different fields (multitrack and multi-stakeholder). The emergence of a peculiar Turkish modus operandi in the countries of SSA, combined with a new narrative, has made Turkey a non-traditional actor in the region following a novel paradigm of sustainability development: the Ankara consensus. This chapter examines specifically the features that characterize the Ankara consensus from an ideational point of view, leaving to the following chapter the task of examining its practical application through the multitrack approach. Their analysis highlights the numerous original traits that distinguish Turkish policy towards Africa from those adopted by other extra-regional actors, both emerging and traditional. Moreover, here, too, it is possible to highlight the persistent tension between foreign and domestic policy.

5.1 The partnership agenda and the development of security dimension

As described in the previous chapters (3 and 4), Turkey initially operated in SSAa similarly to other non-traditional actors (China, Brazil, India), focusing on economic development and humanitarian aid without concern for political issues. Until 2011, Turkey's engagement in Africa was included in the international strategies of the New Partnership for Africa's Development (NEPAD),[1] whose aim has been to bring development and stability through peacekeeping interventions under the auspices of the UN. For the Turkish state, humanitarian aid was and still is a means to strengthen bilateral relations with governments. Furthermore, Turkey used its membership in multilateral organizations and other international bodies, such as AU and OIC, to reach out to Africa, gaining credibility in African eyes. Nevertheless, the year 2011 marked a turning point in Turkish foreign policy, including its African agenda.

It is commonly accepted that the general orientations of foreign policy are affected by the local–global nexus, which has been channellized by the process of state-building.[2] In the case of Turkey, there was a further shift in its foreign policy agenda in 2013. The new shift in Turkish policy was determined by the interplay of factors of different origins, such as the weakening of domestic democratic standards, the slowdown of economic growth and the failure of the regional policy. A determining variable was, once again, the perception of the external environment by foreign policymakers, which changed rapidly following the Arab upheavals of 2011. At the beginning, in the eyes of the Turkish elites, the reshuffling of the political balances in the Middle East seemed to open new windows of opportunity for their regional ambitions, but after a few months it turned out to be a threat to Turkey's security and government stability.[3] Indeed, at the outbreak of the uprisings, Turkey had tried to present itself as a regional order builder in the surrounding region, trying to revive – at least ideationally – the historical and cultural boundaries of the Ottoman Empire. This strategy, heavily influenced by the JDP's conservative identity nexus, tried unsuccessfully to profit from the redistribution of political power in the region following the

[1] The New Partnership for Africa's Development is an economic development programme of the AU. Adopted in 2001, NEPAD aims to provide an overarching vision and policy framework for accelerating economic cooperation and integration among African countries. See www.nepad.org.

[2] Keyman, Fuat E. and Sebnem Gumuscu. 2014. *Democracy, Identity and Foreign Policy in Turkey: Hegemony through Transformation*. London: Palgrave Macmillan.

[3] Özpek, Burak Bilgehan and Yelda Demirağ. 2014. 'Turkish Foreign Policy after the "Arab Spring": From Agendasetter State to Agenda-Entrepreneur State'. *Israel Affairs* 20 (3): 328–46.

reluctance of the great powers to intervene, initially, on a large scale. In less than two years all the inconsistencies of the Turkish agenda emerged, including the failure to export its model to neighbouring countries – democracy, pro-Islamic ruling party, secular institutions and market economy. By contrast, Turkey has internalized several of the matrices of regional instability, most notably the centralization of powers in the hands of a single leader. This triggered a process of Middle Easternization of the Turkish system and institutions – a dynamic highlighted by the progressive shift from an illiberal democracy characterized by electoral hegemony (2012–15) to a regime ever closer to competitive authoritarianism,[4] sanctioned by the constitutional referendum of 2017 that definitively opened a season of personalist government.[5]

The regional crisis and its spillover effects have had implications on Turkey's global ambitions, undermining its credibility and the efficiency of the Turkish state's capabilities to act as an emerging middle power. As a result, the two-year period (2011–13) opened a resilience stage in Turkey's global agenda, entailing changes in its policy towards SSA. In this phase, which ended in 2017, Turkey tried to expand its scope as a global player, taking advantage of the crisis in the established powers and the need for new partners in the Global South, especially among the LDCs. The Turkish state, by doing that, hoped to be able to revitalize its foreign policy and to rehabilitate its international image weakened by the internal illiberal drift and inefficient actions in adjacent crises such as Syria. Indeed, regional and global processes prompted the Turkish foreign policymakers to search for an alternative path in world politics, by focusing their attention on other regions such as Latin America, SSA and Southern Asia. The impossibility of becoming a regional hegemon in the post-Arab Revolution scenario, the constraints of the traditional – and the new Middle Eastern – markets, in addition to the stoppage in the EU membership process, led Turkey to invest, more seriously, time and resources in alternative regions and adopt the good practices in policy areas such as foreign aid, humanitarian assistance, peacekeeping operations and cultural cooperation, among others. Besides the regional and global factors, the ideological preferences of the political coalition – grounded on conservative principles with pragmatic implementation – defined this different route for the Turkish foreign policy towards the Global South. This southern route posits a normative and responsible stance as a middle emerging

---

[4] Özbudun, Ergun. 2014. 'AKP at the Crossroads: Erdoğan's Majoritarian Drift'. *South European Society & Politics* 19 (2): 155–67.

[5] Esen, Berk and Sebnem Gumuscu. 2016. 'Rising Competitive Authoritarianism in Turkey'. *Third World Quarterly* 37 (9): 1581–606.

power by taking a more global and accountable approach of world politics emphasizing the ways to overcome global inequality.[6] By using a set of soft power tools – such as the use of peacekeeping troops, developmental aid, humanitarian activities and public diplomacy – Turkey extended its role in regional and world politics reflecting a concern for justice with an 'ethical foreign policy'.[7]

The trajectory of the Global South has been widely discussed since the end of the Cold War. During the last three decades, many non-DAC countries have begun to redefine their role in the global governance by intensifying their efforts to support various developmental activities undertaken by countries in the Global South. As a result, the world has witnessed an unprecedented growth of what can be called 'South–South' aid, promoting horizontal cooperation based on the principle of equality, partnership and mutual interest.[8] Nowadays, emerging powers, particularly of the Global South, are perceived to have become the agents of change,[9] even if there is evidence that emerging powers do not always have a common vision of development and an orientation to the Global South. They often pursue an active agenda based on their distinct conceptualization of development, which pays attention to such values as social justice, environmental sustainability, democracy and human rights. Foreign aid and development cooperation constitute a relatively small element within the global change, but it is an arena that is revealing of wider patterns and trends in political, economic and cultural power.[10] The behaviour of emerging powers is systemically different from that of traditional ones, in that it refuses to use the dominant language of official development, which tends to rationalize the hierarchical relationship between North and South.[11] Therefore, Turkey is not a single case among the emerging powers, but its approach presents several elements not found in other experiences. The engagement in Somalia has brought to light how the Turkish mould clearly differs from that of both traditional DAC countries and non-DAC

[6] Donelli, Federico and Ariel S. González Levaggi. 2018. 'From Mogadishu to Buenos Aires: The Global South in the Turkish Foreign Policy in the Late JDP Period (2011–2017)'. In *Middle Powers in Global Governance: The Rise of Turkey*, edited by Emel Parlar Dal, 53–73. London: Palgrave Macmillan.

[7] Bayer, Reşat and E Fuat Keyman. 2012. 'Turkey: An Emerging Hub of Globalization and Internationalist Humanitarian Actor?' *Globalizations* 9 (1): 85.

[8] Quadir, Fahimul. 2013. 'Rising Donors and the New Narrative of "South–South" Cooperation: What Prospects for Changing the Landscape of Development Assistance Pogrammes?' *Third World Quarterly* 34 (2): 322–3.

[9] Chaturvedi, Sachin, Thomas Fues and Elizabeth Sidiropoulos, eds. 2012. *Development Cooperation and Emerging Powers: New Partners or Old Patterns?* London: ZED Books Ltd.

[10] Woods, NGaire. 2008. 'Whose Aid? Whose Influence? China, Emerging Donors and the Silent Revolution in Development Assistance'. *International Affairs* 84 (6): 1205–21.

[11] Dreher, Axel, Peter Nunnenkamp and Rainer Thiele. 2011. 'Are "New" Donors Different? Comparing the Allocation of Bilateral Aid Between non-DAC and DAC Donor Countries'. *World Development* 39 (11): 1950–68.

countries. Indeed, the increasing involvement in SSA portrays an example of the novel Turkish orientation towards the Global South.

Since its high-profile intervention during the height of the famine in 2011, Turkey has elevated its level of engagement with Somalia and has committed to robust humanitarian assistance, development aid and civilian capacity to resuscitate the fragile state. Its presence in Somalia as a humanitarian actor first, and then as a political mediator between the conflicting parties and a development initiator, has shifted the focus of Turkish interest towards greater involvement in the political problems of the sub-region. Turkey has assumed more political responsibilities in the HOA, rather than being merely an economic power or donor country. This change has made Turkey a unique extra-regional actor because it combines the traditional political-stability perspective of Western powers with the economic-trade perspective of emerging ones.[12] Turkey's engagement in Somalia has become one of the most visible examples of a rising power's approach to a conflict-affected and fragile country. At the same time, it has given Turkey an opportunity to experiment with its own way of creating relationships and consolidating partnerships with the LDC countries and to project its image as a global rising power. This belief was clearly expressed by the Turkish International Cooperation and Coordination Agency (TİKA), the main Turkish state agency charged with coordinating development assistance and humanitarian aid projects abroad. In 2012, a few months after the Turkish humanitarian intervention in Somalia, the agency's annual report highlighted that

> In 2012, there has been a decrease in the amount of development assistance provided by traditional donors; whereas Turkey's development assistance increased by 98.7% in one year. In this framework, Turkey is now defined as an 'emerging donor' and strengthens its 'donor' role each passing year.[13]

One consequence of the perception of development cooperation as a foreign policy instrument is that Turkish development cooperation is normally accompanied by other public diplomacy measures. This mix has, over time, favoured the formation of a peculiar version of multitrack diplomacy that is analysed in depth in the next chapter. Thus, the Turkish model of engagement in crises and post-crises situations is noted for its emphasis on soft-power attributes such as business interests and cultural affinities, such as the Muslim identity

---

[12] Özkan, 'Turkey's Religious and Socio', 50.
[13] TİKA. 2013. *2012 Annual Report*. Ankara: Turkish Development and Coordination Agency.

The commitment made in Somalia, the increasing popularity acquired throughout the continent and the desire to export a sort of Turkish formula to economic prosperity and political stability convinced Turkey to reformulate its African agenda.

The Second Turkey–Africa Partnership Summit held in Malabo (Equatorial Guinea) in November 2014 established the idea that Turkey's Africa policy had entered a new era. The summit, with the theme of the 'New model of partnership for the strengthening of sustainable development and integration', witnessed Turkey's revised agenda towards Africa. President Erdoğan and Foreign Minister Mevlüt Çavuşoğlu headed the Turkish delegation, which included around 200 business representatives. Some thirty African countries were represented, seven at the presidential level.[14] At the end of the summit, even without a joint communiqué, the participants signed a joint action plan for the five-year period between 2014 and 2019 whereby they decided to elevate their relations to the level of strategic partnership. In other words, the opening-up-to-Africa period was closed, and the relationship entered a new phase under the rubric Turkey–Africa Partnership initiative. This new strategy would further facilitate the consolidation of African ownership of African issues under the motto 'African issues require African solutions'.

During those months, Turkey was already lobbying African countries to get their votes in the non-permanent UN Security Council election for the two-year period from 2015 to 2016. The main argument put forward by the Turkish leaders to support Turkey's candidacy was that a seat for Turkey would be another voice for Africa.[15] On the African side, there were many expectations in relation to the G20 hosted by Turkey in Antalya in 2015. It was expected that Turkey would use its presidency of the G20 as a vehicle to further its interests in SSA and to advocate the cause of the African people, at the summit. Prime Minister Davutoğlu stated in late 2014 that many African governments had asked Turkey to be their 'voice' within the G20, in which South Africa is otherwise the continent's sole representative.[16] In 2016, on the wake of the commitment made during the G20, Turkey organized the first Turkey–Africa Economic and Business Forum. The forum, under the motto of 'Unite, Discover,

---

14 The presidents of Benin, Chad, Equatorial Guinea, Mauritania, Niger, Republic of Congo and Zimbabwe attended, as did the vice presidents of Burundi and South Africa and the prime ministers of Algeria, Gabon and Swaziland. There was also ministerial-level representation from Angola, DR Congo, Ethiopia, Ghana, Kenya, Libya, Morocco, Nigeria, Senegal, Somalia and Sudan. The chairperson of the African Union Commission, Nkosazana Dlamini-Zuma, was also present.
15 Bülent Arınç's speech at the Turkey–Africa Media Forum, Ankara, May 2012.
16 'Turkey committed to a more inclusive G20 for an interconnected world', Daily Sabah, 14 November 2014.

Create', brought together 50 high-level officials and 3,000 businesspeople from Turkey and 49 African countries. Besides economic interests, the consequences of the failed coup d'état of 15 July 2016 led to the choice of organizing a major conference in Istanbul to involve the African political and economic elites, who were traditionally the most exposed to the influence of Gülen's movement.[17] The forum, which was held again two years later (2018), had the aim

> to improve Turkey's commercial and investment relations with African countries and the Continent as a whole; as well as increase the share of Turkish companies in the African geography by providing networking platforms to gather the political leaders and senior decision makers in Africa and Turkey, heads of financial institutions, company executives, investors for new joint ventures, trade partnerships and investments.[18]

The two events, both organized by DEIK under the auspices of the presidency of the Republic and the AU, followed the Africa ownership approach introduced in the Turkish policy towards Africa in Malabo in 2014. To demonstrate the credibility of this approach, the Turkish organizers chose, in the two forum editions, to set up the conference not only from the point of view of Turkish–African relations but also by giving centrality to African issues. Especially at the 2018 forum, the central theme was how to raise awareness among African public and private sectors of the African Continental Free Trade Area. Turkey, in other words, was able to transform a bilateral forum into a platform for effective discussion and debate among African state and non-state actors. The Turkish state has tried to export its idea of partnership through the concrete example of cooperation – an original approach that distinguishes the Turkey partnership experience from others. Indeed, the Africa–Turkey partnership is one of many that the African continent has entered into in order to boost its chances of attaining the aspirations, goals and targets set out in Agenda 2063. Other partnerships exist with the UN and its agencies, the EU, South America, the League of Arab States, the United States, China and Korea.[19]

At the same time, Turkey continued to invest in an ambitious programme to establish diplomatic missions in SSA countries and encouraged the reciprocal opening of embassies in Ankara. Embassies were established in Gambia,

---

[17] The topic will be discussed in more detail in the next chapter.

[18] Turkey–Africa Economic and Business Forum overview document, available on the Forum website, URL: http://www.turkeyafricaforum.org/about-overview.html.

[19] For further information on the different characteristics of the partnerships, see Cumming, Gordon and Tony Chafer, eds. 2011. *From Rivalry to Partnership?: New Approaches to the Challenges of Africa*. Burlington: Ashgate.

Mauritania, Mozambique, South Sudan, Zambia and Zimbabwe (2011); Burkina Faso, Gabon, Namibia and Niger (2012); and Chad, Guinea, Djibouti and Eritrea (2013). When Turkey opened its embassy in Eritrea in 2013, it became the first country in the world to have ambassadorial representation in every country in the HOA. Different Turkish representations in the region have more symbolic than substantial relevance, although trade with these countries has increased in recent years. In this period, one of the main constraints of the Turkish approach towards Africa emerged: the vacuum in knowledge of the sub-Saharan context. Indeed, Turkey has had difficulties in recruiting qualified personnel that would be able to know how to navigate the African context. This deficiency is still evident today; in some representative offices, there are two or at most three Turkish employees. Although there are limits to what these small missions can do to promote Turkish interests, they still allow an ambassador to have personal interaction with Turkish government officials and other elements of society.[20]

In addition to the organization of fora and multilateral meetings, and the frenzied diplomatic activity, the personal diplomacy of President Erdoğan proved to be an essential value. Within a few weeks, the Turkish president met the leaders from a multitude of African countries, including President Ali Bongo Ondimba of Gabon and President Alassane Ouattara of Côte d'Ivoire.[21] In addition, Erdoğan also continued with his trips. During the first two months of 2016 Erdoğan visited some West African countries (Ivory Coast, Ghana, Nigeria) as well as some others in the HOA (Ethiopia, Djibouti, Somalia). While Turkey had long invested in both the consolidation of the area of the Horn and its development, its interests in the West coast of the continent were determined mainly by the aim of consolidating the partnership with the Economic Community of West African States. The president's visit to Nigeria was dictated by the desire to not only increase trade with one of the continent's economic powers but also silence some speculation regarding relations between Turkey and the Islamist group Boko Haram. After the French military intervention in Mali (2013–14), rumours began to circulate about alleged support provided by Turkey to Islamist militias and Salafist groups operating across the borders of Niger, Mali and Nigeria.[22] The government and the state-owned Turkish Airlines

---

[20] Shinn, David. 2015. *Turkey's Engagement in Sub-Saharan Africa: Shifting Alliances and Strategic Diversification*, 6. London: Chatman House. The Royal Institute of International Affairs.

[21] Fehim Tastekin, 'Erdoğan's Africa Tour'. *Al-Monitor*, 28 January 2015.

[22] Among the indiscretions was also the alleged tape posted in YouTube in which the voice supposedly of the Turkish Airlines CEO Mehmet Karataş tells Mustafa Varank, a close adviser to Prime Minister Erdoğan, that he feels guilty about the national carrier's arms shipments to Nigeria, apparently to be utilized by the terrorist groups active in the area such as Boko Haram. Michael Rubin, 'Tape Suggests Turkey Supports Terror'. *Commentary*, 20 March 2014.

attributed the rumours to defamatory propaganda by the Gülen movement's followers;[23] however, Turkey's reputation, already damaged by its ambiguous conduct towards ISIL,[24] lost its international prestige. Despite many Turkish efforts to settle the issue, in spring 2017 the Nigerian authorities detected in the Tin Can port in Apapa (Lagos) a cargo of weapons produced in the United States and Italy but imported from Turkey, intended for organized crime and probably also for some militias.[25]

The security dimension

In the field of security, the traditional foreign policy approach adopted by Ankara had led, especially after 1989, to Turkish involvement in several multilateral operations in Africa under the auspices of the UN. Between 1989 and 2018, the UN launched twenty-four peacekeeping operations in Africa, seven of which are currently underway. Although Turkey played a prominent role in the UN operation in Somalia (UNOSOM II) conducted from March 1993 to March 1995 under the command of Turkish General Çevik Bir, its involvement in other peacekeeping operations in Africa was very limited until 2005. While the Turkish contribution in the past has been limited, with participation in only eight of the twenty-four peacekeeping operations carried out, within the framework of the African agenda promoted by the JDP governments, Turkey has adopted a more active approach as evidenced by the involvement in four of the seven ongoing peacekeeping operations in Africa. In addition to its contribution to UN initiatives, Turkey has taken part in European Union military missions in Africa, including European Union Force Central African Republic (EUFOR RCA) and European Union Training Mission in Mali. Simultaneously with the development of political, trade and humanitarian relations, Turkey has increased its involvement in African security issues. While Turkish involvement in the previous decade was limited to multilateral initiatives such as UN-sponsored peacekeeping operations, since 2011 Turkey has increased its unilateral actions by strengthening its defence and security ties with African countries – among the first initiatives, the mission conducted by Barbaros Turkish Naval Task Force. Consisting of three warships, a logistical ship and 781 staff, it embarked upon a joint military exercise in the Gulf of Guinea organized by the US Africa Command. The Turkish warships also used and tested important weapon

---

[23] 'Turkish Airlines Denies Carrying Weapons to Nigeria'. *Reuters*, 19 March 2014.
[24] Vicken Cheterian, 'Turkey and the "Islamic State"'. *Open Democracy*, 23 September 2014.
[25] 'Illegal Arms Shipped from Turkey Seized in Nigeria'. *Stockholm Center for Freedom*, 24 May 2017.

systems, including Sea Sparrow missiles off South Africa's coast to measure their power and capacity. The fleet visited twenty-four African countries' ports with the objectives of developing relations with Africa, promoting Turkey, providing humanitarian assistance, fighting sea piracy and increasing its international visibility. Turkey carried out such a mission in Africa for the first time since 1866.[26]

A field to which Turkey has actively contributed is maritime security in the Mediterranean Sea, the Red Sea and the Gulf of Aden. Like many other countries, the Turkish Navy also has sent several frigates off the coast of Somalia with the aim of countering sea piracy. According to Sıradağ, 'since Turkey's active contribution to maritime security in Africa began in 2009, the number of attacks and naval hijackings has declined significantly'.[27] Furthermore, since 2007, Turkey has signed a multiplicity of bilateral agreements in the field of defence and security with more than twenty-five African countries, developing police cooperation and training programmes under the International Police Training Cooperation Project. These agreements are in addition to the previously signed counter-terrorism cooperation agreements with Kenya, Tanzania and Uganda. More recently, Turkey has developed special security relations with a number of African countries, including Sudan, Senegal and Somalia.

More recently, Turkish military projection in Africa has increased significantly. Regional and domestic factors have contributed to the increasing Turkish involvement in the African security sector, more specifically in the HOA. In recent years, competition among Middle Eastern powers has increasingly engaged the countries of the Horn. Since the Saudi-led intervention in the Yemeni crisis in 2015, the Red Sea has become a new power arena for the Middle East. A dynamic fostered by the Middle East competition that shows the growing interplay between the two Red Sea shores is the progressive militarization. This trend has been led by the policies of two players whose competition has risen significantly over the last few years: the UAE and Turkey. Actually, since 2017, along with the reshuffling of alliances, there has been a speedy process of militarization of the area through the opening of ME's military bases and outposts.[28] The UAE's and the KSA's attempts to expand their role in

---

[26] Sıradağ, 'Turkey-Africa Alliance: Evolving Patterns in Security Relations'. *African Security Review*, 316. doi: 10.1080/10246029.2018.1550429.

[27] Ibid., 316.

[28] Verhoeven, Harry. 2018. 'The Gulf and the Horn: Changing Geographies of Security Interdependence and Competing Visions of Regional Order'. *Civil Wars* 20 (3): 333–57; Cannon, Brendon J. and Federico Donelli. 2020. 'Asymmetric Alliances and High Polarity: Evaluating Regional Security Complexes in the Middle East and Horn of Africa'. *Third World Quarterly* 41 (3): 505–24.

the wider ME, have, on the one hand, pushed the Gulf powers to double down on their alignments in the Horn – with a burgeoning collaboration that goes beyond narrow security interests – inviting countries to choose their side of the divide. On the other hand, the change in the regional security patterns between 2015 and 2017 has affected the nature of the Turkish presence in Somalia. The worsening of the proxy-war in Yemen and the following rift within the GCC with the emergence of a blockade – the so-called Arab Quartet – opposed to Qatar, a Turkish ally even in Africa, have given Turkey's presence in Somalia a greater geostrategic significance. Therefore, the Turkish presence in Somalia has assumed a greater security dimension after the decision to open a military base in Mogadishu, the largest Turkish base overseas. Although the base (Camp TURKSOM) is formally and legally a military facility for the training of the Somali National Army, in practice it is a full-fledged Turkish military outpost in the region. At Camp TURKSOM some 200 Turkish soldiers were deployed and are currently training 1,500 Somali soldiers, with a target of 10,000 in the long term.[29] Despite the fact that, from a purely legal point of view, Camp TURKSOM is not a military base,[30] the Turkish military training camp in Mogadishu can be considered a Turkish outpost on the continent to such an extent that it is a source of concern to regional rivals such as the KSA and the UAE.[31] The opening of the Turkish military training base in Mogadishu was accompanied by plans to establish a navy outpost in Suakin (Sudan). The small island of Suakin is an ancient Ottoman city of strategic significance both for the control of the Red Sea – it is at the crossroads between Aden Gulf and the Suez Canal – and for its proximity to the holy places of Islam, Mecca and Medina. Turkey and Qatar had reached a trilateral agreement with Omar al-Bashir in December 2017 on a variety of issues including security cooperation and the concession of Suakin, although the core of the agreement was the restoration of old Ottoman buildings on the island, including the redevelopment of an old Ottoman-era port as a tourism hub. Despite official denials, many observers believed that the Sudanese concessions were the prelude to the establishment of a Turkish military base on the island.[32] The threat of a growing Turkish presence in the area alarmed Turkey's

[29] Hussein, Abdirahman and Orhan Coskun, 'Turkey Opens Military Base in Mogadishu to Train Somali Soldiers'. *Reuters*, 30 September 2017.

[30] Rossiter, Ash and Brendon J. Cannon. 2018. 'Re-examining the "Base": The Political and Security Dimensions of Turkey's Military Presence in Somalia'. *Insight Turkey*, 1–22. doi: 10.25253/99.2019211.09.

[31] Telci, Ismail and Tuba O. Horoz. 2018. 'Military Bases in the Foreign Policy of the United Arab Emirates'. *Insight Turkey* 20 (2): 308–25.

[32] See, for example, Tastekin, Fehim. 'Erdoğan's Ottoman Dream Causes Storm in the Red Sea'. *Al-Monitor*, January 2018, URL: https://www.al-monitor.com/pulse/fa/originals/2018/01/turkey

regional rivals such as the KSA, the UAE and Egypt, and also had consequences for the relationship between the latter and the Khartoum government. Turkish projects in Suakin have suffered a setback with the overthrow of al-Bashir even though they have not yet sunk. The Sudanese transitional government and the military apparatus led by General Mohamed Hamdan Dagalo have strengthened their ties with the KSA and the UAE by downgrading relations with Qatar and Turkey. At the same time, the Sudan realignment has favoured the increasing presence of the UAE, which, with the takeover of Port Sudan by the state-owned DP World, has added a further anchor to its security strategy.[33]

While regional developments have played an important role in increasing Turkish military presence in Africa, some domestic changes have been equally important. Notably, the shift of approach in foreign policy has been significant, characterized by a change in the conception of the national role of the FPEs and a gradual shift from soft power to hard power. The increase in Turkish military presence in Africa reflects developments in its foreign policy behaviour. The Libyan and Syrian crisis have shown to Turkish FPEs that 'a cautious "wait and see" approach was not a viable option'.[34] The developments on the Turkish southern border have made Turkey's status more unstable and they have influenced Turkish FPEs' orientation towards their neighbours. The 'order maker' role in the region asserted during the Davutoğlu's era proved to be too optimistic as shown by the worsening of the Syrian civil war. These circumstances have also driven another change in the Turkish foreign policy, from the idea of a 'central country' to one of Turkey as a 'buffer state'. Similar to the Cold War period, Turkey perceives itself as a buffer state. This current conception is security-driven and based on the notion of containment and status quo orientation. Among its determinants are several domestic factors: first, the polarization of liberal and secular factions of the Turkish public and the discontent with the JDP's autocratic drift; second, the conflict between the Turkish state institutions and the Gülen movement erupt in the failed coup attempt in mid-2016; third, the large number of attacks by terrorist groups such as ISIL and TAK (a PKK offshoot) in Turkish cities; and finally, the disappointing results for the government in the June

-sudan-cooperation-sparks-worry-in-gulf.html (accessed 20 April 2020); Amin, Par Mohammed. 'Suakin: "Forgotten" Sudanese Island becomes Focus for Red Sea Rivalries'. *Middle East Eye*, 19 March 2018, URL: https://www.middleeasteye.net/fr/news/suakin-island-sudan-turkey-saudi-arab ia-egypt-394055164 (accessed 20 April 2020).

[33] AA.VV. 'UAE Taking Steps to Gain Control of Sudan's Main Port', *Al-Jazeera*, 20 April 2020, URL: https://www.aljazeera.com/news/2020/04/uae-steps-gain-control-sudan-main-port-200423205443 903.html (accessed 4 May 2020).

[34] Keyman, E. Fuat. 2016. 'Turkish Foreign Policy in the Post-Arab Spring Era: From Proactive to Buffer State'. *Third World Quarterly* 37 (12): 2274–87.

2015 general elections in which JDP saw its majority fading away. The events described here indicate how the domestic sphere is currently characterized by growing challenges to the JDP's role, and depict the increasing polarization among different social and political communities in the country. Accordingly, 'it became increasingly difficult for the JDP to govern with soft measures, and some autocratic tendencies prevailed'.[35] President Erdoğan monopolized the authority within the JDP. His 'one-man' rule has been observed in almost all aspects of Turkish politics including foreign policy, which assumed a peculiar trait of other Middle East regimes: the idiosyncratic variable. As also pointed out by Dawisha (1988), the idiosyncratic variable usually occurred in regimes where power is personalized and concentrated, especially in times of fluidity or crises.[36] Since 2014, Erdoğan has taken the primary role in Turkish foreign policymaking, leaving a limited position to Davutoğlu's circle.[37] Alongside, Turkey had to set aside its ambition to become a regional power, in line with Davutoğlu's grand vision, and embraced a more pragmatic and less ideological foreign policy behaviour.

Since 2015, Turkey has adopted a more securitized foreign policy in which hard power regained supremacy over soft power, which came together with a clear doctrine of pre-emptive action, called the 'Erdoğan doctrine'. The core idea of this new security approach is that, while facing a wide range of external problems and threats, Turkey must adopt preventive policies. This doctrine recalled the 2002 G. W. Bush National Security Strategy of 'pre-emption', defined as pre-emptive and preventive action. The first and clear outcome of such a new pre-emptive approach was the military intervention in northern Syria launched in August 2016 (Euphrates Shield).[38] Yet again, in January 2018 Turkey launched another military operation (Olive Branch) in the Afrin region[39] in order to prevent the consolidation of Kurdish militia positions and to create a safe zone

---

[35] Yesilyurt, Nuri. 2017. 'Explaining Miscalculation and Maladaptation in Turkish Foreign Policy towards the Middle East during the Arab Uprisings: A Neoclassical Realist Perspective'. *Center for Foreign Policy and Peace Research, İhsan Doğramacı Peace Foundation* 6 (2): 65–83.

[36] Dawisha, Adeed. 1988. 'Arab Regimes: Legitimacy and Foreign Policy'. In *Beyond Coercion: The Durability of the Arab States*, edited by Adeed Dawisha and William I. Zartman, 260–75. London: Croom-Helm. For a more in-depth analysis, see also Hermann, Margaret G. 1980. 'Explaining Foreign Policy Behaviour Using the Personal Characteristics of Political Leaders'. *International Studies Quarterly* 24 (1): 7–46; Roberts, Jonathan M. 1988. 'The Importance of Individual and Role Variables'. In *Decision-Making during International Crises*, edited by Jonathan M. Roberts, 160–80. London: Palgrave Macmillan.

[37] Kuru, Ahmet. 2015. 'Turkey's Failed Policy toward the Arab Spring: Three Levels of Analysis'. *Mediterranean Quarterly* 26 (3): 94–116.

[38] The military operation, which ended in March 2017, was carried out with the aim of opposing the ISIL advance and preventing the constitution of an independent Kurdish state in Syria.

[39] A Syrian district near the Turkish border controlled by Kurdish forces.

on the border. The Ankara government decided to conduct such an operation although it would have potentially put itself in direct conflict with the United States and other NATO allies, considering the circumstances a threat to its own national security. An unusual aspect of this new deal in foreign policy is that the new concept of pre-emptive action is being discussed a lot in Turkish media. It seems that the government is working to generate support from the Turkish public by promoting the doctrine of pre-emption and cross-border operations as the sole method of combating the threats. The strategy involves concepts such as the effective use of military force beyond borders when needed, the possible disregard of traditional alliance relations and taking unilateral action independently of the United States and NATO.

Despite various constraints and some difficulties, the Turkish presence on the continent was becoming increasingly widespread. Especially in the HOA, the commitment made in Somalia and the frenetic diplomatic activity had allowed Turkey to earn credit which could be used in the rest of the continent – a situation that would have alarmed regional rivals, particularly the UAE and Egypt, both concerned about the Ankara government's support for the rise of political Islamic movements. At the same time, the Turkish presence and its activism in SSA began to take shape along original lines. Although several traits can be attributed to experiences gained by other extra-regional actors, traditional and non-traditional ones, as a whole, the features of the Turkish approach remain unusual to such an extent that we can refer to Turkey as a hybrid actor in the sub-Saharan context.

5.2 The ideational dimension: Turkey as a neo-Ottoman 'virtuous power'

Today, Turkey's presence in the region has particular characteristics that differentiate it from other external powers. Indeed, Turkish policy in SSA represents a unique model and a break with the traditional mould of conducting foreign policy on the continent by East/West partners such as China, the United States, Russia and other emerging powers. In the wake of the mediation and peacemaking efforts undertaken in Somalia, Turkey has been careful to distance itself from both the traditional donors, especially those associated with colonialism in Africa, and relative newcomers to the continent whose main interests are economic.[40] Turkey is distinguished from other emerging

---

[40] Wasuge, *Turkey's Assistance Model*, 10; see also Cannon, *Turkey in Africa*.

players such as South Korea, India, Brazil or China by a multiplicity of aspects, including a long history of economic and cultural interactions with some African countries and, as emphasized by the European Commission, a tradition of close collaboration and work with OECD and DAC countries. The latter is a key element in understanding Turkey's difference from other emerging players, which, on the contrary, make the absence of links with OECD–DAC countries one of their major strengths as well as a pillar of their own storytelling. In addition to these aspects, there are also the peculiarities, in both practice and storytelling, inherent to Turkey's African agenda, which make the Anatolian country a unique actor of its kind. The practical dimension is analysed accurately in the next chapter and it has been displayed in the multitrack policy. As for the ideational dimension, that is, how Turkey presents itself and its commitment in Africa to the eyes of the African peoples and the international community, it can be discerned in three key themes:

The absence of a colonial past: this aspect was perfectly summarized by the former Turkish president Abdullah Gül, who during a visit to Africa said that Turkey's intent is to bring a 'clean slate with humanist approach to Africa'.[41] If one carefully analyses Gül's sentence it is possible to identify Turkey's double detachment, from traditional powers and from other emerging actors. The term 'clean slate' is an implicit denunciation of Western imperialism. Indeed, by the expression 'clean slate', Gül was alluding to the crucial fact that Turkey has never been a colonizing power in the region[42] – an assertion derived from the reinterpretation of historical memory promoted in Turkey under the tutelage of the JDP government.[43]

From this angle of imperial history, it is in the belief of the current Turkish conservative establishment that the Ottoman period was a golden age in all domains, including areas of North and East Africa, which were an integral part of the Empire rather than lands of exploitation. During his mandate, Gül, together with Erdoğan and other distinguished members of the ruling party, was one of the most active extra-regional leaders in SSA. Through his many speeches made during bilateral visits and multilateral events, some of the recurring topics of the Turkish narrative towards Africa emerged. Among the issues that have been treated with the highest insistence, there was the Turkish will to break away from

---

[41] 'Ottoman Dreaming'. *The Economist*, May 2010.
[42] Abdirahman, 'Turkey's Foray into Africa', 66. See also Rudincová, 'New Player on the Scene', 209.
[43] For a more in-depth discussion of the process of recovery and reworking of the Ottoman heritage by JDP governments, see Uzer, Umut. 2018. 'Glorification of the Past as a Political Tool: Ottoman History in Contemporary Turkish Politics'. *The Journal of the Middle East and Africa* 9 (4): 339–57.

the policies of traditional extra-regional actors, especially European countries. The then Turkish president used to remind the former colonial powers of their responsibilities, asking them to answer for the pain inflicted on the African people during their imperialism. At the same time, Gül was pointing out that Turkey had no past to be ashamed of. Accordingly, Turkey was in a position to set up its relations with African countries from scratch, relying on common interests and the claim of being a truly equal partner. This point was very well clarified during a meeting with Ghanaian officials, when Gül stated:

> We [Turks] are different from Europeans. We do not take away your raw materials. We invest and also bring along technology and qualified work force. We have done so in other African countries. We already began to do so in Ghana as well.[44]

At the same time, the second part of Gül's sentence – 'humanist approach' – was intended to make a difference with other emerging powers interested in Africa. In particular, the expression was addressed to the most active extra-regional player, namely China, known for turning a blind eye to its authoritarian trading partners, which, as long as they exported oil and raw materials, secured Beijing's support on the world stage, in particular the important UN Security Council.[45] The way in which many emerging players operate in the African context is considered by Turkish policymakers to be unscrupulous and aimed solely at achieving their own material interests. On the contrary, the Turkish approach always shows sympathy for the plight of the African people, and it tends to place the interests of both, their own as well as those of the beneficiary country, at the centre. Turkish efforts always place great emphasis on the humanitarian aspect, namely, the improvement of the living conditions of the African people. However, one of the vulnerable traits of the Turkish strategy towards Africa stems from the gap between rhetoric and real action – a constraint that, as McLean pointed out, is evident throughout Turkish foreign policy.[46] Indeed, the narrative that accompanies the official visits of Turkish government figures needs to be questioned, and it should be stressed that these are often nothing more than lip service. Like all the extra-regional actors that are active in Africa, Turkey also has as one of its goals the pursuit of material gains. In most cases, this means political and diplomatic support, the acquisition of contracts for Turkish companies and

---

[44] Abdullah Gül cited in Afacan, Isa. 2013. 'The African Opening in Turkish Foreign Policy'. *Ortadoğu Analiz* 5 (52): 53.

[45] Abdirahman, 'Turkey's Foray into Africa', 66.

[46] Mclean, Wayne. 2015. 'Understanding Divergence between Public Discourse and Turkish Foreign Policy Practice: A Neoclassical Realist Analysis'. *Turkish Studies* 16 (4): 449–64.

the concessions on African natural resources. Therefore, the humanitarian, anti-imperialist, and anti-colonial discourse stressed by Turkish policymakers concerning the African agenda and beyond might represent a counteraction for Turkey at the risk of a backlash. That risk has been exacerbated by the counter-propaganda spearheaded by regional rivals (the UAE, Egypt, the KSA) and the domestic anti-state lobby (Gülen movement) who intend to jeopardize the credit gained by the Ankara government in recent years.

The existence of historical ties: as seen in Chapter 2, Turkey's relations with various regions of the African continent date back to the Ottoman period. As mentioned earlier, the governments led by the JDP have, in these two decades, promoted the general rehabilitation of the Ottoman past, a period of history that long remained silent after the founding of the Republic. If Mustafa Kemal and his political heirs considered the imperial period as an obstacle in the difficult process of westernization of the country, JDP policymakers have perceived it as a treasure, value added to be exploited both domestically and internationally. As previously done in relations with other regions – the Balkans and the Middle East – Turkish authorities have begun to take advantage of the historical similarities as a key for access to the hearts and minds of the African people. Turkish officials do not miss a chance to stress that Turks and many Africans share a similar culture, underpinned by the Ottoman state's historical influence.[47] As Davutoğlu said during a press conference,

> We [Turks] are proud of this [. . .] culturally, we see ourselves as African. We do not have a bad memory with Africa, but a good history to share.[48]

Although the Turkish trend does not end with a romantic reinterpretation of the Ottoman past, many Turkish officers use that same portrayal of history as the bedrock on which to establish the current Turkish–African partnership.

In many official statements and speeches addressed to the African countries, Turkish leaders have repeatedly used episodes from the distant past, elevating them as examples of kinship. Even simple episodes of contact dating back to the Ottoman age are repeated ad nauseam by Turkish officials as if they were evidence of an almost organic relationship. As highlighted by Langan's study,

> the JDP elites have used the Ottoman historical framework to articulate a uniquely Turkish moral mission in global affairs. (Re)interpreting Ottoman

---

[47] Langan, Mark. 2017. *Neo-Colonialism and the Poverty of 'Development' in Africa*, 102. Newcastle: Palgrave Macmillan.
[48] Bilgic and Nascimento, 'Turkey's New Focus on Africa', 2.

history as one of benevolent hegemony, Erdoğan and his ministers have sought
to construct an altruistic identity for modern Turkey.[49]

In addition to these, there are also more famous historical episodes, which,
however, are covered with a new meaning, to prove the natural Turkish solidarity.
Davutoğlu, who devised a substantial part of his foreign policy strategy on the
basis of the Ottoman legacy, used to mention the imperial history during his
visits to Africa as well as during the conferences and meetings with African civil
society – for example, at the Somali Civil Society Gathering in Istanbul, the then
foreign minister addressed the Somali participants thus:

> You are home, Turkey is your motherland, sixteenth century Aḥmad ibn Ibrāhīm
> al-Ghāzī fought occupying forces with Ottoman support.[50]

Or again, at another time, the same Davutoğlu explained the importance of
Somalia for Turkish interests by underlining the Ottoman expeditions to that
country during the sixteenth century. He stated that 'We [Turks] have inherited
these [relations] from the Ottomans'.[51] The Turkish memory not only selectively
takes up episodes from past centuries but also exploits more recent phases of
history by creating original analogies. Above all, the Turkish concern with
legitimizing itself as a country that understands the pain suffered by the African
people has led the Turkish narrative to make a comparison between the colonial
period and the last years of the Ottoman Empire. As a way to create a further
link with the African people, the Turks narrate the partition of the Ottoman
Empire by the European powers as a phase of new imperialism. As a result, the
late Ottoman era is group in with the African events during the late nineteenth
and early twentieth centuries, and it is interpreted by the Turks through the lens
of colonialism. In this interweaving of history, reality and narrative, Turkey not
only has no colonial past to be ashamed of but has also itself been a victim of
colonialism.

The presence of religious bonds: like the historical past in its different
interpretations, religion is also considered a useful tool by Turkish policymakers
to break the distrust of African people. While not often openly expressed, the
religious dimension is present in almost all Turkish activities and initiatives in
SSA. Religion is an element of legitimacy to foster a reliable image. It has allowed
Turkey to open privileged channels in predominantly Muslim countries, in a

---

[49] Langan, 'Virtuous Power Turkey', 1400.
[50] 'Opening Remarks by Foreign Minister of Turkey Ahmet Davutoğlu', Somali Civil Society Gathering,
      Istanbul, 27 May 2012.
[51] Bilgic and Nascimento, 'Turkey's New Focus on Africa', 2.

variety of areas, from humanitarian assistance to business. As depicted well by Özkan and Akgün:

> The Turkish conception of Islamic understanding is compatible with western democratic values, and provides an alternative to that fostered in Africa by a number of other Muslim states.[52]

Turkey includes a religious meaning to its development and humanitarian assistance to the African people. Most of the works carried out by these private non-state actors are promoted as Islamic duties. In the same manner, Turkey's businessmen frequently present Islam as the unifying bond between Africa and Turkey in Muslim states in order to gain advantage over their Western and non-Western competitors, but the field in which Turkey exploits religion most of all is education. Both state agencies and civil society organizations work in this area. Particularly active in the first case is the Diyanet (Directorate for Religious Affairs of Turkey), which organizes meetings[53] and training courses for African imams and young Muslim students. The real importance of this meeting consisted in the creation of a platform for the sharing of experience and knowledge between Turkey and Africa.[54]

Among the civil society organizations, the Gülen movement, between 2005 and 2014, had a special place in the formulation and practical implementation of Turkey's opening to Africa, above all in the education sector through the spreading of schools. Therefore, Gülenist schools had become the leading implementers of Turkey's public diplomacy in Africa, and the first of its kind as a Turkish non-governmental engagement with the continent.[55] The next chapter will analyse the rift between Gülen's movement and the JDP government (2012–14) and the damage it has caused to the Turkish policy in Africa, transforming the movement from a relevant transnational asset to an anti-state lobby. The religious dimension has allowed Turkey to open and consolidate relations with the Muslim-majority countries but, at the same time, it has placed constraint on its African policy. The attention given to Muslim countries has led Turkey to

---

[52] Özkan and Akgün, 'Turkey's Opening to Africa', 538.
[53] In 2006 Diyanet organized a summit meeting with senior African Muslim figures. The 2006 Summit meeting was attended by religious figures from twenty-two African countries, for example, from Chad, Cameroon, Rwanda, Mali and Kenya. Delegates discussed a variety of topics, such as 'Religious Identity in the Globalization Process', 'Religious Education and Opportunities in the Educational Field', and 'The Basic Approaches and Stances in the Conservation of Cultural Heritage'. See Rudincová, 'New Player on the Scene', 210.
[54] Özkan, 'Turkey's "New" Engagements', 123.
[55] See Chapter 6.

direct its investments without a serious evaluation of interest – economic and political – and rather base it on considerations biased by the ideological element.

The three categories listed earlier contribute to shaping, in a flexible way, the ideational dimension of the Turkish approach towards Africa. These, however, are not discrete, but closely connected, feeding each other and, in some cases, overlapping with one another. Indeed, almost all the religious leaders who attended the meetings organized by the Diyanet or other Turkish non-state organizations have repeatedly stressed, positively, the Ottoman legacy in their countries. Consequently, together with the development of relations on religious matters, they wanted the Ottoman element to be highlighted as well. Thus, in addition to the establishment of long-term educational cooperation in Islamic studies through the opening of an international theological school, several African Muslim leaders have called for the construction of Ottoman and Turkish-style mosques in their countries.[56] From the beginning of its involvement in Africa, Turkey has understood that its policy of opening up to the continent would not be complete or sustained without religious connections, which are also directly linked with the Ottoman past in Africa.[57]

Consequently, the two elements – Islam and the Ottoman past – reinforce the idea of 'clean slate'. Whereas the historical past is an obstacle for Western powers, Turkey is able to emphasize its imperial past and use it to retrieve old historical and identity links. Significantly, in terms of Turkish relations with the Global South, the JDP foreign policy elite have stressed, moreover, that the Ottoman Empire never engaged in the full-fledged colonialism of European powers. The anti-colonial discourse has emerged several times in the tones used by the Turkish elite, assuming in some cases an anti-European connotation:

> We [Turks] have never run after only our own interests. We know that states, which only looked after their own interests in the past engendered major damage to Africa. The international community should know that we could only be equal partners in Africa.[58]

The relationship between the Ottoman centre and its peripheral zones is, instead, set forth as having been one of consent, anchored by cultural ties between fellow Muslims as part of a pax-Ottomana.[59] In the Global South, the

---

[56] Kavas, Ahmet. 2006. 'Afrikali Musluman Dini Liderler Istanbul'da Bulustu'. *Dusunce Gundem* 3 (25): 9.

[57] Özkan and Akgün, 'Turkey's Opening to Africa', 538.

[58] See Rudincová, 'New Player on the Scene', 199.

[59] Yanık, Lerna K. 2011. 'Constructing Turkish "Exceptionalism": Discourses of Liminality and Hybridity in Post-Cold War Turkish Foreign Policy'. *Political Geography* 30 (2): 80–9.

neo-Ottoman identity is presented as a benevolent force in contrast to Western hegemony, within an 'anti-colonial' narrative.[60]

It is necessary to emphasize that, since the rise of the JDP to power, the rapprochement with the countries of the neighbouring regions has been supported by recurrent rhetoric rooted in historical-religious elements. The emphasis on the recovery of the Ottoman past prompted many observers, analysts and scholars to label the Turkish proactive foreign policy as 'neo-Ottoman' – a term with a high media impact, especially in the West, which has been repeatedly stigmatized by Turkish elites. According to those who still use it to date, Ankara's strategic choices are part of a neo-imperialist project aimed at restoring the Caliphate's power.[61] Other scholars have, instead, stressed that the neo-Ottoman policies also constitute effective instruments of a nationalist geopolitical strategy that aims to make Turkey the hegemonic power in the region.[62] After 2011 and the reorientation of Turkish global policy, however, it became clear that the 'neo-Ottoman' concept cannot be ascribed to a simple nationalist project. On the contrary, it is wholly a normative enterprise that articulates an explicit moralism in terms of the character of the Turkish nation[63] – an ethical effort that, as Murphy and Wood have pointed out, has seen Davutoğlu and Gül at the forefront of the game. During their years in service both have fed the face of Turkey as a 'virtuous power':

> Foreign Minister Davutoğlu has started to describe the 'ethics' underpinning Turkey's foreign policy framework as being sincere, honest, transparent, trustworthy, neutral, hopeful, inclusive and sharing a common vision. President Gül has also stated that Turkey's framework emphasises human dignity and justice, serving as a unique and 'virtuous power'.[64]

As seen in the previous chapter, Turkey has utilized interventions in Somalia to build the image of a virtuous power and as a 'showpiece' for its potential humanitarian clout throughout SSA. From the JDP elites' perspective, Erdoğan's visit, in a situation of conflict and international isolation, served to underline the apparent ethical qualities of the leader, as well as of the Turkish state. The effort

---

[60] Langan, 'Virtuous Power Turkey', 1403.
[61] See, for example, Colborne, Michael and Maxime Edwards. 2018. 'Erdoğan Is Making the Ottoman Empire Great Again'. *Foreign Policy*.
[62] See, for example, Erickson, Edward J. 2004. 'Turkey as Regional Hegemony 2014: Strategic Implications for the United States'. *Turkish Studies* 5 (3): 25–45; Murinson, Alexander. 2012. 'Turkish Foreign Policy in the Twenty-First Century'. In *Mideast Security and Policy Studies*. Ramat Gan: The Begin-Sadat Center for Strategic Studies – BarIlan University.
[63] Langan, 'Virtuous Power Turkey', 1403.
[64] Murphy and Woods, *Turkey's International Development*, 10.

made in Somalia has strengthened the neo-Ottoman theme by putting Turkish resolve at odds with the West and the EU institutions. This approach was made explicit by Erdoğan in a famous speech at the United Nations General Assembly in September 2011. During his speech, the then prime minister pointed at the former colonial powers deeming them responsible for the difficult situation in Somalia:

> We should not only look into the picture of today, but also the shameful history that has led Somalia into the arms of this great tragedy. Indeed, beneath the tip of this huge iceberg lie great crimes against humanity. In that respect, the situation in Somalia has also revealed the deep wounds inflicted by the colonialist mentality which kept Africa under its hegemony for centuries. As this old colonial mentality ignores places where it has no interest, it is now watching millions of children die in need of a morsel of bread.[65]

Turkey thus was able to exploit the opportunity to project the image of a global power. The lack of a colonial past intertwined with a revisited interpretation of Ottoman events and the religious dimension have shaped the ideological framework on which to base the Ankara consensus.

As Ezgi Guner pointed out, the Turkish presence in Africa and the narrative that accompanies it can be grasped through the prism of the politics of scale. The politics-of-scale metaphor, originally used in human geography[66] and later included in social anthropology studies,[67] represents a form of hierarchy that is not separate or discrete but interconnected. According to Guner, the metaphor is useful to better understand the Turkish policy of opening to and presence in SSA; attention must also be paid to the scalar practices of the state, business and civil society.[68] Since the beginning, the Turkish involvement in Africa has been characterized by three interconnected levels or scalar projects: the legitimization of its presence in the continent, the construction of a multiracial Muslim world and the evocation of a Turkish–African partnership – three distinct dimensions – national, community (Muslim ummah) and global capitalism – which are complementary and which can be found both in the rhetoric and in the Turkish practical approach. These distinctive traits may be encapsulated in a single concept: the Ankara consensus.

[65] Erdoğan, R. T. 'Statement by Recep Tayyip Erdoğan at 66th UN General Assembly'. *Voltaire Network*. New York, 22 September 2011.

[66] See, for example, Flint, Colin. 2016. *Introduction to Geopolitics*. Third edn. Abingdon: Routledge.

[67] See, for example, Carr, Summerson E. and Michael Lempert, eds. 2016. *Scale: Discourse and Dimensions of Social Life*. Oakland: University of California Press.

[68] Guner, Ezgi. 2020. 'The Scalar Politics of Turkey's Pivot to Africa'. *POMEPS Studies – Africa and the Middle East: Beyond the Divides* 40:59–63.

5.3 A mixed paradigm: The Ankara Consensus

At the core of this idea is Turkey's presentation of itself as the continent's natural partner, untainted by a colonial past, promoting a kind of Ankara consensus. Even though it is not a well-defined concept, the Ankara consensus can be conceived of as a new model for the economic, political and social development of the African countries, an alternative to both the so-called Washington consensus[69] – US- and European-dominated neoliberal economic and developmental discourse – and the more recent Beijing consensus as state-led economic growth and prioritization of stability over democracy.[70] In spite of the neoliberal model remaining the most appreciated model and one followed by African leaders, a broader crisis of confidence in it, particularly after the 2008 financial crisis, has paved the way for the rise of the Chinese one.[71] China is now the dominant player in some African states due to its extra-market decision-making, partly based on Africa's abundant natural resources.[72]

Turkey has attempted to promote a middle way, or a third way, through the implementation of a win-win policy in Africa which includes peacebuilding efforts and a policy of mutual empowerment. At the same time, Ankara's idea

---

[69] The Washington Consensus is a set of economic policy recommendations for developing countries that became popular during the 1980s. The term 'Washington Consensus' usually refers to the level of agreement between the IMF, World Bank and the US Department of the Treasury on those policy recommendations. All shared the view, typically labelled neoliberal, that the operation of the free market and the reduction of state involvement were crucial to development in the Global South. Essentially, the Washington consensus advocates free trade, floating exchange rates, free markets and macroeconomic stability. For the Washington Consensus, see Williamson, John. 1989. 'What Washington Means by Policy Reform'. In *Latin American Readjustment: How Much has Happened*, edited by John Williamson. Washington: Institute for International Economics; Tausch, Arno. 2003. 'Social Cohesion, Sustainable Development and Turkey's Accession to the European Union: Implications from a Global Model'. *Turkish Journal of International Relations* 2 (1): 1–41; Babb, Sarah. 2013. 'The Washington Consensus as Transnational Policy Paradigm: Its Origins, Trajectory and Likely Successor'. *Review of International Political Economy* 30 (2): 268–97.

[70] The term has been coined by the US economist Joshua Cooper Ramo in 2004 as opposed to the Washington consensus. It is used to identify a series of economic and social doctrines, born in China after 1978, opposed to the neoliberal policies of development and the influence that these are finding in developing countries. The Beijing Consensus is as much about social change as economic change. It incorporates ideas that not only concern the economy but are also connected with politics and the strengthening of China's political weight at the international level. For the Beijing consensus, see Cooper Ramo, *The Beijing Consensus: Notes on the New Physics of Chinese Power*; McKinnon, Ronald I. 2010. 'China in Africa: The Washington Consensus versus the Beijing Consensus'. *International Finance* 13 (3): 495–506; Lubieniecka, Ewelina. 2014. 'Chinese Engagement in Sub-Saharan Africa: Can the Beijing Consensus be Explained under World-Systems Analysis?' *Fudan Journal of the Humanities & Social Sciences* 7 (3): 433–50.

[71] Hsu, S. Philip, Yu-Shan Wu and Suisheng Zhao, eds. 2011. *In Search of China's Developmental Model: Beyond the Beijing Consensus*. Milton Park: Routledge; Lekorwe, Mogopodi, Anyway Chingwete, Mina Okuru and Romaric Samson. 2016. 'China's Growing Presence in Africa Wins Largely Positive Popular Reviews'. In *Afrobarometer Dispatch*. Afrobarometer.

[72] Eisenman, Joshua. 2012. 'China–Africa Trade Patterns: Causes and Consequences'. *Journal of Contemporary China* 21 (7): 793–810.

neither refuses nor denies benefits and opportunities of global capitalism. Therefore, Turkey seeks to share with African countries its own development paradigm or formula that has proved successful in its own rapid economic growth. This approach recalled what Turkey tried to do in the neighbouring countries of the Middle East region before the Arab upheavals of 2011.[73] Rather than creating new relations of dependence – as the traditional actors, including China, tend to do – Turkey's approach, particularly in states that are trying to get out of crisis situations such as Somalia, tends to focus on political equality, mutual economic development and a long-term social partnership. As pointed out by Cannon,

> Turkey has shown less interest in an attempt to craft expensive, long-term solutions that are short on detail and involve the usual suspects of foreign-funded civil society organizations, NGOs and consultancies. These result in conferences and policy papers but rarely offer anything concrete such as medical facilities or roads.[74]

Although Turkey does not categorize itself as a member of the Global South, its narratives and ways of working are similar to them and partially refer to the SSC. What is now known as SSC derives from the adoption of the Buenos Aires Plan of Action for Promoting and Implementing Technical Cooperation among Developing Countries (BAPA) by 138 UN Member States in Argentina, on 18 September 1978. The plan established a scheme of collaboration among least developed countries, mostly located in the south of the planet. It also established for the first time a framework for this type of cooperation and incorporated in its practice the basic principles of relations between sovereign states: respect for sovereignty, non-interference in internal affairs and equality of rights, among others.[75] In general terms, the SSC refers to technical cooperation, knowledge exchange and financial assistance between pairs of developing countries. It is a tool used by states, international organizations, academics, civil society and the private sector to collaborate and share knowledge, skills and successful initiatives in specific areas such as agricultural development, human rights, urbanization, health and climate change. Also, the aid of emerging donors is frequently not labelled 'aid' but, rather, as a form of SSC, which differs from

[73] Bank, André and Roy Karadag. 2013. 'The "Ankara Moment": The Politics of Turkey's Regional Power in the Middle East, 2007–11'. *Third World Quarterly* 34 (2): 287–304.

[74] Cannon, *Turkey in Africa*, 99.

[75] Modi, Renu, ed. 2011. *South-South Cooperation: Africa on the Centre Stage*. London: Palgrave Macmillan; Gray, Kevin and Barry K. Gills, eds. 2017. *Rising Powers and South-South Cooperation*. London: Routledge.

Western aid because of its lack of conditionality and its 'untied' nature.[76] Turkey's approach has several components ascribable to the SSC. Indeed, the philosophy behind the SSC emerges from the notion of mutual growth, and the underlying principle is to support one another for a win-win partnership on all sides.[77] The main tenets of Turkish assistance efforts reportedly have much in common with the principles of SSC: respect for national ownership, mutual benefit, solidarity, context-specific and demand-driven assistance.[78]

The similarities of the Turkish approach to the principles of the SSC can be assessed more precisely thanks to a framework for assessing the quality of SSC that has been recently developed by the Network of Southern Think Tanks (NeST).[79] The NeST framework defines the quality of the SSC on the basis of a qualitative analysis of the performance of the actors on a number of issues: (a) inclusive national ownership, (b) horizontality, (c) self-sufficiency and sustainability, (d) accountability and transparency, (e) development efficiency. By applying this tool to the Turkish case, it is possible to highlight certain traits of the Turkish approach that make Turkey a kind of hybrid because it mixes SSC tools with traditional donor practices. With regards to inclusive national ownership (a), the Turkish approach indicates respect for non-conditionality, non-interference and respect for sovereignty, as well as demand-led assistance. The horizontality of the aid (b), expressed in terms of mutually beneficial cooperation for both parties, is evident in the Turkish approach both in practice and in the narrative, where concepts such as solidarity, mutual trust and partnership are often stressed. Regarding the self-sufficiency and sustainability (c), it has been explicitly indicated several times as one of the main targets of Turkish aid initiatives in crisis situations. Specifically, fostering self-reliance and sustainability has been declared as one of the most important objectives of Turkish aid to SSA. Emblematic of this approach has been the activism in Somalia where both state agencies (Ministry of Foreign Affairs and TİKA) and

---

[76] Woods, 'Whose Aid? Whose Influence?' 1205–21; Paolo, de Renzio and Jurek Seifert. 2014. 'South–South Cooperation and the Future of Development Assistance: Mapping Actors and Options'. *Third World Quarterly* 35 (10):1860–75, 1864.

[77] Quadir, 'Rising Donors and the New Narrative of "South–South" Cooperation', 321–38.

[78] Fidan, Hakan and Rahman Nurdun. 2008. 'Turkey's Role in the Global Development Assistance Community: The Case of TİKA (Turkish International Cooperation and Development Agency)'. *Southern Europe & the Balkans* 10 (1): 93–111; Öniş, Ziya and Mustafa Kutlay. 2017. 'The Dynamics of Emerging Middle-Power Influence in Regional and Global Governance: The Paradoxical Case of Turkey'. *Australian Journal of International Affairs* 71 (2): 164–83.

[79] NeST was established in 2014, on the sidelines of the Mexico High Level Forum on Effective Development Cooperation. It is a forum of think tanks and academics from the Global South committed to generating, systematizing and sharing knowledge on South–South approaches to international development cooperation. For further information, see http://southernthinktanks.org /index.html.

NGOs have stressed on capacity building, concentration on education through scholarships and building leadership skills, manifestation of the long-term interests through building embassies and consulates, support to institutions and training of state officials, such as diplomats, investing in Mogadishu city through building of roads, developing infrastructure and employing local Somalis in several projects including private sector efforts. As pointed out by Sucuoğlu and Sazak,

> Turkey's efforts have really been remarkable in these areas, and in alignment with SSC principles of solidarity, capacity building and technology/ knowledge transfer, and use of local systems and resources.[80]

On accountability and transparency (d), Turkey is one of the few emerging powers that shares its development assistance data with OECD–DAC, including those related to NGOs, and more sporadically reports to OCHA's financial monitoring services.[81] However, there are many doubts about effective transparency. Reports do not always present a geographical and sectoral breakdown and, as specified in the following paragraph, there is no standardized model for monitoring and evaluating projects in the field. Turkey has not developed quantifiable indicators and targets to measure the real impact and progress of its projects and initiatives. Finally, as far as development efficiency (e) is concerned, the presence in the field of Turkish practitioners – belonging to state and non-state agencies – alongside local communities and indigenous civil society has allowed Turkish actors to be more adaptable to local conditions, needs and desires. In other words, the Turkish approach has proven to hold a higher degree of resilience on the ground.

Compared to other emerging players that are active in Africa following the SSC approach, Turkey includes a religious meaning to its assistance. Turkey, in its development model, also takes some elements from the Arab model, including the religious significance attributed to aid and the close link between aid and foreign policy strategy. As briefly mentioned earlier, most of the works carried out by Turkish NGOs are promoted as Islamic duties.[82] Turkey gives a religious dimension to its assistance and, following the Arab model of development aid, concentrates on Muslim African communities. This is the case in Somalia, which is a member of the Arab League and, as well as Turkey, is also a member

[80] Sucuoğlu, Gizem and Onur Sazak. 2016. 'The New Kid on the Block: Turkey's Shifting Approaches to Peacebuilding'. *Rising Powers Quarterly* 1 (2): 69–91.
[81] https://fts.unocha.org.
[82] Özkan, 'Turkey's Religious', 48.

of the OIC. Arab aid is distinct from the DAC model, as it remains primarily concentrated regionally and is more openly influenced by social solidarity and religious ties. Further, Arab aid has traditionally been very generous, yet also very volatile, both because of the uncertainty of Arab countries' oil and gas export earnings and because of the strategic use of aid in support of their foreign policies. Initially, in the early years of foreign assistance the Arab solidarity was the decisive factor and the primary objective in directing aid. Subsequently, however, aid has become an important foreign policy tool, and the Arab donors have expanded to SSA.[83]

The Ankara consensus takes these two aspects from the Arab model – religious meaning and aid as a foreign policy tool – and puts them together with other elements including an important feature of the Beijing Consensus: the non-conditionality principle. Conditionality refers to the conditions attached to the provision of loans, debt relief or foreign aid by the provider to the recipient, which is usually a sovereign government. In other words, recipient nations must meet certain prerequisites in order to receive aid. The application of clear political and economic conditionalities in aid and assistance to push for normative principles and values, especially in human rights, is one area of divergence between more traditional donors and non-traditional aid providers. Aiming to attract developing nations, China adopted a policy of no political preconditions for receiving aid.[84] Turkey's agenda adheres to the principle of non-conditionality in its support for African countries. By refraining from imposing political conditions, Turkey demonstrates that it is able to engage with recipient governments in a spirit of solidarity while not sacrificing effectiveness and efficiency.[85] By avoiding imposition of conditionality on the beneficiary states, Turkey avoids the resentment from recipient states, and it distances itself from the traditional donors and their development policies – an approach that is visible in the narratives of Turkish officials. For example, in 2012 TİKA director

---

[83] For further details about the Arab model, see Neumayer, Eric. 2003. 'What Factors Determine the Allocation of Aid by Arab Countries and Multilateral Agencies?' LSE Research Online; Villanger, Espen. 2007. *Arab Foreign Aid: Disbursement Patterns, Aid Policies and Motives.* Bergen: Chr. Michelsen Institute; Zimmermann, Felix and Kimberly Smith. 2011. 'More Actors, More Money, More Ideas for International Development Cooperation'. *Journal of International Development* 23 (5): 722–38.

[84] The only political condition required by China to receive its aid is that the recipient state should have no official links with Taiwan. See Huang, Meibo and Ren Peiqiang. 2012. 'China's Foreign Aid and Its Role in the International Architecture'. *International Development Policy* 3 (3). doi: 10.4000/poldev.1004.

[85] Sucuoğlu, Gizem and Onur Sazak. 2016. 'The New Kid on the Block', 69–91.

Serdar Çam underlined the following, with regard to the promotion of human rights:

> Meanwhile we also understand that a considerable number of aid recipient countries are facing human rights violations problems to various degrees. If we [Turks] articulate this issue [conditionality] when dealing with any aid recipient, we would run the risk of punishing the people of that country in need of urgent help. Therefore, as an aid agency, our principle is not to interfere with the domestic policies of certain aid recipients but concentrate on cooperation and coordination when official request of aid is conveyed to our government.[86]

Undoubtedly, Turkey has taken political and security risks by eliminating middlemen and directly delivering its aid to beneficiaries, in cooperation with national and local providers. This kind of approach is not immune to the costs and collateral effects similar to those experienced by other donors, such as rampant corruption on both the part of donor nation and recipient.[87] However, it fits well with the vision of 'African solutions to African problems' that is promoted by a new generation of African leaders and the AU in the last two decades. Furthermore, Turkey's African policy pays lip service to a normative element, on behalf of a more egalitarian world politics, fostered by the narrative of Turkish officials during their visits. By criticizing the development policies of traditional donors, Turkey distances itself from them, emphasizing the novelty of its approach based on a mutually beneficial and sustainable partnership between donor and recipients.[88] During the 2015 Sustainable Development Summit, former prime minister Ahmet Davutoğlu brought forward the Turkish policy on SSA as an example of the driving force for the positive outputs resulting from combining humanitarian and development assistance programmes within a collective strategy. The Ankara consensus is emphasized by the narrative that backs up Turkish activism, strengthening the perception of Turkey as a unique actor in the sub-Saharan context. The Turkish South–South narrative is blended with faith-based elements, humanitarianism and some references to a particular kind of third worldism.

South-South: even though traditionally its sights have been focused on the West – and therefore it has been considered to be close to the global North – Turkey is also aware of its position between the North and the South due to the strong

---

[86] 'Interview with Serdar Çam'. Afronline – The Voice of Africa, 3 August 2012. URL: https://www.afronline.org/?p=26422#more-26422.

[87] Schudel, Carl J. W. 2008. 'Corruption and Bilateral Aid: A Dyadic Approach'. *Journal of Conflict Resolution* 52 (4): 507–28.

[88] Murphy and Woods, *Turkey's International Development*, 10.

identity/security nexus that has characterized its developmental path. Therefore, like other emerging powers, Turkey refuses to use the dominant language of official development, which tends to rationalize the hierarchical relationship between North and South.[89] Furthermore, Turkey displays such rhetoric in every bilateral and multilateral meeting in which it emphasizes that the Turkish goal is to help the African nations in their policy of 'African solutions to African problems'. As President Erdoğan underlined during the Second Economic and Business Forum, 'We [Turks] want to improve our relations, built on mutual respect, in all areas on the basis of win-win and equal partnership'.[90] In spite of this strong SSC rhetoric, Turkey's South–South credentials have not proven to be fully reliable.

Humanitarianism: in a global context, Turkey's humanitarian-oriented approach is used as a way to live up to the expectations of international solidarity and problem-solving initiatives that come with the status of being a rising power. As seen in Chapter 4, since 2008 Turkey's humanitarian diplomacy has grown and its reputation as a humanitarian state rings louder over all of SSA. For the Turkish government, humanitarian aid was and still is a means to strengthen bilateral relations with governments. The religious element is especially evident in the humanitarian dimension of Turkish efforts. Indeed, during the last decade, Turkey's humanitarianism aimed to restore the bond between Turkey and Muslim countries, and it was articulated in relation to a perceived Turkish responsibility towards Muslim communities outside of its borders (the *ummah*). In recent years, however, this focus on the *ummah* has been replaced by an Islamic internationalism which suggests that having cross-border humanitarian engagement is a vessel of Islamic religious identity.[91] Theoretically, it means that even though Turkish NGOs do not discriminate on the basis of religion and ethnic origin in their aid activities, a strong Islamic identity shapes their approach to their actions.[92] The main constraint of this discourse is that this image of a moral state, which Turkey has fed in the international arena, is a mismatch with the decreasing level of democratic standards within the country following the coup attempt in mid-2016.

Third worldism: finally, a sort of Turkish third worldism is traceable to the revision project of global – political and economic – governance institutions and structures, and in particular to the United Nations Security Council,

---

[89] Dreher, Axel, Peter Nunnenkamp and Rainer Thiele. 2011. 'Are "New" Donors Different?' 1950–68.

[90] Erdoğan's speech at the Second Turkey–Africa Economic and Business Forum, hosted by the Ministry of Trade and organized by the Foreign Economic Relations Board of Turkey (DEIK) in collaboration with the African Union (AU), began in Istanbul on 10 October 2018.

[91] Çevik, Senem. 2014. *The Rise of NGOs: Islamic Faith Diplomacy*. USC Center on Public Diplomacy.

[92] Çelik, *Contemporary Turkish Foreign Policy*.

International Monetary Fund (IMF) and the World Bank – a point that was strongly claimed by President Erdoğan:

> In the name of globalization, one growth model has been dictated to different countries. If you want to grow your economy, you need to find the IMF, the World Bank, or an interest rate hike. You cannot go beyond the limits they set for you in the infrastructure projects and defence industry. You must obey the definition of democracy.[93]

In some circumstances, Turkey's rhetoric against globalization seems very harsh, as it considers globalization a new form of Western colonialism and modern slavery.[94] However, statements with a significant media impact are more related to the current anti-Western domestic political discourse rather than true belief. Such discourse does not go against the globalization process and its economic and financial effects, as in the position of the traditional post-Marxist wave, but it implies a broader and deeper criticism of international governance. Yet, this rhetoric does not reflect the nature of traditional third world[95] political movements such as the Non-aligned Movement or the G-77. In the last six years, even though Turkey has been trying to get elected to a non-permanent seat on the UN Security Council – after its successful bid of 2008 – it has been increasingly critical of the UN, labelling the intergovernmental organization as 'unfair'. President Erdoğan and other senior Turkish diplomats use the ethical discourse based on the notion 'the world is greater than five' that finds strong resonance in Africa – a rhetoric that the Turkish president has never missed to emphasize, as during the Justice Forum of 2018 when in his speech he stressed that

> Countries and societies, almost held to ransom by means of overt and covert threats, are being forced to finance this crooked system. As Turkey, we voice our objection to this injustice, unlawfulness and tyranny at every platform. Our motto 'the world is bigger than five' is the biggest-ever rise against global injustice. We will maintain this objection of ours, which draws larger support each passing day, until a more just global order of government is established. We raise the same objection to the crookedness in the field of economy, too.[96]

[93] Baffour Ankomah, 'Turkey and Africa Pledge Co-operation'. *New African*, 20 December 2016. About the Turkey-Africa Business and Economic Forum, see http://www.turkeyafricaforum.org/.

[94] Editorial, 'Globalization New Form of Colonialism, President Erdoğan Says'. *Daily Sabah* (online), 2 November 2016, https://www.dailysabah.com/economy/2016/11/02/globalization-new-form-of-colonialism-president-Erdoğan-says.

[95] By 'Third World' the present study means states in Asia, Africa, Latin America, the Caribbean and other regions that were either full colonies or semi-colonies of Western powers. This definition reflects the category used in Kessler, Meryl A. and Thomas G. Weiss, eds. 1991. *Third World Security in the Post-Cold War Era*. Boulder: Lynne Rienner.

[96] Erdoğan's speech delivered at the Justice Forum held in Istanbul, on 10 January 2018.

This narrative represents a radical critique of the existing status quo in the international system that is inspired by the notions of global good and responsibility. As pointed out by Çevik and Seib, from the Turkish perspective the concept of global governance 'draws its conceptual framework from the guiding principles of achieving inclusivity and outreach'.[97] The call to reform the architecture and representation mechanism of the UN carries a strong message to African leaders and people. At the same time, this anti-systemic discourse is connected to the increasing isolation the Ankara government has faced in the post-Arab Spring era.[98] According to Özcan and Orakçi, thanks to such discourse, together with the horizontal win-win partnership and humanitarian-oriented policy, 'Turkey has been able to handle the distrust and the suspicion present in several African countries during the opening period'.[99] However, despite Turkey's relatively non-Western image in Africa, based on its non-colonial past, and despite its historical, religious and cultural ties with the continent increasing its legitimacy, it is still a non-African state. This situation may create a perception that Turkey is attempting to cultivate an international image by using Africa's vulnerabilities.[100]

Although it may sound provocative, the author has thought it would be useful to formulate a concept that could define the peculiarities of Turkey's agenda in Africa. The notion of the Ankara consensus proves to be particularly useful to encapsulate the multiple traits of the rhetoric and the practice applied in Africa by Turkey. As examined in this chapter and further explored in the following chapter, the paradigm of Turkish engagement in Africa is a mix of different models. In a few years, features that originate from different patterns of involvement in the African and, more generally, in less developed countries have been selected and implemented by the Turkish state to tailor its model of intervention. This has been configured to enhance the specificities of the Turkish development pathway, its identity and its past. Consequently, one of the peculiarities of the Turkish case lies in this mixed paradigm. It is possible to find only within the Ankara consensus a distinctive trait of the Chinese approach (the Beijing consensus) such as the non-conditionality of aid combined with the institution-building activities that are common among the traditional stakeholders within the so-called post-Washington consensus approach or the so-called second-generation reforms.

---

[97] Çevik, Senem and Philip Seib, eds. 2015. *Turkey's Public Diplomacy*. New York: Palgrave Macmillan, Introduction.

[98] Ayata, Bilgin. 2015. 'Turkish Foreign Policy in a Changing Arab World: Rise and Fall of a Regional Actor?' *Journal of European Integration* 37 (1): 95–112.

[99] Özkan and Orakçı, 'Viewpoint: Turkey as a "political"', 343–52.

[100] Akpınar, 'Turkey's Peacebuilding in Somalia', 751.

6

Operationalizing Turkey's multitrack policy

As mentioned in the previous chapter, the substantial distinction between the 'Turkish model' of engagement and that of other extra-regional players is not only in the storytelling but also in the way in which Turkey operates practically in the field. Over the last two decades, Turkey has developed a multi-stakeholder pyramidal framework for intervening in both the African and non-African critical scenarios, such as Somalia, affected by civil war and famine, and in no-crisis contexts in which Turkey seeks to increase its presence and influence. Following the total performance principle, introduced by Davutoğlu, and already considered in the previous chapters, the Turkish state has set up a structure of engagement based on the activities of non-state actors, both governmental and nongovernmental. The concurrent involvement of governmental and nongovernmental non-state actors in the multi-stakeholder framework of intervention in Africa has constituted one of the assets of the Ankara consensus as well as one of the traits that distinguishes the Turkish presence on the continent the most. However, it must be underlined that the relationship between the Turkish state and the Turkish public and civil society organizations is not a unidirectional, but one that is mutually nourished. There are many cases in which organizations belonging to Turkish civil society or the Turkish business sector have acted as forerunners in driving diplomatic relations at the bilateral level. The distinctive Turkish approach has allowed the country to achieve good results in terms of trust-building with local populations and, at the same time, to create connections and networks of informal relationships. As a result, Turkey has developed partnerships and non-dependency relations with African countries, as is usually done by other extra-regional players. After highlighting the main hallmarks of Turkey's unconventional implementation of the multitrack approach – namely bilateral engagement, coordinated activities and direct delivery aid – the chapter discusses the three fields in which Turkey has invested the most in recent years, examining the main actors involved, governmental and nongovernmental.

6.1 A new kind of diplomacy in the globalized world: The multitrack diplomacy

Before proceeding with the analysis of the Turkish case, it is necessary to present a brief overview of how the rising of non-state actors (NSAs)[1] has affected the world politics and diplomacy. By the end of the Cold War, diplomacy experienced a period of great changes, which witnessed the emergence of new kinds of initiatives encompassing international relations and going beyond traditional diplomacy. With accentuated forms of globalization and communication revolution, the scope of diplomacy has moved beyond the traditional core concerns to encompass a myriad of issues. Yet, the number and the types of actors in world affairs have grown enormously and the agenda of international public diplomacy has been altered in line with the changing circumstances. Beyond the framework of state-based actors, there is a wealth of non-state groups emerging as protagonists on the world's political and economic stage.[2] As pointed out by Heine, many sub-national and civil society actors linked up together have favoured the conceptual shift from the old model of an international system based only on independent states – club diplomacy – to one in which states remain the key actors, but they are not the only ones – network diplomacy.[3] The adoption of network diplomacy, also defined as a 'multi-stakeholder model',[4] enables nations to cooperate with NSAs, which now influence the diplomatic playing field.

The role of the state has not diminished, but it has changed or it has been and continues to be restructured.[5] As a consequence, the diversification of actors in the world politics has made an essential revision in the definition of the term 'diplomacy' itself. Recent years have witnessed a strong debate among the scholars belonging to the field of IR as well as diplomatic studies

---

[1] By the term 'NSA', the international relations scholars commonly refer to an entity or group which seeks to have an impact on the internationally related decisions or policy of one or more states. For further details, see Bieler, Andreas, Richard Higgott, and Geoffrey Underhill. 2004. *Non-state Actors and Authority in the Global System*. London and New York: Routledge.

[2] Cooper, Andrew F. and Daniel Flemes. 2013. 'Foreign Policy Strategies of Emerging Powers in a Multipolar World: An Introductory Review'. *Third World Quarterly* 34 (6): 943–62.

[3] The notion of network diplomacy was introduced by Anne-Marie Slaughter who wrote an article in 'Foreign Affairs' in which she argued that the key to a successful foreign policy is the 'networked diplomacy', a type of new diplomacy. According to her, war, business, media, society, even religion, are all networked, so diplomacy in managing international crises requires mobilizing international networks of public and private actors. See Heine, Jorge. 2013. 'From Club to Network Diplomacy'. In *The Oxford Handbook of Modern Diplomacy*, edited by Andrew F. Cooper, Jorge Heine and Ramesh Thakur, 54–69, 54–6. Oxford: Oxford University Press.

[4] Hill, Christopher. 2003. *The Changing Politics of Foreign Policy*. New York: Palgrave Macmillan.

[5] Weiss, Linda. 1997. 'Globalization and the Myth of the Powerless State'. *New Left Review* 225:3.

concerning new and more flexible definitions of diplomacy. Among others, Melissen extended the scope of diplomacy by defining it as 'the mechanism of representation, communication and negotiation through which states and other international actors conduct their business'.[6] This definition appears particularly suitable to explore the key traits of Turkish implementation policy in the African context because the Turkish approach gives emphasis to the role played by NSAs. Indeed, the current Turkish diplomatic landscape, as well as foreign policy agenda, is populated by a growing number, expanding role and increasing influence of NSAs. Such actors might be international organizations, NGOs, MNCs, transnational corporations (TNCs), armed elements seeking to free their territory from external rule, or terrorist groups or even individuals.[7] The importance of NSAs at the international level has intensified over the past thirty years. They have become major partners in the international response to humanitarian emergencies, abuse and violations of human rights, and in the efforts to rebuild and reconcile societies affected by conflicts or natural disasters that prevent normal functioning. The input of NSAs has sometimes been taken into account, but their role has been characterized as primarily discursive, attempting to influence the 'agenda-setting', 'framing', 'lobbying' or 'norm-building' of official policymakers.[8] Recently, there is an emerging literature that studies the role of NSAs in the foreign policymaking apparatus by examining the interaction between official state actors and non-state actors in the foreign policy 'implementation process'. According to the evidence from such research, the NSAs have 'operational responsibilities' in foreign policy actions,[9] and scholars refers to this dynamic as 'privatization of diplomacy'.[10]

With the growing role of NSAs in global affairs, the academic awareness on the concept of unofficial or informal diplomacy has increased substantially – above all, in preventive and post-conflict studies – where official governmental diplomacy – bilateral or multilateral – has some limitations in both practice and

---

[6] Melissen, Jen, ed. 2005. *The New Public Diplomacy: Soft Power in International Relations*, 5. London: Palgrave Macmillan.

[7] The NSAs, however, form a broad category that would be misleadingly defined only by the independence from states and state authority. Indeed, the theoretical purity of this ideal type is muddied by the complexity of reality. This book focuses on NSAs which are in principle autonomous from the structure and machinery of the state and that operate in both the domestic and international fields.

[8] Goldstein, Judith and Robert O. Keohane. 1993. *Ideas and Foreign Policy: Beliefs, Institutions and Political Change*, 301–9. Ithaca: Cornell University Press.

[9] Davidson, Lawrence. 2006. 'Privatizing Foreign Policy'. *Middle East Policy* 13 (2): 134–47.

[10] Hocking, Brian. 2006. 'Multistakeholder Diplomacy: Forms, Functions, and Frustrations'. In *Multistakeholder Diplomacy: Challenges and Opportunities*, edited by Jovan Kurbalija and Valentin Katrandjiev, 147–52. Geneve: DiploFoundation.

theory. Indeed, government-to-government diplomacy, known as track one, is oriented to the short-term results, achieved through power-based, formal and often rigid forms of official interaction.[11] In this debate Davidson and Montville were the first to introduce the term 'track two' or 'citizen diplomacy'.[12] In its original meaning, track two includes a broad spectrum of unofficial contacts, ranging from the most apolitical cultural exchanges to psychologically focused political problem-solving meetings. Later, Montville reconceptualized this kind of diplomacy as

> an unofficial, informal interaction between members of adversary groups or nations that aims to develop strategies, influence public opinion, and organize human and material resources in ways that might help to resolve their conflict.[13]

In other words, citizen diplomacy is characterized as a non-governmental, informal and constructive interaction between citizen groups, aimed at de-escalating conflict by reducing anger, fear and tension, and by improving communication and mutual understanding. Track-two diplomacy is not an alternative method but one that is complementary to official state-based diplomacy. This kind of diplomacy is often needed either to establish the basis for further track one activities or to put into practice a former track one agreement.[14] Government officials participate in such negotiations alongside the non-officials, merely in an informal way. It is an important mechanism in overcoming psychological barriers between adversaries, opening non-official interaction channels. However, as pointed out by Kaye, considering it primarily as a mechanism for the facilitation of track one agreements is misleading and undervalues the real significance of the track-two process itself.[15]

Generally speaking, because of the diversity of track-two diplomatic efforts, this form of diplomacy is further subdivided into new categories by scholars and practitioners. For instance, McDonald expanded track-two diplomacy into four separate tracks. According to this classification, diplomatic efforts of conflict

[11] Jones, Peter. 2015. *Track Two Diplomacy in Theory and Practice*. Stanford: Stanford University Press.
[12] Davidson, William D. and Joseph Montville. 1982. 'Foreign Policy According to Freud'. *Foreign Policy* 45:145–57, 146–50.
[13] Montville, Joseph. 1991. 'Track Two Diplomacy: The Arrow and the Olive Branch: A Case for Track Two Diplomacy'. In *The Psychodynamics of International Relationships: Unofficial Diplomacy at Work*, edited by Vamik D. Volkan, Demtrios Julius and Joseph Montville, 162. Lexington: Lexington Books.
[14] Papa, Michael J., Jeffrey Mapendere and Patrick J. Dillon. 2010. 'Waging Peace through Improvisional Action: Track-Two Diplomacy in the Sudan-Uganda Conflict'. *Southern Communication Journal* 5 (4): 349–69, 353.
[15] Kaye, Dalia Dassa. 2001. 'Track Two Diplomacy and Regional Security in the Middle East'. *International Negotiation* 6:49–77, 50–3.

resolution professionals constitute the track two, business activities constitute the track three, citizen-to-citizen exchange programmes constitute the track four, and media-to-media-based efforts constitute the track five diplomacy.[16] From this categorization, some scholars elaborated the track three diplomacy or soft-track two that is commonly defined as semi-official talks among ordinary citizens or people-to-people diplomacy established by both individuals and private organizations. Others have developed a concept known as track one and a half, referring to unofficial dialogues, during which all or most of the participants from the conflicting sides are officials, or non-officials, but acting under instructions from their respective governments, bridging official and unofficial activities. Finally, Schiff introduced the notion of quasi track one diplomacy in order to differentiate some kind of negotiations from both track two and track one and a half diplomacy.[17]

This brief summary of how diplomacy and the study of diplomacy have developed from the end of the Cold War to the present day has been used as a framework for the development and unconventional use of multitrack diplomacy by Turkey. Indeed, all the above-mentioned new categories of diplomacy are commonly referred to as multitrack diplomacy. The term 'multitrack diplomacy' was popularized by Kumar Rupesinghe and refers to the contributions of a variety of actors at different levels of a conflict that work together effectively to attain peace. It includes official diplomacy but also incorporates a variety of actors such as international institutions, regional organizations, NGOs, civic organizations, religious organizations, the business community and the media, among others. The multitrack diplomacy concept asserts that the individual efforts of a variety of actors can complement one another and combine to form a larger framework of preventive action.[18] Alternatively, multitrack diplomacy has been described as a web of interconnected parts – activities, individuals, institutions, communities – that operate together towards a common goal.[19] The essence of this concept is that combined efforts often prove to be more effective than an individual contribution in preventing conflicts from escalating. Rupesinghe presents six strands of multitrack diplomacy: (1) intergovernmental diplomacy; (2) governmental diplomacy; (3) track-two diplomacy; (4) ecumenical diplomacy;

[16] McDonald, John W. 1991. 'Further Exploration of Track Two Diplomacy'. In *Timing the De-Escalation of International Conflicts*, edited by Louis Kriesberg and Stuart J. Thorson, 201–20. Syracuse: Syracuse University Press.
[17] Schiff, Amira. 2010. 'Quasi Track-One Diplomacy: An Analysis of the Geneva Process in the Israeli–Palestinian Conflict'. *International Studies Perspectives* 11 (2): 93–111.
[18] Rupesinghe, Kumar. 1997. *The General Principles of Multi-track Diplomacy*. Durban: ACCORD.
[19] Diamond, Louise and John W. McDonald. 1997. *Multi-track Diplomacy: A Systems Approach to Peace*. Washington: Kumarian Press.

(5) citizen diplomacy; and (6) economic diplomacy.[20] Therefore, his concept of multitrack diplomacy departs from the standard definition of track-two diplomacy through the detailing of six specific preventive diplomacy tracks and serves to form a more complete theoretical framework.

6.2 The key traits of Turkish unconventional multitrack

As will be illustrated in this paragraph, during the implementation process of foreign policy towards sub-Saharan African countries, Turkey has used the multitrack framework as a method to coordinate the efforts of public and private NSAs (multi-stakeholder approach), enabling it to open and strengthen its relations with several African countries. Its unorthodox interpretation of multitrack has become one of the main tenets of Turkey's strategy towards not only Africa but, more generally, also towards the Global South. First and foremost, the context in which this approach is applied and the aims it characterizes illustrate the Turkish experience. Differing from the traditional understanding, Turkey unconventionally applied multitrack to both crisis and non-crisis scenarios and with the objective of not only ensuring a peaceful environment but also establishing and improving bilateral relations with other countries as part of its soft power strategy. In Turkish foreign policy lexicon, the concept of multitrack is a synonym for multidimensionality, which indicates the ability to operate on different levels and on different fronts, from 'official' diplomatic relations, within international and regional organizations, to transnational people-to- people relations developed by NSAs. During the Fourth UN Conference on the Least Developed Countries held in Istanbul in 2011, Davutoğlu stressed the importance of civil society organizations as a valuable tool for bringing global peace and stability. He underlined that they are an integral part of international relations and that Turkey believes that a strong civil society can grow only through heavy state support, saying 'this is why we [the JDP government] strongly support civil society organizations participating in international affairs'.[21] This shows an approach of coordination between Turkish state and civil society aid agencies.[22] This multi-stakeholder policy is based on the idea that NSAs are not

---

[20] Rupesinghe, *The General Principles*.
[21] Editorial, 'Davutoğlu Says Civil Society Key in Development of LDCs', *Sunday Zaman*, 8 May 2011. http://www.todayszaman.com/news-243200-Davutoğlu-says-civil-society-key-in-devel opment-of-ldcs.html (accessed 1 April 2017).
[22] Cannon, 'Deconstructing Turkey's Efforts in Somalia', 115.

only consumers but also providers of the benefits achieved through diplomatic efforts. Usually, this mode of action is a concert-oriented and participatory approach with a semi-horizontal relationship (go-between) among state agencies and NSAs as well as a penchant for multilateralism.[23] The Turkish multitrack approach, instead, has a strong unilateral character. Ankara rarely takes part in countries' coalitions because it prefers to maintain a wide range of manoeuvres. Another trait that makes the Turkish application of the multitrack approach unconventional is the relationship between the state and NSAs. If Turkey's policy implementation on the ground is a combination of government-coordinated funding, business ventures and humanitarian work pigeonholed in different but connected fields or tracks, the decision-making process remains a governmental monopoly. In other words, there is no participatory inclusion of NSAs. Further, without a defined institutional structure, the ties between the government and the NSAs are ensured by a mix of sharing ideological roots, personal and family relationships and patronage networks. More specifically, Turkish multitrack policy has some characteristics that make Turkey's involvement in the region original and unique. It is possible to highlight some elements, in addition to the multi-stakeholder trait, that typify the Turkish case. Among these are bilateral engagement, coordination activities and the direct delivery of aid.

Bilateral engagement

The multitrack policy highlights that alongside Turkey's growing presence in the major supranational organizations of the last decade, there has been a gradual widening of the foreign policy tools, with the opening of the policy implementation process to a new set of actors.[24] Therefore, as Akpınar has argued, Turkish foreign policy in the preceding decade has changed from a single-track policy and diplomacy, in which the state – official bureaucracy and the military – was the single primary actor, to a multitrack diplomacy, in which numerous actors have become influential. This development has also encouraged Turkey to shift its aid and assistance approach from a multilateral to a more bilateral one. Indeed, traditionally, and until the mid-2000s, Turkey preferred to deliver assistance to African countries through multilateral channels. However, a robust shift has been observed since the second half of the last decade, from multilateral

---

[23] Assanvo, William Taffotien. 2006. 'Multistakeholder Diplomacy in the Context of National Diplomatic Systems'. In *Multistakeholder Diplomacy: Challenges and Opportunities*, edited by Jovan Kurbalija and Valentin Katrandjiev, 141–5. Geneve: DiploFoundation.

[24] Akpınar, 'Turkey's Peacebuilding in Somalia'.

actions towards a bilateral engagement. The multilateral ODA accounted for 2 per cent of Turkey's total ODA in 2014, as opposed to 44 per cent in 2004.[25] Turkey shares this trend with other emerging players, such as India, which over the last decade have chosen to shift their aid from multilateral to bilateral commitments.[26] Even though bilateral engagement with the recipient countries has a number of limits, for example, it lacks a reliable monitoring model to evaluate the impact of specific projects and programmes, it has various and significant advantages. Indeed, it presents the aid provider with the opportunity to better understand, directly engage and build relationships with the national and local actors on the ground. Turkey's preference for bilateral engagement is dictated by its desire to speed up the process of distributing aid and produce tangible results as quickly as possible. In other words, the bilateral approach can ensure greater visibility than is achieved through multilateral modes of engagement.[27] This is particularly important for Turkey, which has long been trying to build up its profile as an influential global player by consolidating its influence and relevance in niche sectors such as humanitarian assistance, development aid and mediation. The flip side of this autonomy in bilateral engagement is the lack of coordination and cooperation with other donors. This is a weak point in Turkish policy. Indeed, Turkey has often failed to coordinate with traditional donors, creating situations of duplication of activities.[28] Moreover, even though the bilateral approach has reduced the time and red tape that inevitably slows down the implementation of commitments made, the limited presence of Turkish practitioners in multilateral platforms and projects has limited Turkey's positive contributions to burden-sharing, humanitarian assistance and development.[29] A further Turkish weakness is that bilateral efforts, unlike multilateral mechanisms, lack a reliable model for monitoring and assessing the impact of specific projects and programmes.[30] Furthermore, Turkey normally has no joint reviews or evaluations of projects with stakeholders in the beneficiary country, and there is a lack of adequate monitoring of public–private partnerships. As pointed out by Birdsall and Kharas, the 'burden reduction' and 'transparency and learning' require high coordination between the donors and beneficiaries for two main reasons: first of all, because multilateral coordination allows to reduce the

---

[25] See OECD Development Cooperation Report 2005. 'Turkey's Official Development Assistance' 2014. URL: http://www.oecd.org/dac/stats/turkeys-official-development-assistanceoda.htm.
[26] For further details about India's approach, see Sinha, Shakti. 2016. *Rising Powers and Peacebuilding: India's Role in Afghanistan*. New Delhi: VIJ Books India PVT.
[27] Sucuoğlu and Sazak, 'The New Kid on the Block', 69–91.
[28] Hausmann and Lundsgaarde, *Turkey's Role in Development Cooperation*, 4.
[29] See Keyman, E. Fuat and Onur Sazak. 2014. 'Turkey as a "Humanitarian State"'. In *POMEAS PAPER*.
[30] Sucuoğlu and Sazak, 'The New Kid on the Block'.

waste of resources, overcrowding and the multiplication of forces, all of them consequences of the lack of communication and cooperation among the different donors and beneficiaries. The second reason is that transparency and learning from experiences are two essential aspects of motivating donors to collect the data needed to assess the scope, breadth and effectiveness of their intervention.[31] In other words, the sharing of critical aspects and results achieved through certain activities allows the donors to improve the intervention mechanisms. The Turkish case shows how the lack of transparency has had consequences for the learning process of the Turkish agencies and institutions involved in aid and mediation.[32]

Coordination activities

Turkish engagement in countries affected by crisis situations – conflicts, humanitarian disasters – has had a significant impact, and strategies are formulated mostly at government level, while their implementation is based on a multi-stakeholder community engagement. The literature explains how citizen-based activities can be very effective in the arduous process of trust-building and in creating a space for dialogue in both conflict and non-conflict scenarios. However, each initiative has a limited but critical impact, and 'to be effective it must be combined with other efforts'.[33] In other words, there must be a coordination among the different actors involved in the field. Such coordination is ascribable to the so-called track one. Track one refers to those elements of official government that engage in diplomatic activities. Due to the wide variety of agencies on the ground, the main challenge for the Turkish state is the coordination and coherence of its initiative. Indeed, coordination efforts are particularly difficult when several independent agencies are competent to negotiate their own intervention mechanisms with central and local governments in the host countries. In order to overcome this constraint, or at least reduce any negative effect thereof, Turkey has developed a two-tier strategy.

At the high political level, Turkey's broad coordination is provided by an institutional framework at the top of which are both the Disaster and Management Presidency (AFAD), previously an agency under the office of

[31] Birdsall, Nancy and Homi Kharas. 2014. *The Quality of Official Development Assistance*, 2–3. Washington: Center for Global Development.
[32] Sazak and Woods, 'Thinking Outside the Compound'.
[33] Rupesinghe, Kumar and Sanam Naraghi Anderlini. 1998. *Civil Wars, Civil Peace: An Introduction to Conflict Resolution*, 115–16. London, Sterling: Pluto Press.

the prime minister re-formed as an agency under the Ministry of Interior, and the Ministry of Foreign Affairs. Although AFAD was established to promote cooperation among government agencies, in practice it has gradually interpreted its mission of planning and coordinating the response to crisis situations more extensively. The widening of competences has led, especially in some scenarios such as Somalia and the Syrian refugee crisis, the AFAD to coordinate the entire activities of Turkish NSAs. Civil society organizations and their actions enjoy support from the state institutional framework. At the same time, they can count on full financial independence. The state's role is in the form of indirect support, that is, it provides the necessary legal authorizations and logistical support.

A more practical level is specifically concerned with operations on the ground. Despite there not being a concept paper or strategy document that informs or constitutes Turkish implementation on the ground, the main role is played by the TİKA with the assistance of Turkish embassies and consulates. After being established in the mid-1990s with the aim of increasing Turkish cooperation with Central Asian Republics, in 2001, TİKA was appointed as the sole coordinator of all Turkish development aid, which had previously been allocated in an uncoordinated manner by a multiplicity of state agencies. TİKA represents an operative branch of Ankara's government with the aim of paving the way for subsequent public and private initiatives in three main areas: humanitarian aid; assistance in the development of the country; and making financial investments to consolidate business.[34] On the ground, this umbrella agency has been set up to manage and coordinate with the various stakeholders. The establishment of a leading agency is not new in the international landscape, especially with regard to development assistance models. Many DAC countries conduct specific assistance programmes through a dedicated independent agency – a structural difference compared to the non-DAC countries which, instead, usually operate through ministries.[35] Turkey, although formally close to the DAC model, is in essence very far away due to the TİKA's political nature. Indeed, although it was conceived as an independent agency, TİKA currently operates under the strict formal control of the Ministry of Culture and Tourism, but informally under the Office of the Presidency of the Republic. Indeed, under the JDP government, TİKA has been transformed 'into a global aid agency in accordance with

[34] Özkan and Orakçı, 'Viewpoint: Turkey as a "political" actor in Africa'; Özkan, Güner and Mustafa Turgut Demirtepe. 2012. 'Transformation of a Development Aid Agency: TIKA in a Changing Domestic and International Setting'. *Turkish Studies* 13 (4): 647–67.
[35] Gore, Charles. 2013. 'The New Development Cooperation Landscape: Actors, Approaches, Architecture'. *Journal of International Development* 25 (6): 769–86.

government policies'.[36] Further, the agency has no institutional decision-making mechanism and it does not operate according to clear and uniform procedures. In the field, TİKA is the pivot of all public and private initiatives. In addition to various ministries – such as the Ministry of Culture and Tourism and the Ministry of National Education and Technological Research Council of Turkey – a notable commitment is also provided by the Turkish Red Crescent (Kızılay), the largest charity in Turkey.[37]

In sub-Saharan African countries, Turkey concentrates primarily on four areas: health, education, infrastructure and the establishment of institutional buildings. For this reason, various ministries such as the Ministry of Food, Agriculture and Livestock, and the Ministry of National Education and Technological Research Council of Turkey have operated on the ground as well. In terms of development, state agencies such as the Foreign Economic Relations Board of Turkey (DEİK) and the Turkish Exporters Assembly (TIM) are cooperating with several private organizations. Among the latter, the Islamic-oriented business association MÜSİAD is active through promotions of fora between Turkish entrepreneurs and their African counterparts – stressing common economic goals, and at the same time exploiting the religious dimension, which is perceived as a legitimate basis for Turkey's involvement.[38] The presence of NSAs (NGOs, charities and businesses) in cooperation with the official diplomacy (ministries and state institutions) on the ground fosters interpersonal dialogue and engagement with local actors. Such a coordinated approach is particularly useful in crisis situations as well as in post-conflict scenarios like Somalia, Sudan and South Sudan since it helps to foster the inclusiveness of all local parties and increase mutual trust. Despite the many coordination efforts made by the Turkish state, in particular on the ground through the strengthening of the TİKA's role and the involvement of Turkish embassies, there are still many cases of overlapping or duplication of efforts.[39]

Direct delivery of aid

In recent years, particularly since 9/11, there has been a sharp increase in attacks by violent NSAs against agencies that operate on the ground. The multiple cases

[36] Çevik, Senem B. 2016. 'Turkey's State-Based Foreign Aid: Narrating "Turkey's Story"'. *Rising Power Quarterly* 1 (2): 55–67, 63.
[37] Genc and Tekin, 'Turkey's Increased Engagement'.
[38] Korkut and Civelekoglu, 'Becoming a Regional Power', 195.
[39] Sucuoğlu and Sazak, 'The New Kid on the Block'.

of violence and kidnapping have generated new concerns for the safety of civilian experts and aid workers in crisis areas. Nowadays, the modus operandi of many conventional aid providers is to nest their representatives in a 'security bubble' from their first day of training at headquarters all the way to the fortresses of their field offices in host countries.[40] As demonstrated by Duffield, this securitization of assistance and the heavily guarded compounds segregate development and peacebuilding actors from the very populations whose needs and interests they are there to prioritize.[41] In areas of heightened insecurity like Afghanistan and Somalia, there has emerged a technique known as remote management, which means that international aid managers manage projects from a distance, in some cases never visiting them at all.[42] For example, Dubai has become a base for aid operations in Afghanistan. By contrast, in high-intensity conflict and counterinsurgency contexts like Syria, Afghanistan and Somalia, Turkish government personnel and NGOs take pride in being present on the ground, and delivering aid directly without using secondary channels:

> Many Turkish NGOs have adopted what they call a 'direct aid' approach, meaning that it is Turkish aid agencies, manned by Turkish staff, who directly oversee the management of aid distribution on the ground, from its arrival in Somalia to its delivery to final beneficiaries.[43]

Many Turkish aid workers believe that this approach distinguishes them from others. It is seen as a means of ensuring that their aid reaches the beneficiaries. It is used to demonstrate to the beneficiaries their difference from traditional donors but also domestically to enhance the commitment and solidarity of the Turkish people. For instance, in the Somali context, Turkey's decision to operate from Mogadishu, while most of the foreign NGOs operate from Nairobi, has improved knowledge of the environment and given Turks the opportunity to explore the Somali market and aid dynamics first-hand.[44] Turkey's presence on the ground, through the direct aid mechanism, has increased its popularity among officials and the people. Moreover, the presence of Turkish actors alongside their counterparts and local communities has enabled these actors to

---

[40] Ibid., 75.

[41] Duffield, Mark. 2010. 'Risk-Management and the Fortified Aid Compound: Everyday Life in Post-Interventionary Society'. *The Journal of Intervention and Statebuilding* 4 (4): 453–74.

[42] Stoddard, Abby, Adele Harmer and Victoria Di Domenico. 2009. 'Providing Aid in Insecure Environments: 2009 Update'. In *Humanitarian Policy Group*. London: Overseas Development Institute.

[43] Achilles, Kathryn and Onur Sazak, Woods Thomas and Auveen Elizabeth Wheeler. 2015. *Turkish Aid Agencies in Somalia: Risks and Opportunities for Building Peace*, 27. Istanbul Saferworld and Istanbul Policy Center.

[44] Donelli, 'Turkey's Presence in Somalia', 44.

become more adaptable to local conditions, needs and wishes.[45] Furthermore, Turkey is able to bypass intermediaries and deliver aid to the final beneficiaries. Indeed, a visible impact of the direct aid practice is that it reduces the cost of aid delivery by eliminating intermediaries, improves both the speed and accessibility of aid efforts and 'facilitates direct contact with populations in these areas, leading to more needs-based solutions'.[46] Finally, NGO's micro-level visible assistance touches people's lives directly, and partially facilitates winning of trust. Unlike the approaches often taken by both Western and non-Western organizations, Turkey's initiative has the merit of involving local people in the activities of its long-term projects. Indeed, some of the Turkish funds end up in real estate (purchases, rents), boosting the local economy. This practice reportedly has empowered and engendered confidence in the local population by signalling that they can be trusted as equal partners.[47] Turkey's decision to operate in this way is not without risk.[48] It has led to the observation that Turkish diplomats, aid workers, businesspeople and others are 'seemingly unhampered by the security concerns that limit western engagement on the ground'.[49] There must be an acknowledgement that Turkish aid, like any other aid, is not neutral, and steps must be taken to mitigate potential bias. While these criticisms can also be lodged against other donors, they are particularly relevant for Turkey, given its preference for bilateralism and the lack of transparency in some aspects of its engagement.[50] Furthermore, Turkey's officials and NGO members have sometimes bypassed state channels – a practice that undermines the trust-building process that they are hoping to foster.[51]

6.3 A multi-stakeholder approach: Sectors and actors

As shown at the beginning of the chapter, with the increasing interconnection between people due to globalization and the volatile nature of the international context, many actors, including NSAs, have a substantial role to play in international relations and diplomacy. A pivotal role in fostering the trust-building process on the ground has been played by NSAs. Their work is part of

---

[45] Sucuoglu and Stearns, 'Turkey in Somalia', 39.
[46] Achilles, et al., *Turkish Aid*, 10.
[47] Murphy and Woods, 'Turkey's International Development', 14.
[48] Cannon, 'Turkey in Africa', 96–7.
[49] Wasuge, *Turkey's Assistance Model*, 22.
[50] Sucuoglu and Stearns, 'Turkey in Somalia', 35–6.
[51] Akpınar, 'Turkey's Peacebuilding in Somalia', 747.

what is known as track-two diplomacy. Commonly summarized by the formula 'diplomacy without diplomats',[52] the track two highlights how private individuals could play important roles in resolving conflicts and in dealing with crisis situations.

From the beginning, Turkey's activities in SSA were immediately distinguished by a sudden increase in Turkish public and private stakeholders – religious groups, NGOs, community groups and other forms of citizen-based entities – and by their close cooperation with their African counterparts.[53] As a result, there has been an increase in Turkey's civilian capacity through the involvement of NSAs in the policymaking process, and on the ground.[54] For instance, Turkey's engagement in Somalia, from the outset, has combined political, developmental, economic and humanitarian support, and has brought together a variety of actors – government officials, aid agencies, CSOs, religious organizations, municipalities and the private sector.[55] These organizations often build relations with their counterparts from the recipient country, turning disparate peace and development processes in priority countries into a uniquely inclusive, participatory process.[56] It is possible to identify three main areas in which Turkish NSAs operate while maintaining coordination or cooperation with the policies of the Turkish state: humanitarian, business and educational.

Humanitarian sector

The action of Turkish NGOs in Africa is particularly related to Turkey's humanitarian assistance. Several NGOs, mainly faith-based NGOs – among others, Human Relief Foundation (İHH), Yeryüzü Doktorları, Dost Eli Foundation, Türkiye Dyanet Foundation, Deniz Feneri, Sema Foundation and Cansuyu – are involved in the so-called humanitarian diplomacy field and are boosting the quality and quantity of Turkish humanitarian assistance. A notable commitment is also provided by the Turkish Red Crescent (Kızılay), the largest charity in Turkey. TİKA's constant presence on the ground has allowed the development of a cooperative engagement, as in the case of the Africa Cataract Campaign initiated by TİKA and İHH, culminating in the opening of several cataract surgery centres. Similar projects have been initiated by TİKA and

52   Homans, Charles. 2011. 'Track II Diplomacy: A Short Story'. *Foreign Policy.*
53   Achilles, et al., *Turkish Aid.*
54   Sancar, Gaye Aslı. 2014. 'Turkey's Public Diplomacy: Its Actors, Stakeholders, and Tools'. In *Turkey's Public Diplomacy*, edited by Philip Seib and Senem B. Çevik, 13–42. New York: Palgrave Mavmillan.
55   Donelli, 'Turkey's Presence in Somalia'.
56   Sucuoğlu and Sazak, 'The New Kid on the Block', 74.

several other NGOs such as Doctors of Hope and Kimse Yok Mu aid foundation – affiliated with the Gülen movement. All of these projects provide free health check-ups, circumcisions and cataract surgeries, as well as free medicines and medical supplies to African people. The efforts and actions of these stakeholders are coordinated from Ankara and on the ground by TİKA.

The cooperation between the Turkish state's policies and the many Turkish NSAs active in Africa is based on a convergence of objectives that arise from shared motivations. The agency's officials, in fact, share ideological roots with most of the NGOs, a cultural proximity that has enabled significant cooperation between the state and the NSAs. Indeed, the majority of Turkish non—governmental aid providers with whom TİKA has cooperated are Islamic charity organizations. Unlike secular NGOs that use rights-based language in their actions, faith-based NGOs use the language of religious duties and obligations when explaining their involvement[57] – a convergence of motivations that in the Turkish case becomes evident in the meaning conferred on some humanitarian initiatives, such as the construction of water wells. Several Turkish faith-based NGOs and TİKA itself have developed many projects to provide water and sanitation services, as a contribution to African countries' development by preventing deaths from water-borne diseases, decreasing the daily burden of carrying water and thus improving the quality of life of the people. For the Muslim NGOs, ensuring access to water also takes on a deeper value, linked to the need to fulfil their religious duties. In Islam, cleanliness is seen as a religious duty, especially in Muslim purification rites (*abdest*).[58]

Among the most active Turkish NGOs in Africa is the İHH, which has been operating on the continent since 1996. The IHH has delivered assistance in the fight against hunger and has opened medical clinics in 140 countries worldwide. The organization's name became famous in 2010 with the so-called 'Mavi Marmara maritime incident' and the consequent cooling of bilateral relations between Turkey and Israel. The ship was rented by an NGO to provide humanitarian aid to Gaza was attacked by the Israeli security forces as it broke the embargo imposed by the Israeli government. The Turkish activists who died in the clashes were IHH volunteers.[59] Despite the controversy surrounding the flotilla, the IHH campaign was successful and contributed to the organization's status as a trustworthy third party in the Muslim world willing to share in the

---

[57] Atalay, 'Civil Society as Soft Power', 176–7.
[58] Ipek and Biltekin, 'Turkey's Foreign Policy Implementation'.
[59] For more on that epidsode, see Makowski, Andrzej. 2013. 'The Mavi Marmara Incident and the Modern Law of Armed Conflict at Sea'. *The Israel Journal of Foreign Affairs* 7 (2):75–89.

burden of moral struggles. At the same time, it strengthened its bond with the Turkish government, which had supported the effort.[60]

However, the Mavi Marmara incident was not the first time that the organization had been at the centre of international concern. Already in 2006, a report published by the Danish Institute for International Studies had highlighted the ties of some of the organization's members with Islamic fighters' cells in Bosnia and Chechnya. Furthermore, the same report pointed out that the IHH maintained an ambiguous attitude towards some al-Qaeda affiliates residing in Europe.[61] However, it is the relations with Hamas that have led several countries to be very suspicious of the organization's activities. Due to these bonds, the IHH has been banned by Israel (2008) and Germany (2010), and it has risked being classified as a terrorist organization by the US Congress as well.

In the African context, the IHH, as well as the Gülen movement, was one of the first active Turkish civil society organizations. The IHH has started to operate in Africa through small and very localized projects; however, its presence on the ground has been proven to be very important to acquire a first knowledge of some areas – for example, Sudan and Somalia – and to establish a first contact with local actors. The organization operates in more than thirty African countries developing both independent projects and in cooperation with initiatives of the Turkish state. The projects implemented by the IHH have often been put on the agenda of meetings between Turkish–African leaders, thus becoming a foreign policy issue. Among its main activities are the construction and maintenance of water wells, assistance to orphans through remote adoption systems and the direct management of orphanages. The name of the IHH in Africa, however, is mainly linked to cataract surgeries and the project called '100 Thousand Cataract Surgeries in Africa' launched in 2007. Cataract is medical condition that affects the lens of the eye and occurs due to the lack of, or unhealthy, nutrition, insufficient health care and equatorial climate conditions. Developed in fourteen African countries, including Ghana, Sudan and Ethiopia, the project had the goal of performing 100,000 cataract operations in ten years. Having reached its target in 2017, IHH has invested not only in direct intervention but also, in cooperation with TİKA and other institutions such as the WHO, in the training of specialized staff.

---

[60] Tabak, Hüsrev. 2015. 'Broadening the Nongovernmental Humanitarian Mission: The IHH and Mediation'. *Insight Turkey* 17 (3): 193–217.

[61] Kohlmann, Evan F. 2006. 'The Role of Islamic Charities in International Terrorist Recruitment and Financing'. In *DIIS Working Paper*. Copenhagen: Danish Institute for International Studies.

Even though religion is not mentioned in its vision and mission statement, as an openly Muslim organization affiliated with the Union of NGOs of the Islamic World, the aids are directed mainly but not exclusively to Muslim communities. It has helped restore Turkey's bonds with the global Muslim community (*ummah*) through humanitarian work in the region. The major achievement of the first humanitarian initiatives undertaken by the IHH was to raise awareness among the Turkish public. Their outreach campaigns characterized by strong impact slogans such as 'Turkish people will open the eyes of 100,000 Africans', and '700,000 people are dying' brought Africa to the attention of all layers of Turkish society. The most important outcome of IHH's campaigns was, as pointed out by Özkan and Akgün,

> to encourage many other institutions, foundations and associations to start activities in Africa. They wanted to know Africa, and the IHH took them to many countries in the continent, sharing its experience with fellow relief and aid organisations as well as Turkish media outlets.[62]

The media campaigns launched by the IHH were an essential component of a broader process of raising Turkish public awareness of African issues – a process instigated and fuelled by the Turkish state within the framework of the general redefinition of Turkey's national role identity and Turkish geographical perception (see 3.1). To encourage the growing involvement of Turkish NSAs, a change was necessary in the Turkish geographical imagination of Africa, no longer considered as a poor and backward place but as a fecund ground full of opportunities. Therefore, Turkey's opening to Africa has also had profound psychological effects on Turkish society. At the same time, one of the main incentives to turn towards Africa came from below, from civil society. In a short time, the Turkish public has become increasingly aware of the many African issues, particularly relating to long-ignored sub-Saharan countries, creating a general interest in the region.[63] Despite the fact that this growing consciousness has not yet translated into in-depth knowledge of the African societies and people, it has developed a widespread sensitivity to African problems. This trend is revealed by the wide public support for fundraisers and relief goods collections allocated to African countries. The attention is usually promoted by citizens-based organizations. In some cases, these have preceded the official political initiatives. For instance, as mentioned before, in the summer of 2011, a widespread campaign in Turkey, led by NGOs such as the İHH, Deniz Feneri Derneği and

---

[62] Özkan and Akgün, 'Turkey's Opening to Africa', 542.
[63] Gökhan and Afacan, 'Turkey Discovers Sub-Saharan Africa'.

Cansuyu Charity, made a considerable contribution by finding substantial resources for relief efforts with a flow of over $365 million in humanitarian aid.[64] Recently, in the spring of 2017, the state-owned Turkish Airlines, the only airline that flies to Mogadishu, backed the campaign #TurkishAirlinesHelpSomalia,[65] in an attempt to draw worldwide attention to the famine in the Somali peninsula. The campaign has had credited with highlighting the famine crisis in Somalia and, at the same time, slyly reaffirming Turkish presence in the HOA. People's participation and feelings have made all these campaigns a somewhat domestic issue for both the Turkish government and society. Many Turkish people feel a deep sense of obligation to help the suffering ones by donating money or helping on the ground as humanitarian, medical and teaching staff.[66] However, it should be noted that such funding campaigns are usually indirectly promoted by the state, engage only a part of the Turkish public and are only for a limited period of time, following a specific agenda and foreign policy priorities.

A distinctive feature that needs to be stressed as regards Turkish religious NGOs that promote humanitarian, development and educational projects in Africa is that these are promoted and implemented in the name of the nation as much as that of the Ummah. Furthermore, concern about the real autonomy of NGOs operating in Africa should also be stressed. Indeed, during the last decade, the transfer of a remarkable amount of public surplus money to Islamist or faith-based humanitarian NGOs close to the JDP's elite eventually turned to government-organized NGOs. The increasing number of organizations' board members who are to some degree linked to the JDP ruling party has increased the risk of their activities being politicized.[67] In other words, the rationale behind the actions of some Turkish NGOs is becoming increasingly political and less humanitarian – a dynamic highlighted after the 2016 failed coup, when the Turkish state shut down many NGOs and took control of others, making them purely political instruments. The lack of autonomy for NSAs might weaken, over the medium term, the effectiveness of the track two, acting as a domestic constraint.

---

[64] Editorial, 'Assessing Turkey's Role in Somalia'.
[65] The Twitter hashtag #TurkishAirlinesHelpSomalia was launched by a French social media celebrity Jerome Jerre. See Lansdown, Sarah. 'Turkish Airlines to Send Supplies to Somalia after Social Media Campaign'. *Huffington Post*, 20 March 2017. http://www.huffingtonpost.com.au/2017/03/19/turkish -airlines-to-send-supplies-to-somalia-after-social-media_a_21902874.
[66] Wasuge, 'Turkey's Assistance Model', 4.
[67] Dan Bilefsky, 'Sponsor of Flotilla Tied to Elite of Turkey'. *The Washington Post*, 15 July 2010.

Business sector

In this field are business associations whose activities pursue the possibilities of using trade as a tool of international political policy. During the opening period (2005–14) trade associations, private companies and businessmen have contributed to the growth of Turkey–Africa relations in a private-led approach, similar to that championed by the United States and the EU. Turkish state institutions supported these activities through official visits and agreements such as the establishment of industrial zones or visa-waiving programmes. At the same time, Turkey has fostered the idea of a Turkish–African partnership through the organization of fora and summits aimed at encouraging business-to-business meetings. As seen earlier, since 2008, it also organizes Turkey–Africa summits every four years, modelled on Chinese forum diplomacy. In a few years, the events have become one of the practical manifestations of the Turkish–African policy, combining the state dimension with the private one. Although the summits are managed and supported by the Turkey–Africa Desk within Turkey's Foreign Economic Relations Board, they place private investors and entrepreneurs at the heart of activities. At the fora, the latter have the opportunity to meet their potential partners and communicate with the assistance of international students from African countries who, thanks to the exchange and scholarship programmes (Türkiye Scholarships) awarded by Turkey's Ministry of Culture and Tourism, have studied in Turkish universities.[68]

As showed in the previous sections, the Turkish opening towards sub-Saharan countries has produced political and economic results, enriching the total trade volume and increasing Turkey's visibility throughout the entire continent. Turkey is close enough geographically to be considered a friendly power by Africans, but at the same time far enough to remain aloof in a way that the Arab states cannot. As Shinn explained,

> Turkish businesses are carving out a niche in construction and in information and communications technology, and Turkish Airlines is becoming prominent as a carrier to the region.[69]

In the last few years, Turkish Airlines (THY), which is 49 per cent state-owned, has rapidly increased its African destinations as well as the number of flights.[70] Behind this increase was the company's willingness to create direct connections

---

[68] Guner, 'The Scalar Politics', 60.
[69] Shinn, *Turkey's Engagement in Sub-Saharan Africa: Shifting Alliances and Strategic Diversification.*
[70] In 2011, Turkish Airlines flew to fourteen African cities. By the end of 2019, it was operating on fifty-two routes from Istanbul across Africa.

that could open up new business opportunities for Turkish entrepreneurs. But in the broader framework of Turkey's strategy towards Africa, THY is not only a carrier to open the country to the continent's markets, but also a soft power tool. The Istanbul-based carrier is probably the leading Turkish national brand that contributes to boosting the reputation of the country and the quality of its services all over the world. In addition to increasing its presence in the continent, THY has contributed to communicating Turkey's message by introducing its guests to Turkish culture and modernity.[71] Nowadays, many of those from the Middle East, Europe and even the Far East who have to go to Africa fly the Turkish carrier.

Among private companies, although an important share of Turkish business in Africa is carried out via large conglomerates such as Koç (the largest Turkish group involved in energy, insurance, banking), Sabanci (cement, energy, banking, telecommunications, textiles) and Doğan or Doğuş (banking, construction, tourism), small–medium enterprises are increasingly acquiring influence and market shares due to the growing role gained in the Turkish economy and the tighter ties with Turkish politicians.[72] An analysis of the main sectors in which Turkish companies operate indicates that the strongest Turkish business presence in Africa is in the construction field. In 2015, forty-three Turkish firms entered the Engineering News Record list of the world's 250 biggest contractors through investment in Africa.[73] In that same year, Öztürk Construction – which currently operates in Guinea, Ghana, Cameroon, Angola, Tanzania, Zambia and Sudan – became the highest-rated Turkish firm, and eighteenth overall, by operating investments in sectors as varied as energy, education, mass housing and healthcare. There are many other Turkish companies involved in mega infrastructure projects in the African countries, for example, the airport in the Senegalese capital Dakar or the new terminal at Ghana's Kotoka International Airport in Accra.[74]

Another sizeable field in which Turkish companies have invested a lot is the textile and garment sector, particularly in some African countries such as Ethiopia, Nigeria and Kenya. For example, Turkish firms have so far invested about $1.2 billion in the textile industry in Ethiopia alone, which is more than the

---

[71] For a deeper analysis of Turkish Airlines' role as a soft power tool, see Sancar, 'Turkey's Public Diplomacy', 13–42.

[72] Augé, Benjamin. 2018. 'The 2016 Failed Coup in Turkey: What Is the Impact on Turkish-African Relations?' In *Notes de l'Ifri*, 14. Paris: Institut français des relations internationales.

[73] http://www.enr.com/toplists/2015_Top_250_International_Contractors1.

[74] Howson, Peter. 2017. 'Turkey Eyes on Africa'. *The Business Year*. URL: https://www.thebusinessyear .com/turkey-2017/turkish-eyes-on-africa/focus (accessed 9 September 2017).

total Chinese investment in the same industry. However, the growing presence of Turkish companies has created the conditions for some frictions with other regional powers such as, for example, South Africa. Turkish businesses are in direct competition with other businesses, many of which have been operating in the region for years. This dynamic has been easily visible in the Mogadishu Airport events. The Favori LLC, a Turkish company, gained control of the airport under opaque circumstances,[75] at the expense of the South African-staffed SKA International Group.[76] Another interesting aspect linked to the track three is that among the business associations, the Islamic-oriented MÜSİAD is active through the promotion of fora between Turkish entrepreneurs and their African counterparts – stressing common economic goals, and also exploiting the religious dimension, which is perceived as a legitimate basis for Turkey's involvement. Turkish businessmen frequently present Islam as 'the unifying bond between Africa and Turkey in order to gain advantage over their competitors'.[77]

There are several doubts about Turkish actions related to this field as well. There is a concern that Turkey is merely following the EU and other countries – mainly BRICS ones – in a 'new scramble' for African markets. From this perspective, 'Turkey is perceived to follow only a mercantilist and interest-oriented logic'.[78] Besides, there is also a concern about the provision of Turkish arms to African countries.[79] In the last decade, the Turkish defence industry company ASELSAN and Turkish Airspace Industries have known impressive revenue gains in SSA. Turkey aims to present itself in Africa as in other areas as a weapons producer with the awareness of being able to acquire more influence, a strategy previously pursued by other countries such as France.

Despite the lack of institutional coordination mechanisms, most of the companies that operate in SSA have patronage relationships with the JDP. Some of them also have family ties with government figures, including President Erdoğan. Although structurally different from the top-down model of other emerging powers like China, even the Turkish case shows how the state has

---

[75] Ali, Ahmed. 2013. 'Turkish Aid in Somalia: The Irresistible Appeal of Boots on the Ground'. *The Guardian*, 20 September 2013. URL: https://www.theguardian.com/global-development-professionals-network/2013/sep/30/turkey-aid-somalia-aid-effectiveness (accessed 20 September 2017). However, to ensure more transparency the Turkish government amended the deal with Favori LLC after it was dogged by accusations of corruption and lack of competition in the awarding of contracts.

[76] The UN Monitoring Group for Somalia and Eritrea accused Favori LLC of paying senior members of the SFG a $1.8 million 'Initial Premium Fee' to remove SKA from the airport.

[77] Korkut and Civelekoglu, 'Becoming a Regional Power', 195.

[78] Langan, 'Virtuous Power Turkey', 1409.

[79] Rubin, Michael. 2014. 'Did Turkey Arm Boko Haram?'. American Enterprise Institute. URL: http://www.aei.org/publication/did-turkey-arm-boko-haram.

enough power leverage to control and constrain the activism of economic NSAs abroad.

Education sector

According to Rupesinghe's multitrack model, track five is related to the educational field and track seven to the religious dimension. The primary task of the educational component is to transfer information about the home country to the target, while track seven deals with the beliefs and peace-oriented actions of spiritual and religious communities. To better understand Turkey's engagement in SSA, it is appropriate to treat these two fields together because, compared to other emerging non-Western powers that are active in Africa, Turkey gives a religious dimension to its efforts – either as an element of legitimacy to foster a reliable image, on one hand, or as it constitutes a dimension of tension and even dispute with both local groups and other extra-regional actors on the other. The gradual rehabilitation of the religious dimension in Turkish foreign policy must be included in its multidimensional nature, as a tool of its soft power, especially so in Africa. This dynamic has been initiated by Turkey's diplomatic rediscovery of the Muslim world and reaffirmed by the role assumed abroad by the Directorate for Religious Affairs (Diyanet). The Diyanet until recently did not have a role in foreign policy and focused solely on the domestic religious needs of Muslims.[80] On a broader level, Diyanet also hopes to contribute to the development of religious education and to a quality environment for praying in Africa, and has established mosques to this end. Religion has thus become a most distinctive aspect of Turkey's involvement in Africa. It has made Turkey unique in comparison to other emerging actors, as its policy extends beyond the humanitarian and economic fields.[81]

Since 2006, Turkey has organized three African summits of Muslim religious leaders, which helped introduce the African participants to the Turkish model of state–religion relations and Islamic education. In Africa Diyanet acts through its non-profit foundation *Türkiye Diyanet Vakfı* and promotes the spread and development of Sunni-Hanafi education (the so-called Turkish Islam) through the opening of Turkish religious schools – Imam-Hatip – materials distribution and the organization of meetings between African religious leaders and their

---

[80] For further information on the Diyanet development, see Öztürk, Ahmet Erdi. 2018. 'Transformation of the Turkish Diyanet Both at Home and Abroad: Three Stages'. *European Journal of Turkish Studies* 27. doi: https://doi.org/10.4000/ejts.5944.

[81] Özkan, 'Turkey's Religious and Socio-Political Depth in Africa', 48.

Turkish counterparts. Since the colonial period, European education systems, particularly the French one, have been considered the best in Africa. However, access to these schools has long been reserved only for the elite, for a matter of fee, and they have worked especially well in countries with a strong Christian presence, where the missionary service has allowed access even to those who could not afford it. In African countries with a Muslim majority, the demand for alternative education systems capable of transmitting Islamic values to children has thus gradually increased. This process has led to the emergence of several parallel and competing education systems.

In this context, the spread of Turkish schools, Imam-Hatip, has been rapid and branched. These have proved to be very effective in bridging the gap between religious and scientific teaching. The Imam-Hatip, thanks to their original conception in the secular Kemalist environment, offer a synthesis between the traditional religious teaching and the scientific-positivist of the Western style. The Imam-Hatip represent an exclusively Turkish educational system, where Islamic studies are combined with modern sciences.[82] This approach distinguishes them from traditional Islamic *madrasas* and makes them more adaptable to different contexts (in many African countries, for example, the language of instruction remains French or English). The characteristics of the Turkish schools allowed the system to be widely accepted as 'the best available educational system in the Islamic world for creating a new generation that remains pious but that is more tolerant, interactive and moderate in its readings of the world'.[83]

In the field of education, the Turkish Ministry of National Education also has worked intensively in Africa by allocating several types of grants for African students and distributing material for African schools. Since 2010, over 5,000 students from sub-Saharan countries have been awarded scholarships to study in Turkey. Alongside the Diyanet and the Education Ministry efforts, faith-based NGOs have also increased their presence in SSA. Traditional religious groups actively promote projects in Africa. They generally focus on the educational field, most commonly religious schools, high schools and vocational schools that emphasize education.

Among the most active are the Aziz Mahmud Hüdayi Foundation and Suleymancılar. The Aziz Mahmud Foundation has offices in seventeen sub-Saharan African countries, from where it manages operations in more than forty countries on the continent. In addition to humanitarian interventions,

---

[82] For further information about the Imam-Hatip, see Ozgur, R. 2012. *Islamic Schools in Modern Turkey: Faith, Politics, and Education.* New York: Cambridge University Press.

[83] Özkan, 'Turkey's Religious and Socio-Political Depth in Africa', 49.

the foundation, following its mission statement 'Fighting Against Poverty and Ignorance', implements long-term projects. Among these, in addition to assistance in cases of humanitarian emergency, there is special attention to orphans and families, and other initiatives with considerable religious value such as the construction of new mosques and prayer houses and the supply of food for the *iftar* dinner during the holy month of Ramadan. The involvement of the Turkish public in the foundation's initiatives is consistent, both through donations – in the form of *zakat al-mal*, financial atonements (*fidya*) and zakat alfitr – and through voluntary service. However, the foundation's main activity remains education. It runs Imam-Hatip schools, Koran courses and colleges where graduates can work as teachers. Through the flexibility of their approach, Aziz Mahmud's schools in Africa are structured on the model of traditional Turkish schools, but with minor differences depending on the environment in which they are being implemented.

The other very active civil society organization is the Suleymancılar. The group is composed of students and followers of the teachings of the Sufi master and Islamic philosopher Süleyman Hilmi Tunahan (1888–1959) belonging to the Nakşibendi tariqa order. The organization, despite operating mainly out of the spotlight, is also highly committed to Africa, especially in the field of Islamic education.[84] In particular, it promotes the spread of Turkish Islam against what it sees as deviant currents such as Wahhabism and Shiism.[85]

An issue that is not yet adequately explored concerns the racial element of the Turkish religious dimension. A common trait of discourses and practices of governmental and non-governmental actors that rely on religious values concerns the constant reference to the Islamic principle of racial egalitarianism. As underlined by Guner,

> conjuring of the scale of the ummah is, then, at the same time conjuring of race. In other words, imagining a multiracial Muslim world is conditioned on the racialization of Muslims as white and black. The scalar and racial politics of ummah-making, furthermore, lay the ideological groundwork for the conjuring of the Turkish–African 'partnership'.[86]

Over the last fifteen years, Turkey has progressively opened up to SSA. The Ankara government, having acquired an important role as a humanitarian actor

---

[84] Ibid.
[85] For further information on the Suleymancılar, see Lord, Ceren. 2018. *Religious Politics in Turkey: From the Birth of the Republic to the AKP*. Cambridge: Cambridge University Press.
[86] Guner, 'The Scalar Politics', 63.

and trading partner, has in recent years increased its interest in African political issues. This development was the outcome of a meticulous trust-building policy characterized by the simultaneous commitment of governmental and non-governmental actors. However, this multi-stakeholder approach is not without risks. One of the main pitfalls of such a policy is that NSAs do not always seek the same interest of the political agenda. In some cases, from being a very important asset in a state's soft policy, it can become a constraint and even a threat to the state itself. This parabola is well illustrated by the path taken by one of the most powerful and best entrenched Turkish NSAs in Africa: the Gülen movement.

7

The Gülen movement in Africa

From Turkish transnational asset to anti-state lobby

As seen in the previous chapter, one of the main traits of the unconventional Turkish engagement of a multitrack approach to Africa has been the joint use of state agencies and NSAs belonging to civil society. As mentioned, in a few cases these NSAs even preceded the policies of the Turkish state. In other words, they acted as forerunners. Their established presence within the African context has also led them to become one of the main drivers of the development of a Turkish policy for Africa. Their experience gained on the ground and the Turkish state's need to start from scratch has led to its outsourcing some sectors of its public diplomacy. Therefore, these NSAs have become transnational assets of Turkish politics. Among these, the most important and active in Africa for almost twenty years has been the Hizmet, better known as the Gülen movement. The domestic struggle between the Hizmet, now considered by the Turkish authorities as a terrorist organization, and the state institutions, deflagrated in the 15 July coup attempt, has highlighted the vulnerability of Turkey's foreign policy agenda towards Africa. The multi-stakeholder structure set up in a coordinated and hierarchical way, on one side, has provided a sharing of the engagement on the ground but, on the other side, has allowed some of the NSAs involved to promote and consolidate their agenda without any control by government agencies. The case of the Gülen movement shows how the link between the foreign and domestic policy is continuous and fluid, and how the involvement of NSAs quickly backfires, especially in those countries where there is still a low level of social cohesion and high political polarization. The chapter, after examining the steps of the rapid growth of the movement's network and its international projection through public diplomacy, analyses the role played by the organizations linked to the movement in the Turkish policy towards Africa. Finally, the chapter's last section analyses the repercussions of the struggle between the Gülen movement and the Turkish state following the failed coup in 2016 on Turkey's African agenda.

7.1   From the işık evler to power: The long march through the institutions of Fethullah Gülen

In a 2008 survey, conducted jointly by *Foreign Policy* and *Prospect* magazines, Fethullah Gülen was identified by the interviewees as the most important living intellectual in the world. In announcing the poll results, *Foreign Policy* described Gülen as,

> an inspirational leader to millions of followers around the world and persona non-grata to many in his native Turkey, where some consider him a threat to the country's secular order.[1]

The Hizmet is an Islamic transnational religious and social organization that has developed a multisectoral network in Turkey and abroad. The movement's founder, the Islamic preacher Muhammed Fethullah Gülen, started as a voluntary teacher in the Koranic school of Kestanepazarı, near Izmir. Fethullah Gülen was born in Erzurum in eastern Turkish Anatolia on 27 April 1941 into a family of devout and scholarly Muslims. Since the early years of activity, the sermons of the *hoca* (master) acquired peculiar and unmistakable traits. Among these, one of the key aspects was belief in the need for interfaith dialogue – a quest for dialogue directed solely at whom the Koran defines as the People of the Book, namely, Jews and Christians. In 1976, Gülen opened his first *işık evler* (light houses). It was an off-site student hostel that also offered scholarships for the poorest. The hostel was a meeting place where informal semi-clandestine discussions about the Koran could take place. Later Gülen encouraged some of his first adherents to follow his example and to open light houses, which soon became the basis of the Gülen movement.[2]

During the second half of the 1970s, after a few months in prison Gülen significantly increased his followers, and began to address in his sermons issues related less to spirituality. Specifically, the tone of his speeches adopted a strong nationalist accent. In doing so, the preacher began to progressively

---

[1]   'Meet Fethullah Gülen, the World's Top Public Intellectual'. *Foreign Policy*, 4 August 2008. URL: https ://foreignpolicy.com/2008/08/04/meet-fethullah-gulen-the-worlds-top-public-intellectual/.

[2]   Tee, Caroline. 2016. *The Gülen Movement in Turkey: The Politics of Islam and Modernity*. London, New York: I.B. Tauris.

distinguish himself from his mentor Said Nursi, who had rejected any form of political commitment. According to Nursi's works, which were the basis of the Nur Cemaati or Nurculuk,[3] the believers had to concentrate their efforts on the complex reconciliation between science and faith while ignoring political issues.[4] However, like Nursi, Fethullah Gülen also, until the second half of the 1990s, avoided active politics and adopted a gradualist approach centred on a bottom-up Islamization of society. Over the years, thanks to a patient strategy, based on dissimulation and finalized in the achievement of medium- and long-term goals, the Hizmet grew significantly. Unlike other Turkish-Islamic communities, the Gülen movement renounced public expressions of its Muslim identity, ordering its members to adopt a secular custom and lifestyle to prepare for 'the long march through institutions'.[5]

Over the next twenty years, Gülen established himself as the most prestigious and powerful successor to the traditions of Said Nursi. Exploiting the favourable post-1980 coup environment, in particular the military's adoption of Turkish-Islamic synthesis as a state ideology, Gülen widened the activities of his movement to a multiplicity of spheres of society. Specifically, thanks to the general acquiescence of the state institutions, the group strengthened its presence within Turkish society by enhancing its main instrument of proselytism: the *dershane*. Dershane were private prep-schools that Turkish students attended in order to obtain high scores in the national centralized university entrance exam. Founded and managed by mostly Islamic communities, from the 1980s onwards they became an almost exclusive monopoly of the Gülen movement. The preparatory schools became widespread meeting places, introducing new mechanisms of coexistence and interpersonal exchange in Turkish society. The

---

[3] Nurculuk is a religious philosophy that came to be organized around Said Nursi (1878–1960) and his writings are called Risale-i Nur (Letters of Light). A wide circle of students of Risale-i Nur supported the development of Nurculuk. However, after the death of the religious leader, Nurculuk was dispersed and three independent groups were formed: Group of New Asia, Kırkıncı Hoca and his supporters, and the neo-Nurcu under the leadership of Fethullah Gülen. See Mardin, Şerif. 1989. *Religion and Social Change in Modern Turkey: The Case of Bediuzzaman Said Nursi.* Albany: State University of New York Press.

[4] Said Nursi developed his own method of teaching by combining religious and modern sciences, which had previously been taught separately. His belief was that modern sciences would strengthen the truths of religion, with religion representing the heart and conscience and science representing reason, but with both being necessary conditions for true progress. In Nursi's teaching method, heart and reason must work together, so he opposed the common viewpoint that religion is incommensurate with science. For a further analysis, see, Balci, Bayram. 2003. 'Fethullah Gülen's Missionary Schools in Central Asia and their Role in the Spreading of Turkism and Islam'. *Religion, State and Society* 31 (2): 151–77.

[5] Yavuz, Hakan M. and John L. Esposito, eds. 2003. *Turkish Islam and the Secular State: The Gülen Movement.* New York: Syracuse University Press; Miller, Christopher L. and Tamer Balci, eds. 2012. *The Gülen Hizmet Movement: Circumspect Activism in Faith-based Reform.* Cambridge: Cambridge Scholar Publishing.

Gülen movement, taking advantage of these informal networks, was able to take root rapidly throughout the country, constituting a real parallel community, whose members developed a strong communitarian feeling in which Islam was a source of mutual solidarity and brotherhood. Moreover, these schools were the main recruitment channel of the movement that could thus begin to have many followers within the institutions and state bodies.

Although the community does not have a formal structure, Gülen's supporters have established various formal organizations in order to integrate it into the country's formal systems. These include an international chain of schools and student dormitories, a communications web that includes newspapers, journals, television and radio channels and companies and finance institutions. With the aim of avoiding confrontation with the state, Gülen publicly dissociated himself from any platform of political Islam, including the parties of Necmettin Erbakan. When the Islamist party led by Erbakan came to power in 1995, Gülen increased his public appearances. He gave several interviews to important Turkish and international media, thus making his ideas on topical issues better known. From these public appearances, the distinction between Erbakan and Gülen emerged clearly, equivalent to that between 'political Islam' and 'cultural Islam'. These interviews give the impression of a moderate figure who respects his nation and state, and who admires Picasso's work, as well as the poems of the socialist Turkish poet, Nazım Hikmet. Gülen fostered a Turkish media narrative that promoted him and his movement as a modern and moderate nationalist alternative to Erbakan's party and his political aspirations based on Islamic community (*ummah*). Even more important, Fethullah Gülen, who before 1995 was known only by a small circle of religious believers, become a character increasingly known in Turkey and at the centre of public attention.

The post-modern coup (1997), however, seemed to stop the rise of the Hizmet. In parallel with the repression of political Islam (Welfare Party), Islamist business also came under closer scrutiny by the secular state elite, especially the military. The Hizmet, as an influential Islamist movement, was also under intense investigation and pressure. The movement ended up being investigated in June 1999 when several videos showed Fethullah Gülen advising his followers employed within the bureaucracy to keep their religious identities hidden. In one the preacher said,

> the existing system is still in power. Our friends who have positions in the legislative and administrative bodies should learn its details and be vigilant all the time so that they can transform it and be more fruitful on behalf of Islam

in order to carry out a nationwide restoration. However, they should wait until the conditions become more favourable. In other words they should not come out too early.[6]

As a consequence, the Ankara State Security Court filed a lawsuit against Fethullah Gülen in 2000. In the proceedings against him, Gülen was charged with undermining the secular order of the country. The prosecution defined Gülen as 'the strongest and most effective Islamic fundamentalist in Turkey', who 'disguises his methods with a democratic and moderate image'.[7] Gülen moved to the United States (apparently for health reasons) and remained there in self-imposed exile. Meanwhile, the military continued to watch closely the activities of his community closely, especially in education. By the end of the 1990s, Fethullah Gülen became well known, not only throughout Turkey but also internationally. Despite the push to spread among the ranks of the Turkish bureaucracy, the movement invested capital and energy in the management of about 2000 schools in 160 countries. In a few years the movement had begun to extend its network outside the Turkish borders. The first area of interest was Central Asia. During the late-1980s, Gülen advised his followers to 'prepare to help those countries that would soon gain their independence, most of which were Turkish in origin and language'.[8] Following the collapse of the Soviet Union, in line with the Turkish state's orientation towards the Turkish-speaking republics of Central Asia, Fethullah Gülen encouraged the members of the community to open the first schools of the movement in Azerbaijan and Kazakhstan (1992). Since then, the Hizmet educational model has continued to spread throughout Central Asia. Apart from this activity in Central Asia, Gülen followers were also opening schools in former Soviet republics in Eastern Europe, such as Bulgaria, Romania, Moldova, Ukraine and Georgia, while other volunteers were establishing schools in the Asia-Pacific region, including the Philippines, Cambodia, Australia, Indonesia, Thailand, Vietnam, Malaysia, South Korea and Japan. As a result, by the 2000s, Gülen's educational network had spread to countries all over the world, from Azerbaijan to Ukraine, Albania to Macedonia, the Netherlands to Canada, Australia to South Africa, and Japan to Taiwan.[9] To support its philanthropic activities, the movement used the tools

---

[6] Gülen's speech quoted in Turam, Berna. 2007. *Between Islam and the State: The Politics of Engagement*, 87. Stanford: Stanford University Press.
[7] Taş, Hakkı. 2017. 'A History of Turkey's AKP–Gülen Conflict'. *Mediterranean Politics* 23 (3): 395–402.
[8] Ebaugh, Helen Rose. 2010. *The Gülen Movement*, 43. New York: Springer.
[9] Ibid., 43–4.

of a market-oriented economic model to build a financial empire, making it one of the richest religious communities in Turkey. The movement had several media companies that were capable of generating profits. These included seven television channels, seven radio channels, two newspapers, a press agency and five magazines. The empire also includes affiliates such as an insurance company (*Işık*) and a participation bank (*Bank Asya*). Finally, an employers' association, the Business Life Cooperation Association (İŞHAD), and the Confederation of Businessmen and Industrialists of Turkey (TUSKON), an umbrella organization of seven business federations, were established by businesspeople within the community in 1993 and 2005, respectively.[10] In particular, the latter has played a primary role in opening up the connecting channels between Turkey and several African countries.

The 2002 JDP victory in the elections transformed the Turkish political scenario. Following the amendments to the anti-terrorism law introduced by the ruling JDP on 5 May 2006, the Ankara Criminal Court acquitted Fethullah Gülen of his attempt to change Turkey's secular regime. Despite public perception that there was an intrinsic partnership between the JDP and the Hizmet at this time, the relationship could best be described as a strategic alliance in the pursuit of mutual benefit. The renewed political and strategic affinity allowed both groups to put aside their differences. The bond was as functional as it was natural for the purposes of the common struggle against domination that the secular elite maintained over the institutions, in particular the bureaucracy, the judiciary and the Army. Furthermore, the JDP and the Gülen movement shared the ambitious aim of promoting a cultural revolution capable of unhinging the Kemalist hegemony and replacing it with an ideological apparatus structured along the Islamic-conservative axis. While the JDP benefited from the human capital educated by the movement in the state bureaucracy, the Hizmet found an opportunity to expand further into the social, economic and bureaucratic sectors. From this moment until the end of 2013, the Gülen movement began to contribute actively to the promotion of Turkey's interests and the Turkish brand abroad. For several years, associations and movement members had been used to working abroad with the aim of making proselytes and spreading Gülen's ideas. The strategic alliance with the JDP allowed the Hizmet to move with more freedom and to acquire an institutional role, making it one of the main players in the Turkish state's public diplomacy.

[10] Başkan-Canyaş, Filiz and F. Orkunt Canyaş. 2016. 'The Interplay between Formal and Informal Institutions in Turkey: The Case of the Fethullah Gülen Community'. *Middle Eastern Studies* 52 (2): 280–94.

The strategic alliance between the JDP and the Hizmet began to show the first indications of breaking in 2010, due to the tensions between Turkey and Israel following the Mavi Marmara incident.[11] However, it was in 2013 that the relationship worsened. The Undersecretary of the National Intelligence Organization (MIT), Hakan Fidan, was called to testify as part of an investigation into the Turkish state's negotiations with the PKK. In response, in November 2013, the JDP government announced its decision to close the dershanes, most of which were owned by the Hizmet. The preparatory schools for the university entrance examinations were one of the main sources of funding for the movement and the primary channel for recruitment. It was a clear attack on the movement's educational organizations by the state. Within a month of the government's decision to close the dershanes, about thirty people, including senior bureaucrats and businessmen, and the sons of three JDP ministers, were arrested on charges of corruption. Prime Minister Erdoğan described the corruption investigation as 'a dirty work' against the government, accusing Fethullah Gülen and his followers of creating a 'parallel state', infiltrating key state institutions such as the judiciary and police forces and organizing the operation in alliance with 'dark foreign forces' to overthrow the government.[12]

The corruption scandal generated instability in the JDP government and struck a blow to Erdoğan's image. The event highlighted the transformation of the Hizmet and the presence of a hidden tension with the ruling party.

As well pointed out by Taş,

> The struggle against the secular establishment and the immense power they eventually reached politicized the Gülen Movement considerably and transformed it into something beyond their self-projection as a faith-based civic society movement. Considered along with allegations of evidence fabrication, wiretapping, and blackmail during the judicial investigations, the intimidation and pursuit of those criticizing Gülen resulted in the motto 'the one who touches, burns'.[13]

Since 2014, the Turkish state has been implementing a policy of pressuring and, if possible, closing down the movement's organizations within the country and abroad. Simultaneously, several thousand police officers, judges and public prosecutors considered sympathetic to Gülen were rotated or dismissed. The

---

[11] In contrast to the JDP's full-fledged support for the flotilla and condemnation of the Israeli attack, Gülen and his media criticized this initiative as an unlawful and counterproductive breach of Israeli authority.

[12] Başkan-Canyaş and Canyaş, 'The Interplay between Formal and Informal', 285.

[13] Taş, 'A History of Turkey's AKP–Gülen Conflict', 399.

strategic alliance definitively ended in 2016 following the failed coup attempt on 15 July, which, according to the Turkish state, was orchestrated by the Hizmet. According to Ankara's indictments, the Gülen movement, since 2016 identified by the acronym FETÖ (Fethullah Gülen Terrorist Organization),[14] was not only the perpetrator of the 15 July coup but also the one behind the recent atrocities and turmoil, including the 2006 assassination of priest Santoro and the 2013 Gezi Protests.

7.2 The Gülen movement's public diplomacy in Africa

After the failed coup attempt of 15 July 2016, Africa became yet another theatre of internecine fighting. Indeed, in SSA, between 2003 and 2014, the Gülen movement held a special place in the formulation and implementation of Turkey's public diplomacy, mainly in the education sector, by means of a network of several schools. For many years, Turkey had taken advantage of that network, using it to achieve many political and economic gains. Within the framework of the multitrack approach, a key role was played by the Gülen movement. Thanks to its considerable presence in the state apparatus and to the knowledge it had gleaned on the African continent, it quickly became Turkey's most active and representative NSA, especially in the field of public diplomacy. As it had done with some faith-based NGOs in the field of humanitarian aid, the Turkish state outsourced a significant part of its diplomacy to the Hizmet. As mentioned before, the Gülen movement began to operate in Africa in the mid-1990s. Later, after its initial period of low-profile activity, the movement rapidly expanded its network in Africa, thanks to the proactive policy promoted by the JDP. Following the policy it had adopted in other regions (the Balkans, Europe, Central Asia), the movement founded 'dialogue' or interfaith centres in key African cities. For instance, the Turquoise Harmony Institute was established in South Africa, the Kilimanjaro Dialogue Center in Tanzania, the Respect Foundation in Kenya and the Ufuk Dialogue Foundation in Nigeria. These organizations openly propagated the teachings of Fethullah Gülen. They have been active in interfaith dialogue

---

[14] The acronym FETÖ gained wide currency, referring to the Gülen movement and sometimes to Fethullah Gülen himself. Before the coup attempt, FETÖ was first used in a secret security report, dated 4 March 2015. Written by Deputy Chief of the National Police Department Zeki Çatalkaya, the report referred to FETÖ/PYD (Gülenist Terror Organization/Parallel State Structuring). Unlike the limited scope of the term 'parallel state', the term FETÖ designated all followers (and even sympathizers) of Gülen as part of a terrorist organization. Taş, 'A History of Turkey's AKP–Gülen Conflict', 401.

and have especially close relations with the Catholic and Anglican Churches. The name Gülen never appears on the centres, and this sort of 'camouflage' is one of the peculiar features of the movement and its affiliated organizations and has been so since its establishment in the 1970s. This ambiguous identification derives from the informality of the movement and its culture of secrecy, which has taken on different forms over time. Although Fethullah Gülen supported the establishment of schools, he always denied the existence of an 'organic' and direct relationship between himself and these institutions, or that the schools were run by him.[15] While the movement leader justified his cautious attitude by saying that he would be ashamed to take merit for initiatives initiated and managed by others, in reality, this discretion denotes Gülen's willingness to keep his profile as low as possible. Gülen has also repeatedly denied the use of its own funds or the movement's resources to institute these schools, claiming that there was investment from business enterprises, particularly Turkish businessmen with interests in those countries. These precautions meant that in the eyes of the local population, the schools did not appear as schools of the Gülen movement, but simply as Turkish schools. In other words, in many areas, especially in SSA where there was no Turkish presence, the Gülen-affiliated schools became the country's business card, the first direct contact of the local population with Turkey.

Since its first engagement in Africa in 1994, the movement has been known to operate in fifty-four African countries, becoming the backbone of Turkish public diplomacy on the continent. Indeed, Turkey's activity in Africa, most notably in SSA, has largely depended on Gülenist organizations working in four key fields: humanitarian aid, business, media and education. Gülenist engagement in Africa was driven, at least initially, by genuine concern, but after 2016, it became clear that its activities were a front for the advancement of the movement's long-term strategic interests in the region and for the expansion of its own network.

Gülenist followers settled in many African countries. They were mostly *fethullahçı* (Gülen-related) businessmen belonging to the Gülenist umbrella association, the TUSKON, lobbyists from the interreligious dialogue platforms and expatriate administrators and teachers in Gülen schools, which became the centres of gravity for these followers in SSA.[16] Cultural policy was the field in which the movement had decided to invest the most, a choice in line with the long-term strategy it pursued within Turkey. Gülenist cultural activities in Africa

---

[15] Başkan-Canyaş and Canyaş, 'The Interplay between Formal and Informal', 290.
[16] Angey, Gabrielle. 2018. 'The Gülen Movement and the Transfer of a Political Conflict from Turkey to Senegal'. *Politics, Religion & Ideology* 19 (1): 53.

officially began in 1994 with the opening of the first Gülen-inspired schools in Tangier. Later, in 1997, the Hizmet opened the first one in Senegal, followed by schools a year later in Kenya, Tanzania and Nigeria.[17] Since then, the movement has been at the forefront of educational projects, with nearly 110 Gülen-inspired primary, middle and secondary schools operating in Africa, in addition to a university in Abuja.

Initially, the projects leveraged religious affinity – schools were opened in African countries that are predominantly Muslim or have a Muslim minority of at least 10 per cent. Gülenist followers seemed to be the modern-day version of Protestant missionaries who heeded the call to spread the movement's power and influence simultaneously. The only exceptions are South Africa and Angola, which still have Gülenist schools despite having very small Muslim minorities. However, from the outset, the schools established by the Gülenists were not presented as belonging to a transnational Islamic network, but, rather, as local organizations with no global ties. As such, until 2013, they were not often identified by African students, their parents or the African authorities as belonging to such a network.[18]

In a short time, Gülen-inspired schools became very popular among the African upper middle class. What made these institutions so attractive was both their curricula and their high standard of education – often higher than that of local schools – and their adherence to the UN Sustainable Development Agenda. The aim of the movement was to promote an education that combined the intellectual and moral aspects (*zihinsel ve ahlaki*) of learning, and to provide a system of values, knowledge and religion to Muslim and non-Muslim students. The schools did not offer Muslim education or religion classes but, rather, followed the national curriculum and supplemented it with Fethullah Gülen's theological and ethical teachings. Indeed, the school's programmes had to be approved by the authorities of the national education system, with history and geography courses generally taught by local teachers. The language of instruction was the official language of the African country in which the school was located, such as English, French, Portuguese or Arabic. Turkish was also offered as one of the foreign language course options. The idea was that, through studying in foreign languages, these students would be able to obtain good jobs in foreign companies and study at foreign universities.[19] In so doing, the schools widened their catchment area and became a real alternative to both Western secular

---

[17] Shinn, *Hizmet in Africa*.
[18] Angey, 'The Gülen Movement', 54.
[19] Balci, 'Fethullah Gülen's Missionary School', 160.

schools (mainly French ones) and traditional religious schools.[20] As Gabrielle Angey pointed out in a study of the Gülen-affiliated schools in Senegal, their success was due to their ability to offer international teaching and to rely on the reputation of their collaborators as conscientious teachers.[21]

Although these schools do not have a curriculum that heavily emphasizes religion, they still teach religious values and the message of the community through informal arrangements. That is, in this education model, they teach science formally in the classrooms, while teaching religion informally outside the classrooms, thereby combining science and religion, as advised by Gülen based on Nursi's understanding of education. A distinguishing feature of these schools is that they are geared to the upper middle classes of the local population. In attempting to cater to that cohort, they used to allocate scholarships to the children of senior African bureaucrats, gaining leverage with local officials. Gülenist schools were soon seen by African leaders as the perfect environment in which to shape future elites and a very appealing choice for both their sons and daughters. This elitist approach has contributed to the reinforcement of existing social inequalities in several African countries. The aim of the Gülen movement was to create a network among the future African leadership in order to expand its base and nurture its economic interests. The schools became a place in which contacts with the local establishment could be established and consolidated, preparing the ground for businessmen close to the movement. The intention was to create a network useful to both the movement and its members. Therefore, the Gülenists established a symbiotic relationship between the entrepreneurs and the parents of the children who attended the schools. Most of the parents occupy important positions in the state bureaucracy. Indeed, due to the high-quality education these schools offered, many bureaucrats and administrators preferred to send their children there.[22] Parents also used their influence to help these schools when political or cultural problems emerged, or to encourage the establishment of new schools in other regions of their countries. In addition to indoctrination and network expansion, the schools were – and some still are – used by the movement to recruit new members in order to infiltrate the public service. This policy allowed the movement to gain influence within the institutions of many African countries following the Turkish 'deep state' model. Although the schools were fee-based and the tuition fees were medium to high,

[20] Hendrick, Joshua D. 2013. *Gülen: The Ambiguous Politics of Market Islam in Turkey and the World*, 167. New York: New York University Press.
[21] Angey, 'The Gülen Movement', 56.
[22] Balci, 'Fethullah Gülen's Missionary School', 160.

attracting mainly the sons and daughters of the elite, there was a well-developed scholarships system for the poorer families.

The teachers had a central role to play. These, within the schools of Gülen, had to act as role models for all students. In general, teachers were recruited within the movement. They had received their own education in the Gülenist schools and had been guests of the movement's dormitories or *işık evler*. In this way, as noted by Turam,

> the community aims to ensure that its schools' teachers already have close relations with the community, making them ready to act in its service. The advantage is that, given this loyalty, they voluntarily work in countries with harsh physical conditions, such as Siberia, or [. . .] countries with limited infrastructure, such as in Africa and the new post-Soviet countries in Central Asia.[23]

In addition to indoctrination and network expansion, the schools were – and some still are – used by the movement to recruit new members in order to infiltrate the public service. This policy allowed the movement to gain influence within the institutions of many African countries following the Turkish 'deep state' model.

The second field in which the Hizmet emerged as a particularly active transnational actor was the humanitarian one. The Gülen movement had its own global welfare arm known as Kimse Yok Mu Solidarity and Aid Association, later called Kimse Yok Mu (KYM). This was a charitable, non profit organization established in 2002 by volunteers who were inspired by the ideas of Fethullah Gülen. The basis for the foundation of the association was laid in the days following the 1999 Marmara earthquake, when Samanyolu TV, owned by Gülen, promoted a fundraising campaign to support the population. The reaction of the Turkish public to the campaign launched by the TV channel was so strong that the Samanyolu group executives were persuaded to separate the activity of collecting and organizing aid from its media structure. In 2004 the KYM became an NGO and an international humanitarian aid association. KYM was officially granted 'public interest group' status by the decision of the council of ministers in 2006. The status gives the association authorization to collect funds and aid without permission.[24]

---

[23] Turam, *Between Islam and the State*, 71.

[24] The authorization allows Kimse Yok Mu to give donation receipts to donors that they might declare the receipt as an expenditure (100 per cent of it is allowed to be declared) during tax-return calculation if the donation is in the form of either food, cloth, fuel for heating or cleaning materials. In cash donations, the donor can be exempt up to 5 per cent of the determined tax amount. In this way, while the association was coming to an advantageous position in the collection of money and in kind, at the same time, the donors were motivated to make more donations.

Gradually, the Gülen-affiliated charity acquired a central role in aid efforts and tried to invest in permanent projects in Turkey and abroad. Due to the acute needs of many Africans, the charity, like other Turkish NGOs, began to engage in multiple activities. In particular, the association gave priority to sub-Saharan African countries both for urgent humanitarian reasons and for increasing the presence of the Hizmet network in the area of the HOA. The KYM's popularity among the Turkish public reached its peak during the months of the famine that struck Somalia in 2011. Since then, the organization's name has been associated with the many projects started in Africa. In 2013, the KYM distributed about $17.5 million worth of assistance to forty-three countries in SSA. In addition to is fieldwork in Somalia, the charity launched very extensive programmes in Sudan, Uganda, Ethiopia and Kenya, where it built several complexes including a hospital, a soup kitchen, a dormitory and an orphanage. Especially in Sudan, the KYM focused on people in need of cataract surgery. Like the initiatives in the educational field, the humanitarian commitment also helped the movement gain the trust and sympathy of African officials and the public.

The third field in which the movement succeeded in making its mark felt in SSA was the economic one. As mentioned, the Hizmet's operative arm in the business realm was TUSKON. A non-governmental and non-profit umbrella organization with its headquarters in Istanbul, TUSKON represents the Turkish business sector.[25] The organization was founded by seven regional business associations in 2005, one of whose primary objectives was to increase trade with developing regions, including Africa. Before 2017, TUSKON represented more than 30,000 companies. It was the most important Turkish organization engaged in trade and investment promotion in Africa. In order to fulfil this purpose, TUSKON organized numerous trade ties and business exchanges between companies in Turkey and several African countries. The tool most used by the association to make itself known in a particular geographical area was the organization of regional summits. The events, such as the Turkey–Africa Foreign Trade Bridge, created links and stimulated Turkish small- and medium-sized enterprises to engage in international trade. Another powerful tool of the organization was the ability to have access to the political and economic elites of African countries thanks to the Hizmet's networks. This allowed the organization to establish and support associations in African capitals, managed by both Turks and residents, to facilitate 'business'. TUSKON was a pioneer in Turkey's opening up to new markets. During the bilateral visits of Turkish

---

[25] Hendrick, *Gülen: The Ambiguous*, 167.

officials to Africa, TUSKON organized meetings with local entrepreneurs, acting as gatekeepers of Turkish diplomacy in unknown contexts. The role of the trailblazer was also recognized by the government, which never lagged in its support for the association's initiatives. According to Ahmet Davutoğlu, at the time demiurge of Turkish foreign policy, at the start of the new African policy TUSKON was 'in charge of increasing economic exchanges with Africa, while other employers' associations specialized in different geographical regions'.[26] This observation highlights the leading role that the Gülen movement played in the Turkish policy of opening towards Africa.

TUSKON's commercial and economic initiatives were never detached from the movement's goals: broadening its network and increasing its influence within state institutions. For this reason, to further consolidate its presence on the ground in Africa and to increase its membership, the movement promoted the opening of several business organizations that followed Gülenist principles. Their primary task was to organize African business delegations to Turkey and to host visiting Turkish business delegations. Furthermore, TUSKON members also actively supported the opening of Gülen-affiliated schools and humanitarian projects developed by KYM and other charities related to the movement.[27]

Finally, in order to reach and indoctrinate an increasing number of people, the movement invested a lot in the media and was especially effective in doing so. The Gülen-affiliated media empire based in Turkey and the United States (New Jersey) reached out to Africa. It had a variety of print and TV outlets based in Turkey and outside the country that promoted its message. Furthermore, the dialogue centres in Africa distributed print media and tried to expand the movement's television operation across the continent. In 2012, the movement began Ebru Africa TV, which broadcasts in English from Kenya. Later, in 2014, it launched the internet-based Arabic-language Hira TV. Newspapers played an important role as well. Before they were shut down by the government after the failed coup attempt, the movement's historical organs – the Turkish-language *Zaman* and the English-language *Zaman Today* – were the only Turkish newspapers read in Africa. Several other publications, such as the English-language magazine *The Fountain*, the Arabic-language *Hira* and the French-language *Ebru* magazine targeting French-speaking African countries, were also distributed.

---

[26] This is the case for TUSIAD for Europe or MÜSIAD for the Persian Gulf region. See Davutoğlu, 'Turkey's New Foreign Policy Vision'.
[27] Özkan and Akgün, 'Turkey's Opening to Africa', 540.

From a broader perspective, Ankara also enjoyed the benefits of the movement's engagement in several African countries, taking advantage of the links established by the Gülenists to strengthen the Turkish presence. From the start, the efforts to spread Turkish cultural values and educational standards were closely linked to Gülen, his world view and his operations. Over time, Gülenist organizations and schools have become the main conduit for Turkish soft power, enabling Ankara to establish and maintain relations with African states. However, rather than a coordinated or planned strategy, it was a convergence of interests that resulted in a win-win relationship. Gülenist schools were seeking legitimacy through the support of Turkish officials, while Ankara was using the schools as cultural ambassadors. To some extent, Turkey outsourced a significant part of its public diplomacy in Africa to the Gülen movement as well as part of its humanitarian diplomacy to Islamic NGOs. Evidence of the relevance of the Gülen-affiliated schools and of their conformity with the African agenda of the Turkish state were the words of praise showered by President Uhuru Muigai Kenyatta of Kenya during a bilateral meeting with the then Turkish president Abdullah Gül in 2014. Kenyatta said:

> We believe that Turkey's investments in Kenya are extremely positive. We want even more Turkish investors and Turkish companies to come to Kenya and reach out to the whole of Africa, beyond the Kenyan market.[28]

What the Kenyan president did not know was that the growing strife between the Turkish executive and the movement was exacerbating to the point that a few months later the Turkish state would begin to put pressure on the African country to shut down the Hizmet schools.

7.3 The implications of the 2016 failed coup attempt: The African battleground

As demonstrated, between 2005 and 2014, the Gülen movement had a special place in the formulation and practical implementation of Turkey's opening to Africa, especially in sub-Saharan countries. However, the rift between the JDP government and the Hizmet triggered conflict within Turkish institutions, with repercussions beyond its borders. The transnational nature of the Hizmet, after being a key non-government asset in the reshaping of Turkish foreign policy for

---

[28] 'Kenyan President Hails Gülen-Inspired Schools in His Country'. *Hurriyet Daily News*, 8 April 2014.

over ten years, began to constitute the major threat to the country's image and policies abroad. Since 2014, the Turkish government has been implementing a policy of pressuring and, if possible, closing down the movement's organizations within the country and abroad. This was a radical change of route that the newly elected President Erdoğan had foreseen in his speech at the Second Turkey–Africa Summit, held in Equatorial Guinea from 19 to 21 November 2014. With the aim of warning the many African leaders and officials present at the event, Erdoğan said:

> I notice that several vicious structures are trying to come between Turkey and some African countries under the guise of non-governmental organizations or education volunteers. We follow them carefully. We hope that our friendly heads of states and governments will be more sensitive to such organizations, which venture into developing secretive structures in each country they operate in and whose spying activities are becoming increasingly more apparent. I would like to emphasize here that we are ready to share any kind of information and conduct a joint struggle against organization or organizations constituting a serious threat in each country, including Turkey, where they operate under the mask of education or humanitarian assistance.[29]

In those words, it is already possible to glimpse the scale of the oncoming struggle between the Turkish state and the movement led by Fethullah Gülen. Without ever mentioning the Gülen movement, the Turkish president stressed the presence of shadow or vicious structures rooted within Turkish institutions, which were threatening, from the ground up, relations between Turkey and several African countries. According to Erdoğan, the mutual concern implied greater cooperation between Turkish authorities and its African counterparts in order to eradicate the Gülenist threat. Pressure on the Gülen movement's network and activities increased when the Turkish government listed it as a terrorist group, calling it FETÖ, just weeks before the failed coup attempt conducted by the movement's affiliates.

In the months following the coup, an intense diplomatic campaign warned the African authorities of the 'terrorist threat' represented by the Gülen movement, considered a security threat to both Turkey and the host regimes. During bilateral meetings and multilateral events, Turkish officials did not miss a single opportunity to warn their African counterparts. Four months after the failed

---

[29] Speech by Recep Tayyip Erdoğan, President of the Republic of Turkey, at the Second Turkey–Africa Summit, in Malabo, Equatorial Guinea 2014, quoted in Angey, 'The Gülen Movement', 57. The original text is available at http://afrika.mfa.gov.tr/21-november-2014-speech-by-HE-recep-tayyip -Erdoğan-the-president-of-the-republic-of-turkey.en.mfa.

coup, again addressing the African leaders and key businessmen who attended the Turkey–Africa Economic and Business Forum held in Istanbul (2016), the Turkish president warned:

> Anti-FETÖ fight is our common cause. International solidarity is imperative in the fight against international terror. Unless we can ensure solidarity today, this threat becomes much greater tomorrow. While you are helping us in this fight, we will cooperate with you to prevent any possible gap. We will exert every effort to protect our children studying at FETÖ-linked schools and their parents from any victimization.[30]

It became evident that the main target of Ankara's neutralization efforts was the network of Gülenist educational institutions – preparatory schools for university examinations, universities, high schools and dormitories – both in Turkey and abroad. Undoubtedly, the global Gülenist school system was and still is an important source of revenue and new followers for the movement, and, above all, a wellspring for the indoctrination of future generations. The latter is one of the main reasons Turkey's government perceives it as a genuine threat to its own security as well as the security of the host states. As President Erdoğan said:

> This organization [FETÖ], which caused the depravation of the young generations and robotized them by exploiting religious concepts, poses a major threat not only to Turkey, but to all countries it is present in.[31]

As a consequence of the 15 July coup, Ankara had to engage even further in the conflict abroad, counteracting Gülenist propaganda and its recruitment machinery. For this purpose, Turkey has been exerting pressure on African leaders to shut down all activities related to the movement, especially the revenue-generating organizations.[32] Concurrently, the Turks had to promptly redefine their African policy on the ground, developing new tools for their own transnationalization.[33] Additionally, Turkey modified its multi-stakeholder

---

[30] Speech by Recep Tayyip Erdoğan, President of the Republic of Turkey, at the Turkey–Africa Economic and Business Forum, Istanbul, Turkey 2016. Parts of his speech are available at https ://www.tccb.gov.tr/en/news/542/58861/president-Erdoğan-addresses-turkey-africa-economic-an d-business-forum#.

[31] Ibid.

[32] In other regions, long before the Turkish Government tried to close the schools, other countries acted alone, suspecting the network's foreign connections. In 2000, Uzbekistan closed all schools associated with Gülen operating there, and similar measures were taken in Russia, where only seven of the fifty schools operating until 2008 remained. All are now firmly under the supervision of the Ministry of Education in the Turkish-speaking Muslim region of Tatarstan.

[33] Angey, 'The Gülen Movement', 66–7.

approach by setting up its own para-public structures that were able to integrate with other private actors.

To counter the spread of schools abroad, and to replace them where possible, Turkey set up the Maarif[34] Foundation, a hybrid public–private structure of international scope, tied to the Ministry of Education. It is a predominantly governmental structure, but as a foundation, it receives private funds and public subsidies and is exempted from paying tax. This foundation was tasked with the following international mission:

> To award scholarships in all educational processes from preschool to University education, to open facilities such as educational organizations and dormitories, to train educators to be assigned to these organizations including domestic organizations, to conduct scientific research, and to carry out research and development studies, publish academic works and develop methods and conduct other educational activities which are in accordance with the laws and regulations of that country which these are operated in order to service and improve formal and informal education by taking common human values and knowledge as a basis.[35]

Defending the bill on the Maarif Foundation in Parliament on 16 June 2016, İsmet Yılmaz, the minister of education, stressed that the foundation is state-owned and will serve as the arm of his ministry abroad in the provision of educational services. During the parliamentary debate, Yılmaz repeatedly pointed out how the initiative was a proof of the Turkish state's ambition to project greater power in the world. The minister also said the foundation would operate in places from the Balkans to China (Xinjiang Uyghur Autonomous Region) and from Somalia to Canada.[36]

Since its establishment, Maarif has aroused many doubts and concerns, due to its direct link with the executive – Erdoğan has appointed the key members of the administrative board; its financial support – partly from public sources and partly from donations and grants from a wide range of private donors including the Gulf countries; its semi-public structure – the boundaries between the public and private sectors are blurred; and its role in taking over the management of schools once affiliated to the Gülen network. Undoubtedly, Maarif has

---

[34] Maarif is a Osmanli term with Arabic origins, and it means education and instruction.
[35] Abstract from the official law establishing the Maarif Foundation, available at http://turkiyemaarif .org/kurumsal/vakif-kanunu/.
[36] İsmet Yılmaz quoted in Abdullah Bozkurt, 'Turkey's Maarif Foundation: Erdoğan's Trojan horse', Stockholm Center for Freedom, Commentary Paper, 5 September 2017. Available at https://stockho lmcf.org/commentary-turkeys-maarif-foundation-Erdoğans-trojan-horse/.

become in a very short time an important semi-governmental instrument of public diplomacy able to overcome, partially, the mistrust towards the Ankara government and counter the Gülenists' propaganda. As mentioned earlier, in the eyes of several communities in SSA, the Gülen-affiliated schools were Turkish. Therefore, part of Maarif's effort is to promote a different narrative than the one spread by the Hizmet, projecting a new image of Turkey that is still unknown to many in Africa. As pointed out by the chairman of the Maarif Foundation, Birol Akgün,[37] 'the foundation has the long-term aim to create a reputable and world-renowned brand and spread it all around the world' and for this purpose 'it has been working abroad within the framework of Turkey's strategic priorities by consulting with relevant ministries and other state institutions'.[38] Yet, in another interview the same head of the foundation declared that the Maarif's main objective was to replace schools linked to the alleged 'terrorist group' (the Gülen movement) with educational establishments representing Turkey around the world.[39] However, taking control of Gülenist schools abroad is complicated, because before it can do so, the Maarif Foundation has to wait until the local authority bans the movement. Following the 2016 coup, the first African country that has agreed to transfer the Gülen-affiliated schools to the Turkish government was Somalia. The Somali example, determined by the strong bond between the two countries established in recent years, was followed by other states including the Republic of Guinea which transferred its nine schools with their 1,000 students to the Maarif Foundation, Nigeria (eight schools, 1,200 students), Morocco (2,500 students), the Republic of Congo, Niger and Chad. The dissymmetric power relations that these African countries have with the Turkish economy would make it easier for the Turkish state to transfer its repression against the Gülen movement.[40]

Conversely, other countries whose political and economic strength is comparable to Turkey's have been notably reluctant to comply with Turkish demands. In these cases, the persistent Turkish requests to shut down Gülenist schools have led to tensions with local governments and threatened existing

---

[37] Birol Akgün was previously head of the IR department at the Ankara Yıldırım Beyazit University. He has co-authored several academic works on Turkey's expanding foreign policy in SSA. Thus, the head of the Maarif Foundation is an international relations specialist who is knowledgeable about foreign policy in Africa and about the Gülen movement's activities in the region.

[38] The full text of the interview given to the Anadolu news agency on 23 September 2017 is available at https://www.aa.com.tr/tr/turkiye/turkiye-maarif-vakfi-baskani-prof-dr-akgun-200-civarinda-okul-fetonun-kontrolunden-cikti/917404.

[39] Birol Akgün's interview given to Daily Sabah, 12 February 2017, full text available to https://www.dailysabah.com/politics/2017/02/13/maarif-foundation-head-we-aim-to-offer-an-education-that-reflects-turkish-vision-promote-turkish-language.

[40] Angey, 'The Gülen Movement', 60.

ties. For example, South Africa has allegedly been pressured to close its Gülen-affiliated schools. However, South African President Jacob Zuma has pledged his continued support to the Star College group, which runs the movement's schools that cater to approximately 3,000 South African students. The schools have been in the country for fifteen years. Besides South Africa, other African countries have also created difficulties for Turkish diplomacy by refusing to intervene against the schools affiliated to the Hizmet movement – such as Ethiopia, which plays a central political role in the stability of the HOA. Although the government of the then prime minister, Hailemariam Desalegn had shown solidarity and support to President Erdoğan during the coup d'état, none of the six schools active in the country were transferred to Maarif's control. Instead, these were sold to private investors. Because of their level of development in comparison to some of their neighbours, South Africa and Ethiopia are less impressed by Turkish promises of investment than they are by the benefits of advanced education. In other cases, however, the denial was dictated by the involvement of local politicians in the management of these schools as investors or simply as parents of pupils. This is the case, for instance, of Mozambique where the network of Gülen-affiliated schools, Söğüt Turkish, was supported by the current minister of defence, Atanasio Salvador Mtumuke, a close associate of President Filipe Nyusi. Even though the latter is an economic partner of all the institutions opened in the country, the president has sent one of his sons to one of the Söğüt Turkish institutions. Consequently, pressure from Ankara to Maputo to take control of these schools have not worked and have created different tensions. These stances have long-term consequences for bilateral relations. Indeed, if from the Turkish point of view the refusal to transfer Gülenist schools is interpreted as a complicity with the movement, the African counterparts perceive Turkish pressure as undue interference.

Other factors make the Maarif Foundation's task even more complicated. Over the years, Gülenist schools have built up a high standard of education and a good reputation that will be difficult to match in the short term. Another issue of concern is the schools' personnel. Gülenist teachers and administrative staff were driven by an almost missionary zeal. They were committed to proselytizing and strengthening the power of their movement. The Maarif Foundation aims to replace the staff of the Gülenist institutions with civil servants who can apply to be relocated abroad, and graduate students who, having failed the national exam for teacher training, can be hired on short-term contracts for these posts. Though the new Turkish teachers might be motivated and professional, it is doubtful that they will have the same deep sense of commitment as the Gülenists. For these reasons, countering the anti-state propaganda promoted by the Gülenists will take considerable time and resources.

In the economic field, pressure by the state on TUSKON forced it to cut back dramatically on its efforts to promote business relations in SSA and elsewhere. In fact, the organization's trade and business promotion efforts in Africa have effectively been shut down. The leaders of TUSKON and the 187 member companies were then accused of belonging to a terrorist organization. The president of the organization, Rizanur Meral, fled abroad, and an executive order forced the closure of 196 local associations related to the Gülen movement.[41] Furthermore, Gülen-supporting businesspeople also operate in several independent and informal associations in various African countries. Examples include the South African Turkish Business Association, the Association of Businessmen and Investors of Nigeria and Turkey and the Ethio-Turkish Entrepreneur Association. These organizations continue to exist in the aftermath of the failed coup attempt. In some cases, their activities have been curtailed and their websites are no longer functioning. However, some are actually recruiting new members as Gülen supporters in Turkey are fleeing, and some are relocating to Africa. Turkish firms have not always replaced the now-defunct businesses belonging to the entrepreneurs affiliated to the movement. This has created a vacuum filled by other regional and extra-regional countries. More important, the fight against the Gülenist network has affected Ankara's access to African markets that are particularly relevant for Turkey's exports, as well as its access to Africa's natural resources. In order to contain the damage, Turkey has begun to support an increased presence of the MÜSIAD, the group of Anatolian entrepreneurs, traditionally very close to the JDP government – a tie clearly expressed after the 15 July failed coup when MÜSIAD was mainly at the forefront of the marches to defend President Erdoğan and his government.[42] The MÜSIAD's delegations have increased visits to SSA in order to counterbalance TUSKON's role. Moreover, MÜSIAD branches have been set up in several African countries to replace TUSKON's presence. However, as previously seen, TUSKON enjoyed the network and the many contacts of the movement that allowed it to move with greater freedom than other associations. This is clearly a constraint. In order to overcome this limit, the agenda of MÜSIAD is backed by the DEIK and by several newly-

---

[41] Ege, Y., M. Kimaci and M. Aydoyen. 2017. 'Business Network on Trial for Links to Turkish Coup'. *Anadolu Agency*, 23 October 2017.

[42] Yankaya-Péan, Dilek. 2017. 'Étude des reconfigurations patronales de la dérive autoritaire en Turquie entre contestation, domination et crise'. *Mouvements* 90 (2): 38–47.

established organizations, among them also the Turkish–African Business Association (TABA)[43] and the Africa Turkey Trade Center (ATTC). The TABA is an umbrella organization established in 2012 with the aim of facilitating the development of Turkish economic activities in Africa. In a few years, TABA has organized more than 200 events, which include sectoral and trade visits of delegations, conferences, seminars, B2B/B2G meetings and trilateral fora. The organization is particularly addressed to young Turkish entrepreneurs, and for this reason its structure is much more flexible and dynamic than the MÜSIAD. To be as efficient as possible, the TABA's board is principally composed of specialists of geographical areas or of the main languages spoken in Africa. Recently, the organization has involved some ex-African diplomats such as the former Kenyan ambassador in Ankara – a choice that may help to better understand the complex African scenario and partially compensate for the lack of a rooted network such as the one on which TUSKON relied. The ATTC is a Konya-based consultancy organization founded by several distinguished members of MÜSIAD including the current president, Lütfi Şimşek. Similar to TABA, its objective is to put Turkish businessmen in contact with African partners. After the failed coup, ATTC has increased its efforts to try to gain substantial shares of the African market, partially left empty with the shutdown of TUSKON's affiliates. Ankara's efforts have also extended to the financial sector. In 2009, the Gülenist Bank Asya purchased a stake in an Islamic banking group in West Africa. In 2015, after the Turkish authorities effectively took control of Bank Asya, it was forced to sell the Dakar-based Tamweel Africa Holding, which promotes Islamic finance in SSA, to the Saudi-based Islamic Corporation for the Development of the Private Sector.[44]

The dynamics triggered by the failed coup d'état in 2016 show how deeply the Gülenist network had been able to infiltrate the power chambers of several African states. Today, despite Ankara's best efforts, Gülenist propaganda and networks continue to promote a counter-narrative and attempt to discredit Turkey's image on the continent. Indeed, even though nearly all Gülen-affiliated media activity inside Turkey has been shut down or taken over by the state, its media efforts outside Turkey are not flourishing, but they are surviving. These emphasize the Gülenist philosophy and take a harsh line against the Turkish state and the JDP government. The presence of the

---

[43] Türk Afrika İş Adamları Derneği.
[44] Ebru Tuncay, 'Turkey's Bank Asya to Sell Senegal-based Tamweel Africa Holding Stake'. *The Africa Report*, 9 January 2015. Available at https://www.theafricareport.com/3530/turkeys-bank-asya-to-sell-senegal-based-tamweel-africa-holding-stake/.

movement's affiliates and followers is creating a kind of Gülenist diaspora in Africa that operates as a lobby against the Turkish government. Furthermore, the ties established by the *fethullahçı* with the African ruling elites have also created resistance to Ankara's counteroffensive. The trust gained over the years has allowed the affiliates of the movement to persuade several African elites and to influence their decisions. African authorities have reacted differently depending on their diplomatic weight and the extent of their economic relations with Turkey. The African countries with weaker official relations with Turkey, have, indeed, been more reluctant to give up the assistance and aid they have received from the movement. Over the medium term, pressure from Ankara might dampen relations and in the worst-case scenario, lead to their rupture. At the same time, the Gülen movement's lobbying efforts in Africa have the potential to damage or even reverse Turkey's gains on that continent. Indeed, the consequences of the domestic political warfare between Ankara and the movement may partly affect Turkey's humanitarian efforts and public diplomacy, compromising its reputation in the region. Therefore, from summer 2016 onwards, the need to tackle the Gülen movement, which has well-established cells and networks in the region, was among the reasons that led Turkey to increase its involvement in SSA. In addition, the Turkish state, which had outsourced its public diplomacy to a NSA for more than ten years, has been forced to rebuild and redesign it from scratch. As pointed out by Benjamin Augé:

> The Turkish government's fight against this movement since 2013, and more exclusively since the failed 2016 coup, has forced the diplomatic corps to fully mobilize itself to either take over the schools, or close them and create new employers' networks. This has recently resulted in a dramatic upheaval in the actors responsible for the relationships between Turkey and most African countries. These actors had taken about ten years to build and solidify themselves and are now leaderless. This re-organization is also a waste of time for Turkish diplomacy, which is slaving away to implement the purge of the Gülenist networks that have managed to invest in Africa.[45]

After nearly four years of the failed coup d'état, diplomatic efforts and media campaigns promoted by the Turkish state to present the hidden sides of the Gülen movement to African states seem to have achieved partial success. On the one hand, the number of states that has chosen to transfer the administration of the Gülen-affiliated schools to Maarif Foundation has increased, but on the

---

[45] Augé, 'The 2016 Failed Coup in Turkey', 25.

other hand very few of them have accepted to recognize the Gülen movement as a terrorist organization. In the immediate future, Turkey should move cautiously in its relations with African states and refrain from exerting excessive pressure or it could jeopardize the attainments of the last fifteen years. If this occurs, Ankara may face setbacks in its access to the natural resources that make up the largest share of Turkey's imports from Africa.

Conclusions

As discussed in the book's chapters, there is a complex set of factors explaining why the Turkish policy towards Africa, especially SSA, has grown over the past fifteen years. The research aimed to highlight how these factors are intertwined, and how Turkey's foreign policy choices towards Africa are the outcomes of input coming from the domestic sphere and elements that are outside of it. Notably, through the adoption of a mostly but not exclusively NCR approach, the study has argued that the environment surrounding Turkey has provided favourable conditions for an enlargement of the foreign policy spheres. However, neoclassical realists reject the idea of neorealism in which it is argued that systemic pressures will immediately affect the behaviours of units. They believe that the extent of systemic effects on states' behaviour depends on relative power as well as internal factors of states in an anarchical system. Concerning the case study, among the trends that have made the international environment more permissive is the nascent role of middle and great emerging powers in the international political economy in the post-Cold War context. The definitive opening of the global economy has intensified competition for resources and the search for new markets, thereby placing the focus back on regions that are still poorly integrated into the market, especially Africa. The increasing presence of non-Western actors such as China, India, South Korea and Brazil in Africa provides some clues about the state-to-system linkages. As underlined by Robert Mason, while the growing economic roles of China and others in Africa represent a challenge to the existing development paradigm that needs to be evaluated in the long term, the realignment of global power to favour emergent actors also bears serious consideration.[1]

However, the permissive international environment would not be sufficient to explain the rapid growth of the Turkish presence in Africa. Since 2005, Turkey has, indeed, become one of the most active extra-regional stakeholders after being practically absent from the continent. Equally determinant has been the country's internal transformation, which began with the rise of a new elite

---

[1] Mason, 'Patterns and Consequences', 12–13.

who, following the JDP's election victory in 2003, launched a radical shift in Turkey's foreign policy. The rapid involvement of a new generation of foreign policy makers or FPE with a different background compared to the previous establishment has favoured the development of a new strategy able to overcome the constraints of the traditional post-Second World War Turkish strategic culture. Specifically, the shaping of a new international posture and the revision of the national role identity has allowed Turkey to take a proactive stance towards regions that had been ignored for a long time. Among them, Africa was given a special place.

The speed at which Turkey has spread its presence in Africa – especially towards SSA – starting from almost zero in the region has been remarkable. Turkey, like other emerging powers, depends on a growing engagement with external markets to sustain its economic growth. Turkish efforts towards Africa simultaneously advance Turkey's national economic interests and its aims to acquire international power and prestige. The role played by Turkey's social actors such as trade associations, civil society organizations and the media has been significant, too. Indeed, the growing interest of Turkish FPEs in Africa has matched the new awareness of Africa among the Turkish public. After being considered a deprived and backward region for many decades, the African continent has assumed relevance in Turkish eyes as a space for potential material and prestige gains. The involvement of non-governmental actors in foreign policy has been one of the trademarks of the new course launched by the JDP governments. However, in Africa more than in other regions, non-governmental actors have been the determinant in the trust-building relationships with local communities. Besides, there have been many cases where Turkish NGOs or associations have been the forerunners and real drivers of diplomatic commitment. This relationship of complementarity and cooperation between governmental and non-governmental actors has experienced several changes over the years. The autonomy enjoyed by many non-governmental actors was a key asset when, during the first decade of its opening to Africa, Turkey adopted a disorderly approach to the continent intended merely to increase its presence. Thereafter, due to the overlapping of activities and the weak control of the authorities over private initiatives, Turkey has progressively configured a coordination structure for the various actors involved on the ground – a circumstance that became evident following the failed coup d'état in 2016.

As examined in the course of this book, Turkish foreign policy towards Africa has experienced two phases: the first one, known as the opening period, in which Turkey has worked mainly in the field of diplomacy and economy; and a second phase in which Turkish engagement on the continent has also assumed a political dimension while at the same time enhancing its humanitarian commitment. The mediator role and the institution-building commitment assumed by Turkey in the Somali crises have paved the way for Turkish involvement in African political issues. The constant interaction between the domestic political dynamics and the international context has determined the development of the Turkish policy in Africa. Furthermore, this interplay has led to the progressive development of a unique approach to Africa that distinguishes the Turkish policy from both that of other emerging powers and that pursued by traditional extra-regional players. Through the reference to elements belonging to each other's approaches, Turkey has moulded its way of intervention whose fulcrum has become the promotion of a particular development formula for African countries and, more generally, for the Global South. The Turkish assistance model, defined by the author as the Ankara consensus, combines development, peacebuilding and business with emotive emphasis on humanity, the needs of the Global South and Islamic humanitarianism. Over the years, the Turkish state has nourished these traits both in its narrative and in the effective implementation of its policies towards Africa.

The ability developed by Turkey to move through Africa in an intermediate zone between emerging players and the traditional Western powers is a unique feature for the context. Such a double-track policy and its practical operationalization on the ground through a coordinated multitrack approach marks Turkey's engagement in SSA in comparison to other external powers, bearing out its uniqueness. The Ankara consensus is a mix of different paradigms and intends to portray Turkey as an extra-regional actor different from the rest. In the last few years, features that originate from different patterns of involvement in the African continent and, more generally, in less developed countries have been selected and implemented by the Turkish state to tailor its model of intervention.

The singularity of the case study is provided by the Turkish approach, which combines characteristic elements of the traditional Western players' policies with the peculiarities that have been implemented by emerging stakeholders. While from a scientific point of view, these peculiarities make the Turkish policy in Africa an interesting topic of study, from a political angle they have contributed to the revival of Turkey on the international scene. As a regional power with global interests and ambitions, Turkey has leveraged the credit it has acquired in Africa to promote a third way that balances the secular institutional structure, the Muslim faith and the global capitalism – a paradigm that reflects the desire of the current conservative JDP establishment, and especially of President Erdoğan, to place Turkey at the forefront of the global ummah through leadership, instead of *imperio*. In other words, Turkey as 'a city upon a hill' for the Muslims of the world, but not only for them. Indeed, the Turkish approach to development also generates interest in many non-Muslim African and non-African states that see the experience of Turkish economic growth as a source of inspiration. The originality of the Turkish development model or the Turkish formula places Ankara in a middle position, namely, as a gateway between the North and the Global South – a role that Turkey has shown a willingness to explore, in particular in the African context. Such developments are inevitably entangled with Turkish domestic politics. Like the phase of opening to Africa, the so-called second period of the creation of political relations and a Turkish model for sustainable development is the outcome of the interaction between the domestic and international spheres. Turkey's growing international fame, mainly in the countries of the Global South, is particularly useful to contrast the widespread image of Turkey, no longer as a 'model' country but mainly as a 'paradoxical' example. Indeed, soon after the Arab upheavals, the idea of the Turkish model has been replaced by the so-called 'Turkish paradox', a simultaneously embracing and abusing democracy. Today, Turkish foreign policy, including the African agenda, not only responds to the same illiberal logic but has also become a tool to pursue domestic aims. Over the last few months, a third phase of Turkish policy in Africa seems to be beginning, marked by a growing securitization of its own initiatives. Although the humanitarian and development aid dimension has not disappeared, the African context, especially but not exclusively the HOA, has become a new arena of regional contention. Turkey's active involvement in the Libyan civil war, which was preceded by the opening of a military outpost in Somalia and the plan to establish a similar one in Sudan, suggests that the Turkish presence in Africa is also assuming a military dimension which, until a few years ago, was limited to joint exercises and participation in multilateral operations. The development of a different approach, likewise determined by multiple factors, needs to be monitored in the coming years because it may once again shift the Turkish presence on the continent. For the moment, the Turkish military presence in Africa corresponds more to the logic of competition for leadership in the Middle East than to a comprehensive security agenda for Africa. Following the rift within the Gulf Cooperation Council, the growing overlap of Middle Eastern security interactions with those of Eastern Africa, especially the HOA, has triggered a process of 'middle-easternization' in which alliances and rivalries mix crosswise, generating a highly explosive environment.[2]

---

[2] Cannon and Donelli, 'Asymmetric Alliances and High Polarity'.

Although the new engagement of Turkey in Africa is unquestionable, its real weight in the current and future regional balance should not be overestimated. During the last decade, Turkey has acquired a new political, economic and cultural space of influence in several African countries. However, Turkish efforts should be evaluated in light of the fact that the Turkish policy has several limits. Many doubts remain about Turkey's ability to maintain the same commitment, in terms of material capabilities, in the light of a latent fragility of its economic, financial and political system. The real risk is that there may be a situation similar to that in Afghanistan where, following the outbreak of the Syrian crisis, Turkey, which had invested heavily in the state- and institution-building process, had to drastically reduce the resources previously allocated in order to redirect them to closer emergencies. Consequently, the presence of a gap between expectations and actual capabilities is one of the main limits to the global actor profile that Turkey seeks to carve out. There is a risk of incurring the power paradox described by John Ravenhill (1998) regarding the cycles of the so-called middle powers. According to Ravenhill, when the policymakers of an emerging power overestimate their own power capabilities and opt for overambitious foreign policy strategies, a paradox of power is generated that damages the international image of the country and undermines its regional credibility.[3] In other words, due to excessive ambitions expressed through excessive rhetoric, far from real capability, these states entrap themselves in a series of bold promises and goals that they cannot fulfil. On the contrary, if Turkey was able to balance the expectations with the real capabilities in a forward-looking approach, it could contribute effectively to the strengthening of cooperation and to an increasingly open and multipolar global order. In doing so, Turkey would succeed in establishing itself as a global player.

Another limit derives from the Turkish narrative which is strongly idealized, generating a fundamental contradiction with the internal reality of the country. The political context is increasingly polarized by the figure of President Erdoğan, which has generated a real rift within Turkish society between those who support him and those who contest him. Inevitably, the lack of cohesion leads to a further weakening of capabilities abroad as well as having an impact on the country's economy. Particularly in times of economic trouble, it may become difficult for the Turkish executive to justify the financial efforts in Africa in the eyes of the population.

---

[3] Ravenhill, John. 1998. 'Cycles of Middle Power Activism: Constraint and Choice in Australian and Canadian Foreign Policies'. *Australian Journal of International Affairs* 52 (3): 309–28.

Another element of domestic policy with significant implications for the African agenda of Turkey concerns the clash with the Gülen movement, considered by the Turkish authorities to be responsible for the failed coup in 2016. As shown in Chapter 7, the policy of countering the movement and its network in Africa has generated tensions between Turkey and several African countries, jeopardizing the bonds built in previous years.

A further constraint concerns both Turkish policymakers and the Turkish public in general, and it is their lack of knowledge of Africa. Although there has been a substantial increase in interest over the last two decades, as witnessed by the establishment of several research and study centres, Turkey still lacks Africanists and university curricula that promote a comprehensive and in-depth scientific knowledge of Africa and its peoples. The training of FPEs and field workers who acquire knowledge of the historical, anthropological and cultural peculiarities of African countries may help Turkey to rationalize resources by launching targeted initiatives and efforts. The scholarship policy for African students implemented by the Turkish state has proven to be very useful for this purpose. Beyond its relevance as a public diplomacy tool, the study periods of the young students from African countries in Turkish universities have allowed a daily exchange with Turkish students, promoting the knowledge of African culture and mitigating, even if partially, the widespread phenomenon of racism.

To conclude, the future of relations between Africa and Turkey will inevitably depend on the future developments within the country. Nevertheless, the seeds planted in these two decades have allowed Turkey to shape relations on a new basis. The mutual knowledge and the convergence of interests have fostered the overcoming of old biases by opening up channels in a variety of fields. Turkey, with all the constraints of its policies, has been able to gain significant credit in the eyes of the African peoples. In order to avoid squandering it all, Turkey will necessarily have to adopt a more rational and comprehensive approach to Africa, trying to operate in line with its own specificities and possibilities. Over the weeks following the outbreak of the Covid-19 crisis, competition between Middle Eastern rivals has shifted into the humanitarian field such as delivering full medical equipment packages of beds, ventilators, surgical face masks, face shields and other useful materials. The aid is more important in Somalia where the health system is very fragile and unable to effectively counter the eventual spread of the virus. Although nowadays the state's priority is to deal with the emergency, some doubts are arising about Turkish engagement in Somalia and, more generally, in Africa. The Turkish economy, which even before the crisis highlighted several weaknesses, would face an inevitable backlash, exacerbated by two military campaigns in Syria and, to a lesser extent, in Libya. The resilience of the Turkish economy will probably determine the future of Turkey's foreign policy. A slow recovery in production and exports will compel the Turkish state to reallocate resources, by reducing investment in hard power and, to a higher degree, in humanitarian diplomacy and development aid. Therefore, it is to be expected that there may be a progressive downsizing of Turkey's global projection, with a consequent shift of resources in its neighbourhood. Notwithstanding, one issue to be considered is that the Turkish agenda in Africa has not developed dependency relationships, but has sought to establish cooperative or even partnership relationships. As a result, many of the bonds established in recent years by Turkey with African countries may be maintained even in the face of a drastic reduction in resources allocated for the continent. Therefore, the risk of extreme volatility in the commitment made in Africa due to the Turkish economy's performance may be partly mitigated by Turkey's particular multitrack approach on the ground. The involvement of non-governmental actors examined in Chapter 6 has led to the establishment of people-to-people relationships that have prevented the risk, which many emerging players active in Africa are experiencing, of generating new dependency relationships.

Having said this, the speed at which Turkey has spread its presence in SSA, starting from an almost zero-presence in the region, has been remarkable. Yet, it is irrefutable that Turkey's policy towards Africa has achieved good results, in terms of material and political gains, making it an interesting case study that needs to be looked at in its future development. Indeed, the book has sought to provide a first glimpse of a topic of study that would necessarily need to be explored in depth.

Bibliography

Abdirahman, Ali. 2013. 'Turkey's Foray into Africa: A New Humanitarian Power?' *Insight Turkey* 13 (4): 65–73.

Abdulleh, Jabril I. 2008. 'Civil Society in the Absence of a Somali State'. In *Somalia: Current Conflicts and New Chances for State Building*, edited by Heinrich Böll Foundation, 70–87. Berlin: Heinrich Böll Stiftung.

Acharya, Amitav. 2007. 'The Emerging Regional Architecture of World Politics'. *World Politics* 59 (4): 629–52.

Achilles, Kathryn, Onur Sazak, Thomas Woods and Auveen Elizabeth Wheeler. 2015. *Turkish Aid Agencies in Somalia: Risks and Opportunities for Building Peace*. Istanbul: Saferworld and Istanbul Policy Center.

Afacan, Isa. 2013. 'The African Opening in Turkish Foreign Policy'. *Ortadoğu Analiz* 5 (52): 46–54.

Akpınar, Pınar 2013. 'Turkey's Peacebuilding in Somalia: The Limits of Humanitarian Diplomacy'. *Turkish Studies* 14 (4): 735–57.

Aksan, Virginia H. 2007. *Ottoman Wars: An Empire Besieged*. Abingdon: Routledge.

Aktürk, Şener. 2015. 'The Fourth Style of Politics: Eurasianism as a Pro-Russian Rethinking of Turkey's Geopolitical Identity'. *Turkish Studies* 16 (1): 54–79.

Alden, Chris. 2005. 'China in Africa'. *Survival – Global Politics and Strategy* 47 (3): 147–64.

Altunışık, Meliha B. 2014. 'Geopolitical Representation of Turkey's Cuspness: Discourse and Practice'. In *The Role, Position and Agency of Cusp States in International Relations*, edited by Marc Herzog and Philip Robins, 25–40. London: Routledge.

Ambrosio, Thomas. 2012. 'The Rise of the "China Model" and "Beijing Consensus": Evidence of Authoritarian Diffusion?' *Contemporary Politics* 18 (4): 381–99.

Amineh, Mehdi Parvizi. 2007. *The Greater Middle East in Global Politics: Social Science Perspectives on the Changing Geography of the World Politics*. Leiden: Brill.

Angey, Gabrielle. 2018. 'The Gülen Movement and the Transfer of a Political Conflict from Turkey to Senegal'. *Politics, Religion & Ideology* 19 (1): 53–68.

Antkiewicz, Agata, ed. 2008. *Emerging Powers in Global Governance: Lessons from the Heiligendamm Process*. Waterloo: Wilfrid Laurier University Press.

Apaydin, Fulya. 2012. 'Overseas Development Aid Across the Global South: Lessons from the Turkish Experience in Sub-Saharan Africa and Central Asia'. *European Journal of Development Research* 24 (2): 261–82.

Aras, Bülent. 2007. 'Turkey and the Middle East: Frontiers of the New Geographic Imagination'. *Australian Journal of International Affairs* 61 (4): 471–88.

Aras, Bülent. 2009. 'The Davutoğlu Era in Turkish Foreign Policy'. *Insight Turkey* 11 (3): 127–42.

Aras, Bülent. 2012. 'Turkey's Mediation and Friends of Mediation Initiative'. *Turkey Policy Brief Series (TEPAV)*, 5.

Aras, Bülent, Kenan Dağci and M. Efe Çaman. 2009. 'Turkey's New Activism in Asia'. *Alternatives: Turkish Journal of International Relations* 8 (2): 24–39.

Argun, Selim. 2000. 'The Life and Contribution of the Osmanli Scholar, Abu Bakr Effendi: Towards Islamic thought and Culture in South Africa'. MA Thesis, Johannesburg University.

Arıboğan, Deniz Ülke. 2004. 'Opening the Closed Window to the East: Turkey's Relations with East Asian Countries'. In *Turkish Foreign Policy in Post-Cold War Era*, edited by Idris Bal, 401–20. Boca Raton: Brown Walker Press.

Arrighi, Giovanni and Beverly J. Silver. 2006. *Caos e governo del mondo. Come cambiano le egemonie e gli equilibri planetari*. Milano: Mondadori Bruno.

Assanvo, William Taffotien. 2006. 'Multistakeholder Diplomacy in the Context of National Diplomatic Systems'. In *Multistakeholder Diplomacy: Challenges and Opportunities*, edited by Jovan Kurbalija and Valentin Katrandjiev, 141–5. Geneve: DiploFoundation.

Atalay, Zeynep 2013. 'Civil Society as Soft Power: Islamic NGOs and Turkish Foreign Policy'. In *Turkey between Nationalism and Globalization*, edited by Riva Kastoryano, 165–86. New York: Routledge.

Augé, Benjamin. 2018. 'The 2016 Failed Coup in Turkey: What Is the Impact on Turkish–African Relations?' In *Notes de l'Ifri*. Paris: Institut français des relations internationales.

Ayata, Bilgin. 2015. 'Turkish Foreign Policy in a Changing Arab World: Rise and Fall of a Regional Actor?' *Journal of European Integration* 37 (1): 95–112.

Ayers, Alison J. 2013. 'Beyond Myths, Lies and Stereotypes: The Political Economy of a "New Scramble for Africa"'. *New Political Economy* 18 (2): 227–57.

Aynte, Abdihakim. 2012. *Turkey's Increasing Role in Somalia: An Emerging Donor?* Doha: Al Jazeera Centre for Studies.

Babb, Sarah. 2013. 'The Washington Consensus as Transnational Policy Paradigm: Its Origins, Trajectory and Likely Successor'. *Review of International Political Economy* 30 (2): 268–97.

Bacik, Gökhan and Isa Afacan. 2013. 'Turkey Discovers Sub-Saharan Africa: The Critical Role of Agents in the Construction of Turkish Foreign-Policy Discourse'. *Turkish Studies* 14 (3): 483–502.

Bagdonas, Özlem Demirtaş. 2012. 'A Shift of Axis in Turkish Foreign Policy or A Marketing Strategy?. Turkey's Uses of Its "Uniqueness" vis-à-vis the West/Europe'. *Turkish Journal of Politics* 3 (2): 111–32.

Bal, Idris. 2018. *Turkey's Relations with the West and the Turkic Republics: The Rise and Fall of the Turkish Model*. Abingdon: Routledge.

Balci, Bayram. 2003. 'Fethullah Gülen's Missionary Schools in Central Asia and their Role in the Spreading of Turkism and Islam'. *Religion, State and Society* 31 (2): 151–77.

Balci, Bayram and Bertrand Buchwalter. 2001. *La Turquie en Asie centrale: la conversion au réalisme: 1991–2000*. Istanbul: Institut Français d'études Anatoliennes Georges Dumézil.

Bank, André and Roy Karadag. 2013. 'The "Ankara Moment": The Politics of Turkey's Regional Power in the Middle East, 2007–11'. *Third World Quarterly* 34 (2): 287–304.

Barnes, Cedric and Harun Hassan. 2007. 'The Rise and Fall of Mogadishu's Islamic Courts'. *Journal of Eastern African Studies* 1 (2): 151–60.

Barnes, Sandra T. 2005. 'Global Flows: Terror, Oil & Strategic Philanthropy'. *Review of African Political Economy* 32 (104/105): 235–52.

Barrett, Roby Carol. 2007. *Greater Middle East and the Cold War: US Foreign Policy Under Eisenhower and Kennedy*. London: I.B. Tauris.

Başkan-Canyaş, Filiz and F. Orkunt Canyaş. 2016. 'The Interplay between Formal and Informal Institutions in Turkey: The Case of the Fethullah Gülen Community'. *Middle Eastern Studies* 52 (2): 280–94.

Bayer, Reşat and E. Fuat Keyman. 2012. 'Turkey: An Emerging Hub of Globalization and Internationalist Humanitarian Actor?' *Globalizations* 9 (1): 73–90.

Baylis, John, Steve Smith and Patricia Owens, eds. 2008. *The Globalization of World Politics*. New York: Oxford University Press Inc.

Bein, Amit. 2017. *Kemalist Turkey and the Middle East*. Cambridge: Cambridge University Press.

Belder, Ferit and Samiratou Dipama. 'A Comparative Analysis of China and Turkey's Development Aid Activities in Sub-Saharan Africa'. In *Middle Powers in Global Governance: The Rise of Turkey*, edited by Emel Parlar Dal, 231–53. London: Palgrave Macmillan.

Bereketeab, Redie. 2013. *The Horn of Africa: Intra-State and Inter-State Conflicts and Security*. London: Pluto Press.

Bieler, Andreas, Richard Higgott and Geoffrey Underhill. 2004. *Non-state Actors and Authority in the Global System*. London and New York: Routledge.

Bilgic, Ali and Daniela Nascimento. 2014. 'Turkey's New Focus on Africa: Causes and Challenges'. *NOREF Policy Brief.*

Bilgin, Pinar and Ali Bilgic. 2011. 'Turkey's "new" Foreign Policy toward Eurasia'. *Eurasian Geography and Economics* 52 (2): 13–195.

Binder, Andrea. 2014. 'The Shape and Sustainability of Turkey's Booming Humanitarian Assistance'. *Revue Internationale de Politique de Développement* 5 (2). doi: https://doi.org/10.4000/poldev.1741.

Binder, Andrea, Claudia Meier and Julia Steets. 2010. 'Humanitarian Assistance: Truly Universal? A Mapping Study of Non-Western Donors'. In *Global Public Policy Institute Research Paper*. Berlin: Global Public Policy Institute.

Birdsall, Nancy and Homi Kharas. 2014. *The Quality of Official Development Assistance*. Washington: Center for Global Development.

Bölükbaşı, Suha. 1988. *The Superpowers and the Third World: Turkish–American Relations and Cyprus*. Maryland: University Press of America.

Bozdaglioglu, Yucel and Max Novick, eds. 2003. *Turkish Foreign Policy and Turkish Identity: A Constructivist Approach*. New York: Routledge.

Bradbury, Mark. 2008. *Becoming Somaliland*. London: Progressio.

Bradbury, Mark, Adan Yusuf Abokor and Haroon Ahmed Yusuf. 2003. 'Somaliland: Choosing Politics over Violence'. *Review of African Political Economy* 30 (97): 455–78.

Bradbury, Mark and Sally Healy. 2010. *Endless War: A Brief History of the Somali Conflict*. London: Conciliation Resources.

Brooks, Stephen G. 1997. 'Dueling Realisms'. *International Organization* 51 (3): 445–77.

Brown, Carl L. 1984. *International Politics in the Middle East: Old Rules, Dangerous Game*. Princeton: Princeton University Press.

Brown, William. 2010. 'A Question of Agency: Africa in International Politics'. *Third World Quarterly* 33 (10): 1889–908.

Brummett, Palmira Johnson. 1994. *Ottoman Seapower and Levantine Diplomacy in the Age of Discovery*. Albany: State University of New York Press (SUNY).

Bulhan, Hussein A. 2004. 'Somaliland in Ruin and Renewal: The Story of Somaliland'. In *Conflict Analysis Regional Report*. Hargeysa: Centre for Creative Solutions.

Burrows, Mathew J. and Jennifer Harris. 2009. 'Revisiting the Future: Geopolitical Effects of the Financial Crisis'. *The Washington Quarterly* 32 (2): 27–38. doi: 10.1080/01636600902772604.

Çağaptay, Soner. 2014a. 'The New Davutoğlu'. *Foreign Affairs*.

Çağaptay, Soner. 2014b. *The Rise of Turkey: The Twenty-First Century's First Muslim Power*. Lincoln: Potomac Books.

Candar, Cengiz and Fuller Graham E. 2001. 'Grand Geopolitics for a New Turkey'. *Mediterranean Quarterly* 12 (1): 22–38.

Cannon, Brendon J. 2016a. 'Deconstructing Turkey's Efforts in Somalia'. *Bildhaan: An International Journal of Somali Studies* 16 (14): 98–123.

Cannon, Brendon J. 2016b. 'Turkey in Kenya and Kenya in Turkey: Alternatives to the East/West Paradigm in Diplomacy, Trade and Security'. *Africa Journal of Political Science and International Relations* 10 (5): 56–65.

Cannon, Brendon J. 2017. *Turkey in Africa: Lessons from Somalia*. Rising Powers in Global Governance Project.

Cannon, Brendon J. and Federico Donelli. 2020. 'Asymmetric Alliances and High Polarity: Evaluating Regional Security Complexes in the Middle East and Horn of Africa'. *Third World Quarterly* 41 (3): 505–24.

Carmody, Pádraig. 2011. *The New Scramble for Africa*. Cambridge: Polity Press.

Carpintero, Oscar, Ivan Murray and Josè Bellver. 2016. 'The New Scramble for Africa: BRICS Strategies in a Multipolar World'. *Research in Political Economy* 30: 191–226.

Carr, Summerson E. and Michael Lempert, eds. 2016. *Scale: Discourse and Dimensions of Social Life*. Oakland: University of California Press.

Casale, Giancarlo. 2010. *The Ottoman Age of Exploration*. Oxford, New York: Oxford University Press.

Çelik, Nihat and Emre İşeri. 2016. 'Islamically Oriented Humanitarian NGOs in Turkey: AKP Foreign Policy Parallelism'. *Turkish Studies* 17 (3): 429–48.

Çelik, Yasemin. 1999. *Contemporary Turkish Foreign Policy*. Westport, London: Praeger.

Cem, Ismail. 2001. *Turkey in the New Century*. Ankara: Rustem.

Cevik, Senem. 2014. *The Rise of NGOs: Islamic Faith Diplomacy*. USC Center on Public Diplomacy.

Çevik, Senem B. 2016. 'Turkey's State-Based Foreign Aid: Narrating "Turkey's Story"'. *Rising Power Quarterly* 1 (2): 55–67.

Çevik, Senem and Philip Seib, eds. 2015. *Turkey's Public Diplomacy*. New York: Palgrave Macmillan.

Chamberlain, M. E. 2010. *The Scramble for Africa*. Third edn. London, New York: Routledge.

Chaturvedi, Sachin, Thomas Fues and Elizabeth Sidiropoulos, eds. 2012. *Development Cooperation and Emerging Powers: New Partners or Old Patterns?* London: ZED Books Ltd.

Christensen, Steen Fryba and Li Xing, eds. 2016. *Emerging Powers, Emerging Markets, Emerging Societies: Global Responses*. New York: Palgrave Macmillan.

Cinar, Kursat. 2013. 'Turkey and Turkic Nations: A Post-Cold War Analysis of Relations'. *Turkish Studies* 14 (2): 256–71.

Clapham, Christopher. 1996. *Africa and the International System: The Politics of State Survival*. Cambridge: Cambridge University Press.

Clarke, Walter S. and Jeffrey I. Herbst. 1997. *Learning from Somalia: The Lessons of Armed Humanitarian Intervention*. Oxford: Westview Press.

Colborne, Michael and Maxime Edwards. 2018. 'Erdoğan Is Making the Ottoman Empire Great Again'. *Foreign Policy*.

Cooper, Andrew F. and Daniel Flemes. 2013. 'Foreign Policy Strategies of Emerging Powers in a Multipolar World: An Introductory Review'. *Third World Quarterly* 34 (6): 943–62.

Cooper Ramo, Joshua. 2004. *The Beijing Consensus: Notes on the New Physics of Chinese Power*. London: Foreign Policy Centre.

Cornelissen, Scarlett. 2009. 'Awkward Embraces: Emerging and Established Powers and the Shifting Fortunes of Africa's International Relations in the Twenty-First Century'. *Politikon: South African Journal of Political Studies* 36 (1): 5–26.

Cumming, Gordon and Tony Chafer, eds. 2011. *From Rivalry to Partnership?: New Approaches to the Challenges of Africa*. Burlington: Ashgate.

Curtis, Lisa. 2008. *China's Expanding Global Influence: Foreign Policy Goals, Practices and Tools*. Washington: The Heritage Foundation.

Danforth, Nicholas. 2008. 'Ideology and Pragmatism in Turkish Foreign Policy: From Ataturk to the AKP'. *Turkish Policy Quarterly* 7 (3): 83–95.

Davidson, Basil. 1968. *History in Africa*. London: The Macmillan Company.

Davidson, Lawrence. 2006. 'Privatizing Foreign Policy'. *Middle East Policy* 13 (2): 134–47.

Davidson, William D. and Joseph Montville. 1982. 'Foreign Policy According to Freud'. *Foreign Policy* 45: 145–57.

Davutoğlu, Ahmet. 2001. *Stratejik Derinlik. Türkiye'nin Uluslararası Konumu*. İstanbul: Küre.

Davutoğlu, Ahmet. 2008. 'Turkey's New Foreign Policy Vision: An Assesment of 2007'. *Insight Turkey* 10 (1): 77–96.

Davutoğlu, Ahmet. 2012a. 'A New Vision for Least Developed Countries (LCDs)'. In *Vision Papers*. Ankara: Center for Strategic Research.

Davutoğlu, Ahmet. 2012b. 'Principles of Turkish Foreign Policy and Regional Political Structuring'. *Turkey Policy Brief Series: TEPAV-ILPI* 3:1–9.

Davutoğlu, Ahmet. 2013a. 'Turkey's Humanitarian Diplomacy: Objectives, Challenges and Prospects'. *Nationalities Papers: The Journal of Nationalism and Ethnicity* 41 (6): 865–70.

Davutoğlu, Ahmet. 2013b. 'Turkey's Mediation: Critical Reflections from the Field'. *Middle East Policy* 20 (1): 83–90.

Dawisha, Adeed. 1988. 'Arab Regimes: Legitimacy and Foreign Policy'. In *Beyond Coercion: The Durability of the Arab States*, edited by Adeed Dawisha and William I. Zartman, 260–75. London: Croom-Helm.

DeGhetto, Kaitlyn, Jacob R. Gray and Moses N. Kiggundu. 2016. 'The African Union's Agenda 2063: Aspirations, Challenges, and Opportunities for Management Research'. *Africa Journal of Management* 2 (1): 93–116.

Deringil, Selim. 2000. 'Les Ottomans et le partage de l'Afrique, 1880–1900'. In *The Ottomans, the Turks and World Power Politics*, edited by Selim Deringil, 101–30. Istanbul: Gorgias Press & The Isis Press.

Desai, Radhika 2013. *Geopolitical Economy: After US Hegemony, Globalization and Empire*. London: Pluto Press.

Diamond, Louise and John W. McDonald. 1997. *Multi-track Diplomacy: A Systems Approach to Peace*. Washington: Kumarian Press.

Dietz, Ton, Kjell Havnevik, Mayke Kaag and Terje Oestigaard, eds. 2011. *African Engagements: Africa Negotiating an Emerging Multipolar World*. Leiden: Brill.

Dodd, Clement. 2010. *The History and Politics of the Cyprus Conflict*. London: Palgrave Macmillan.

Donelli, Federico. 2015. 'Turkey's Presence in Somalia a Humanitarian Approach'. In *The Depth of Turkish Geopolitics in the AKP's Foreign Policy: From Europe to an Extended Neighbourhood*, edited by Alessia Chiriatti, Emidio Diodato, Salih Dogan, Federico Donelli and Bahri Yilmaz, 35–51. Perugia: Università per Stranieri Perugia.

Donelli, Federico. 2017. 'A Hybrid Actor in the Horn of Africa: An Analysis of Turkey's Involvement in Somalia'. In *The Horn of Africa Since the 1960s: Local and International Politics Intertwined*, edited by Aleksi Ylönen and Jan Záhořík, 158–70. London: Routledge.

Donelli, Federico and Ariel S. González Levaggi. 2016. 'Becoming Global Actor: The Turkish Agenda for the Global South'. *Rising Power Quarterly* 1 (2): 93–115.

Donelli, Federico and Ariel S. González Levaggi. 2018. 'From Mogadishu to Buenos Aires: The Global South in the Turkish Foreign Policy in the Late JDP Period (2011–2017)'. In *Middle Powers in Global Governance: The Rise of Turkey*, edited by Emel Parlar Dal, 53–73. London: Palgrave Macmillan.

Downs, Roger M. and David Stea, eds. 1973. *Image and Environment: Cognitive Mapping and Spatial Behavior*. Chicago: Aldine.

Dreher, Axel, Peter Nunnenkamp and Rainer Thiele. 2011. 'Are "New" Donors Different? Comparing the Allocation of Bilateral Aid Between nonDAC and DAC Donor Countries'. *World Development* 39 (11): 1950–68.

Duffield, Mark. 2010. 'Risk-Management and the Fortified Aid Compound: Everyday Life in Post-Interventionary Society'. *The Journal of Intervention and Statebuilding* 4 (4): 453–74.

Ebaugh, Helen Rose. 2010. *The Gülen Movement*. New York: Springer.

Ehteshami, Anoushirvan. 2014. 'Middle East Middle Powers: Regional Role, International Impact'. *Uluslararası İlişkiler* 11 (42) :29–49.

Eisenman, Joshua. 2012. 'China–Africa Trade Patterns: Causes and Consequences'. *Journal of Contemporary China* 21 (7): 793–810.

Eligür, Banu. 2014. *The Mobilization of Political Islam in Turkey*. Cambridge, New York: Cambridge University Press.

Elmi, Afyare Abdi. 2010. *Understanding the Somalia Conflagration: Identity, Islam and Peacebuilding*. London: Pluto Press.

Emiralioglu, Pinar. 2014. *Geographical Knowledge and Imperial Culture in the Early Modern Ottoman Empire*. Abingdon: Ashgate.

Erdoğan, Recep Tayyip. 2011. 'The Tears of Somalia'. *Foreign Policy*. URL: https://foreign policy.com/2011/10/10/the-tears-of-somalia/.

Erickson, Edward J. 2004. 'Turkey as Regional Hegemony 2014: Strategic Implications for the United States'. *Turkish Studies* 5 (3): 25–45.

Erşen, Emre and Seçkin Köstem, eds. 2019. *Turkey's Pivot to Eurasia: Geopolitics and Foreign Policy in a Changing World Order*. Abingdon: Routledge.

Esen, Berk and Sebnem Gumuscu. 2016. 'Rising Competitive Authoritarianism in Turkey'. *Third World Quarterly* 37 (9): 1581–606.

Eyrice Tepeciklioğlu, Elem. 2012. 'Africa's Growing Importance in Global and Turkish Politics and Turkish–African Relations'. *Ankara Üniversitesi Afrika Çalışmaları Dergisi* 1 (2): 59–94.

Eyrice Tepeciklioğlu, Elem. 2015. 'What Is Turkey Doing in Africa? African Opening in Turkish Foreign Policy'. *Centre for Policy and Research on Turkey (ResearchTurkey)* 4 (4): 95–106.

Eyrice Tepeciklioğlu, Elem. 2016. 'African Studies in Turkey'. *Uluslararası İlişkiler* 13 (50): 3–19.

Falk, Richard. 2018. 'Through a Glass Darkly: The Past, Present, and Future of Turkish Foreign Policy'. In *Middle Powers in Global Governance*, edited by Emel Parlar Dal, 35–51. Abingdon: Palgrave Macmillan.

Fidan, Hakan and Rahman Nurdun. 2008. 'Turkey's Role in the Global Development Assistance Community: The Case of TIKA (Turkish International Cooperation and Development Agency)'. *Southern Europe & the Balkans* 10 (1): 93–111.

Fırat, Melek. 1997. *1960–71 Arası Türk Dış Politikası ve Kıbrıs Sorunu*. Ankara: Siyasal Kitabevi.

Fırat, Melek and Ömer Kürkçüoğlu. 2002. 'Ortadoğu'yla İlişkiler'. In *Türk Dış Politikası (1919 - 1980)*, edited by Oran Baskın, 785–9. İstanbul: İletişim Yayınları.

Flint, Colin. 2016. *Introduction to Geopolitics*. Third edn. Abingdon: Routledge.

Foulon, Michiel. 2015. 'Neoclassical Realism: Challengers and Bridging Identities'. *International Studies Review* 17: 635–61.

Friedberg, Aaron L. 2010. 'Implications of the Financial Crisis for the US–China Rivalry'. *Survival: Global Politics and Strategy* 52 (4): 31–54.

Fukuyama, Francis. 1989. 'The End of History?' *The National Interest* 16: 3–18.

Gamble, Andrew. 2010. 'A New World Order? The Aftermath of the Financial Crisis'. *Political Insight* 1 (1): 17–19. doi: 10.1111/j.2041-9066.2010.00008.x.

Gause, Gregory F. 2014. *Beyond Sectarianism: The New Middle East Cold War*. Doha: Brookings Institute Center.

Genc, Savas and Oguzhan Tekin. 2014. 'Turkey's Increased Engagement in Africa: The Potential, Limits and Future Perspective of Relations'. *European Journal of Economic and Political Studies* 7 (1): 87–115.

Gizem, Sucuoglu and Jason Stearns. 2016. 'Turkey in Somalia: Shifting Paradigms of Aid'. In *Research Report*. South African Institute of International Affairs.

Göksel, Oğhuzan. 2016. 'The End of Military Tutelage in Turkey and the Re-Making of Turkish Foreign Policy under the AKP'. In *Democratic Peace across the Middle East: Islam and Political Modernization*, edited by Yakub Halabi, 46–73. London, New York: I.B. Tauris.

Goldman, Emily O. 2011. *Power in Uncertain Times: Strategy in the Fog of Peace*. Stanford: Stanford University Press.

Goldstein, Judith and Robert O. Keohane. 1993. *Ideas and Foreign Policy: Beliefs, Institutions and Political Change*. Ithaca: Cornell University Press.

Göle, Nilufer. 1997. 'Secularism and Islamism in Turkey: The Making of Elites and Counter-Elites'. *The Middle East Journal* 51 (1): 46–58.

Gore, Charles. 2013. 'The New Development Cooperation Landscape: Actors, Approaches, Architecture'. *Journal of International Development* 25 (6): 769–86.

Gözen Ercan, Pınar, ed. 2017. *Turkish Foreign Policy: International Relations, Legality and Global Reach*. Cham: Palgrave Macmillan.

Gray, Kevin and Barry K. Gills, eds. 2017. *Rising Powers and South-South Cooperation*. London: Routledge.

Gray, Kevin and Craig N. Murphy, eds. 2014. *Rising Powers and the Future of Global Governance*. Milton Park: Routledge.

Grondin, David and Charles-Philippe David, eds. 2016. *Hegemony or Empire?: The Redefinition of US Power under George W. Bush*. London, New York: Routledge.

Guerrero, Dorothy-Grace and Firoze Manji, eds. 2008. *China's New Role in Africa and the South*. Oxford: Fahamu.

Gullo, Matthew T. 2012. *Turkey's Somalia Adventure: The Quest for Soft Power and Regional Recognition*. London: Research Turkey.

Guner, Ezgi. 2020. 'The Scalar Politics of Turkey's Pivot to Africa'. *POMEPS Studies – Africa and the Middle East: Beyond the Divides* 40: 59–63.

Gürkaynak, Esra Çuhadar. 2007. 'Turkey as a Third Party in Israeli–Palestinian Conflict'. *Perceptions* 7 (1): 89–108.

Haar, Roberta. 2010. 'Explaining George W. Bush's Adoption of the Neoconservative Agenda after 9/11'. *Politics & Policy* 38 (5): 965–90.

Haas, Richard. 2008. 'The Age of Nonpolarity: What Will follow U.S. Dominance'. *Foreign Affairs* 87 (3): 44–56.

Hagan, Joe and Margaret G. Hermann. 2002. *Leaders, Groups, and Coalitions*. Hoboken: Blackwell Publishers.

Hale, William. 2000. *Turkish Foreign Policy, 1774–2000*. Portland, London: Frank Cass.

Halper, Stefan and Jonathan Clarke. 2004. *America Alone: The Neo-Conservatives and the Global Order*. Cambridge: Cambridge University Press.

Han, Aslan Davut and Selcuk Bahadir. 2016. 'Africa in Turkey's Foreign Policy Agenda: Trade, Economic and Military Cooperation'. *Kwartalnik Naukowy Uczelni Vistula* 4 (50): 139–48.

Hansen, Stig Jarle. 2012. *Al-Shabaab in Somalia: The History and Ideology of a Militant Islamist Group 2005–2012*. Oxford: Oxford University Press.

Harkavy, Robert. 2001. 'Strategic Geography and the Greater Middle East'. *Naval War College Review* 54 (4): 36–53.

Harper, Mary. 2012. *Getting Somalia Wrong: Faith, War and Hope in a Shattered State*. Chicago: Zed Press.

Harroff-Tavel, Marion. 2005. 'La diplomatie humanitaire du comité international de la Croix-Rouge'. *Relations Internationales* 121 (Spring): 73–89.

Hasan, Yusuf Fadl. 2007. 'Some Aspects of Turco-African Relations with Special Reference to the Sudan'. *Middle East and African Studies* 2.

Haşimi, Cemalettin. 2014. 'Turkey's Humanitarian Diplomacy and Development Cooperation'. *Insight Turkey* 16 (1): 127–45.

Hausmann, Jeannine. 2014. 'Turkey as a Donor Country and Potential Partner in Triangular Cooperation'. In *Discussion Paper*. German Development Institute.

Hausmann, Jeannine and Erik Lundsgaarde. 2015. *Turkey's Role in Development Cooperation*. Tokyo: United Nations University Centre for Policy Research.

Hazar, Numan. 2000. 'The Future of Turkish–African Relations'. *Dış Politika* 25 (3–4): 107–14.

Hazar, Numan. 2015. 'Turkey's Policy of Outreach to Africa: An Assessment'. *Journal of Business Economics and Political Science* 4 (7): 3–11.

Heine, Jorge. 2013. 'From Club to Network Diplomacy'. In *The Oxford Handbook of Modern Diplomacy*, edited by Andrew F. Cooper, Jorge Heine and Ramesh Thakur, 54–69. Oxford: Oxford University Press.

Helman, Gerald B. and Steven R. Ratner. 1992–93. 'Saving Failed States'. *Foreign Policy* (89): 3–20.

Hendrick, Joshua D. 2013. *Gülen: The Ambiguous Politics of Market Islam in Turkey and the World*. New York: New York University Press.

Hermann, Charles F. 1990. 'Changing Course: When Governments Choose to Redirect Foreign Policy'. *International Studies Quarterly* 34 (1): 3–22.

Hermann, Margaret G. 1980. 'Explaining Foreign Policy Behaviour Using the Personal
    Characteristics of Political Leaders'. *International Studies Quarterly* 24 (1): 7–46.

Hess, Andrew C. 1973. 'The Ottoman Conquest of Egypt (1517) and the Beginning
    of the Sixteenth- Century World War'. *International Journal of Middle East Studies*
    4 (1): 55–76.

Hess, Andrew C. 2011. *The Forgotten Frontier: A History of the Sixteenth-Century
    Ibero-African Frontier*. Chicago, London: University of Chicago Press.

Hill, Christopher. 2003. *The Changing Politics of Foreign Policy*. New York: Palgrave
    Macmillan.

Hocking, Brian. 2006. 'Multistakeholder Diplomacy: Forms, Functions, and
    Frustrations'. In *Multistakeholder Diplomacy: Challenges and Opportunities*, edited by
    Jovan Kurbalija and Valentin Katrandjiev, 13–29. Geneve: DiploFoundation.

Höhne, Markus V. 2006. 'Political Identity, Emerging State Structures and Conflict in
    Northern Somalia'. *Journal of Modern African Studies* 44 (3): 397–414.

Holsti, Kal J. 1970. 'National Role Conceptions in the Study of Foreign Policy'.
    International Studies Quarterly 14 (3): 233–309.

Holt, Peter Malcolm. 1961. *A History of the Sudan: From the Coming of Islam to the
    Present Day*. London: Weidenfeld and Nicolson.

Homans, Charles. 2011. 'Track II Diplomacy: A Short Story'. *Foreign Policy*.

Hsu, S. Philip, Yu-Shan Wu and Suisheng Zhao, eds. 2011. *In Search of China's
    Developmental Model: Beyond the Beijing Consensus*. Milton Park: Routledge.

Huang, Meibo and Ren Peiqiang. 2012. 'China's Foreign Aid and Its Role in the
    International Architecture'. *International Development Policy* 3 (3). doi: 10.4000/
    poldev.1004.

Hughes, Edel. 2011. *Turkey's Accession to the European Union: The Politics of Exclusion?*
    London, New York: Routledge.

Hughes, James H. 2010. 'China's Place in Today's World'. *The Journal of Social, Political,
    and Economic Studies* 35 (2): 167–223.

Huntington, Samuel P. 1993. 'The Clash of Civilizations'. *Foreign Affairs* 72 (3): 22–49.

Huntington, Samuel P. 1999. 'The Lonely Superpower'. *Foreign Affairs* 78 (2): 35–49.

Hurst, Steven. 2005. 'Myths of Neoconservatism: George W. Bush's "Neo-conservative"
    Foreign Policy Revisited'. *International Politics* 42 (1): 75–96.

ICG. 2012. 'Assessing Turkey's Role in Somalia'. In *ICG Africa Briefing*. International
    Crisis Group.

IFRC. 2009. *IFRC Annual Report 2009*. Nairobi: International Federation of Red Cross
    and Red Crescent Societies.

Ikenberry, G. John. 1989. 'Rethinking the Origins of American Hegemony'. *Political
    Science Quarterly* 104 (3): 375–400.

Ikenberry, G. John and Annie-Marie Slaughter. 2006. *Forging a World of Liberty under
    Law: U.S. National Security in the 21st Century*. Princeton: Princeton University Press.

İnalcık, Halil and Donald Quataert. 1994. *An Economic and Social History of the
    Ottoman Empire, 1300–1914*. Cambridge: Cambridge University Press.

Ipek, Volkan. 2017. 'Turkey's Foreign Policy towards Sub-Saharan Africa'. In *Turkish Foreign Policy*, edited by Ercan P. Gözen, 217–35. London: Palgrave Macmillan.

İpek, Volkan and Gonca Biltekin. 2013. 'Turkey's Foreign Policy Implementation in Sub-Saharan Africa: A Post-international Approach'. *New Perspective on Turkey* 49: 121–56.

Iyigun, Murat. 2015. *War, Peace, and Prosperity in the Name of God: The Ottoman Role in Europe's Socioeconomic Evolution*. Chicago, London: University of Chicago Press.

James, Patrick. 2009. 'Elaborating on Offensive Realism'. In *Rethinking Realism in International Relations: Between Tradition and Innovation*, edited by Annette Freyberg-Inan, Ewan Harrison and Patrick James, 45–62. Abingdon: Routledge.

Jervis, Robert. 2009. 'Unipolarity: A Structural Perspective'. *World Politics* 61 (1): 188–213.

Jones, Peter. 2015. *Track Two Diplomacy in Theory and Practice*. Stanford: Stanford University Press.

Kaarbo, Juliet. 2015. 'A Foreign Policy Analysis Perspective on the Domestic Politics Turn in IR Theory'. *International Studies Review* 17: 189–216.

Kadayifci-Orellana, Ayse S. 2016. 'Turkish Mediation in Somalia for Peace and Stability'. In *Turkey as a Mediator: Stories of Success and Failure*, edited by Doga Ulas Eralp, 99–124. Lanham: Lexington Books.

Kai, Jin. 2017. *Rising China in a Changing World: Power Transitions and Global Leadership*. London: Palgrave Macmillan.

Kanat, Kilic, Ahmet Tekelioglu and Kadir Ustun, eds. 2015. *Politics and Foreign Policy in Turkey: Historical and Contemporary Perspectives*. Ankara: SETA.

Kapteijns, Lidwien. 2013. *Clan Cleansing in Somalia: The Ruinous Legacy of 1991*. Philadelphia: University of Pennsylvania Press.

Kara, Mehtap and Ahmet Sozen. 2016. 'Change and Continuity in Turkish Foreign Policy: Evaluating Pre-AKP and AKP Periods' National Role Conceptions'. *Uluslararası İlişkiler* 13 (52): 47–66.

Karaca, Salih Z. 2000. 'Turkish Foreign Policy in the Year 2000 and Beyond: Her Opening Up Policy to Africa'. *Dis Politika* 25 (3–4): 115–19.

Kardaş, Şaban. 2010. 'Turkey: Redrawing the Middle East Map or Building Sandcastles?' *Middle East Policy* 17 (1): 115–36.

Kardaş, Şaban. 2012. 'From Zero Problems to Leading the Change: Making Sense of Transformation in Turkey's Regional Policy'. *TEPAV-ILPI Turkey Policy Brief Series* 5 (1): 1–8.

Katzenstein, Peter J., ed. 1978. *Between Power and Plenty: Foreign Economic Policies of Advanced Industrial States*. Madison: University of Wisconsin Press.

Katzenstein, Peter J. 2005. *A World of Regions: Asia and Europe in the American Imperium*. Ithaca: Cornell University Press.

Kavas, Ahmet. 2006. 'Afrikali Musluman Dini Liderler Istanbul'da Bulustu'. *Dusunce Gundem* 3 (25): 9–10.

Kaye, Dalia Dassa. 2001. 'Track Two Diplomacy and Regional Security in the Middle East'. *International Negotiation* 6: 49–77.

Kelman, Ilan. 2011. *Disaster Diplomacy: How Disasters Affect Peace and Conflict*. London: Routledge.

Kennedy, Paul. 1987. *The Rise and Fall of the Great Powers: Economic Change and Military Conflict from 1500 to 2000*. New York: Random House.

Kepel, Gilles. 2000. *Jihad: expansion et déclin de l'islamisme*. Paris: Gallimard.

Kessler, Meryl A. and Thomas G. Weiss, eds. 1991. *Third World Security in the Post-Cold War Era*. Boulder: Lynne Rienner.

Keyman, E. Fuat. 2010. 'Globalization, Modernity and Democracy: Turkish Foreign Policy 2009 and Beyond'. *Perceptions* 15 (3–4): 1–20.

Keyman, E. Fuat. 2016. 'Turkish Foreign Policy in the Post-Arab Spring Era: from Proactive to Buffer State'. *Third World Quarterly* 37 (12): 2274–87.

Keyman, E. Fuat and Ahmet İçduygu. 2003. 'Globalization, Civil Society and Citizenship in Turkey: Actors, Boundaries and Discourses'. *Citizenship Studies* 7 (2): 219–34.

Keyman, E. Fuat and Onur Sazak. 2014. Turkey as a 'Humanitarian State'. In *POMEAS PAPER*.

Keyman, E. Fuat and Sebnem Gumuscu. 2014. *Democracy, Identity and Foreign Policy in Turkey: Hegemony through Transformation*. London: Palgrave MacMillan.

Kiniklioglu, Suat. 2010. 'Turkey's Neighbourhood and Beyond: Tectonic Transformation at Work?' *The International Spectator* 45 (4): 93–100.

Kirişci, Kemal. 2009. 'The Transformation of Turkish Foreign Policy: The Rise of the Trading State'. *New Perspectives on Turkey* 40: 29–57.

Klare, Michael and Daniel Volman. 2006. 'America, China & the Scramble for Africa's Oil'. *Review of African Political Economy* 33 (108): 297–309.

Kohlmann, Evan F. 2006. 'The Role of Islamic Charities in International Terrorist Recruitment and Financing'. In *DIIS Working Paper*. Copenhagen: Danish Institute for International Studies.

Koops, Joachim A., Norrie MacQueen, Thierry Tardy and Paul D. Williams, eds. 2015. *The Oxford Handbook of United Nations Peacekeeping Operations*. Oxford: Oxford University Press.

Korany, Bahgat. 2010. *The Changing Middle East: A New Look at Regional Dynamics*. Cairo, New York: The American University in Cairo Press.

Korany, Bahgat. 2013. 'The Middle East Since the Cold War'. In *International Relations of the Middle East*, edited by Louise Fawcett, 79–93. Oxford: Oxford University Press.

Korany, Bahgat and Hillal Dessouki, eds. 2008. *The Foreign Policies of Arab States: The Challenge of Globalization*. Cairo: American University in Cairo Press.

Korkut, Umut and Ilke Civelekoglu. 2013. 'Becoming a Regional Power While Pursuing Material Gains: The Case of Turkish Interest in Africa'. *International Journal* 68 (1): 187–203.

Kösebalaban, Hasan. 2011. *Turkish Foreign Policy: Islam, Nationalism, and Globalization, Middle East Today*. New York: Palgrave Macmillan.

Krasner, Stephen D. 2001. *Problematic Sovereignty: Contested Rules and Political Possibilities*. New York: Columbia University Press.

Kubicek, Paul. 2002. 'The Earthquake, Civil Society, and Political Change in Turkey: Assessment and Comparison with Eastern Europe'. *Political Studies* 50 (4): 761–78.

Kubicek, Paul. 2005. 'The European Union and Grassroots Democratization in Turkey'. *Turkish Studies* 6 (3): 361–77.

Kurşun, Zekeriya, ed. 2013. *Osmanlı'dan Günümüze Afrika Bibliyografyası*. İstanbul: Ortadoğu ve Afrika Araştırmacıları Derneği Yayınları.

Kuru, Ahmet. 2015. 'Turkey's Failed Policy toward the Arab Spring: Three Levels of Analysis'. *Mediterranean Quarterly* 26 (3): 94–116.

Kuzmanovic, Daniella. 2012. *Refractions of Civil Society in Turkey*. New York: Palgrave Macmillan.

Laçiner, Sedat. 2009. 'Turgut Özal Period in Turkish Foreign Policy: Özalism'. *USAK Yearbook of International Politics and Law* 2: 153–205.

Langan, Mark. 2017a. *Neo-Colonialism and the Poverty of 'Development' in Africa*. Newcastle: Palgrave Macmillan.

Langan, Mark. 2017b. 'Virtuous power Turkey in sub-Saharan Africa: The "Neo-Ottoman" challenge to the European Union'. *Third World Quarterly* 38 (6): 1399–414.

Layne, Christopher. 2012. 'The Global Power Shift from West to East'. *The National Interest* 119: 21–31.

Lee, Margaret C. 2006. 'The 21st Century Scramble for Africa'. *Journal of Contemporary African Studies* 24 (3): 303–30.

Lefebvre, Jeffrey A. 2018. 'Iran scramble in Sub-Saharan Africa'. *Insight Turkey* 21 (1): 133–50.

Lekorwe, Mogopodi, Anyway Chingwete, Mina Okuru and Romaric Samson. 2016. 'China's Growing Presence in Africa Wins Largely Positive Popular Reviews'. In *Afrobarometer Dispatch*. Afrobarometer.

Lemke, Douglas. 2002. *Regions of War and Peace*. Cambridge: Cambridge University Press.

Lewis, Ioan M. 2002. *A Modern History of the Somali: Nation and State in the Horn of Africa*. Athens: Ohio University Press.

Li, Anshan. 2010. 'African Studies in China: A Historiographical Survey'. In *Chinese and African Perspectives on China in Africa*, edited by Axel Harneit-Sievers, Stephen Marks and Sanusha Naidu, 2–24. Kampala: Pambazuka Press.

Li, Anshan and April Funeka Yazini. 2013. *Forum on China–Africa Cooperation: The Politics of Human Resource Development*. Oxford: Africa Institute of South Africa.

Li, Minqi. 2009. *The Rise of China and the Demise of the Capitalist World-Economy*. New York: Monthly Review Press.

Liew, Leong. 2005. 'China's Engagement with Neo-liberalism: Path Dependency, Geography and Party Self-Reinvention'. *The Journal of Development Studies* 41 (2): 331–52.

Lobell, Steven E. 2009. 'Threat Assessment, the State, and Foreign Policy: A Neoclassical Realist Model'. In *Neoclassical Realism, the State and Foreign Policy*, edited by

Jeffrey W. Taliaferro, Steven E. Lobell and Norrin M. Ripsman, 42–74. Cambridge: Cambridge University Press.

Lord, Ceren. 2018. *Religious Politics in Turkey: From the Birth of the Republic to the AKP*. Cambridge: Cambridge University Press.

Lubieniecka, Ewelina. 2014. 'Chinese Engagement in Sub-Saharan Africa: Can the Beijing Consensus be Explained under World-Systems Analysis?' *Fudan Journal of the Humanities & Social Sciences* 7 (3): 433–50.

Makowski, Andrzej. 2013. 'The Mavi Marmara Incident and the Modern Law of Armed Conflict at Sea'. *The Israel Journal of Foreign Affairs* 7 (2): 75–89.

Mangala, Jack, ed. 2010. *Africa and the New World Era: From Humanitarianism to a Strategic View*. New York: Palgrave Macmillan.

Manners, Ian. 2007. *European Cartographers and the Ottoman World, 1500–1750: Maps from the Collection of O. J. Sopranos*. Chicago: Oriental Institute Publications of the University of Chicago.

Marchal, Roland. 2004. 'Islamic Political Dynamics in the Somali Civil War'. In *Islamism and Its Enemies in the Horn of Africa*, edited by Alexander De Waal, 114–45. London: Hurst.

Marchal, Roland. 2009. 'A Tentative Assessment of the Somali Harakat Al-Shabaab'. *Journal of Eastern African Studies* 3 (3): 381–404. doi: https://doi.org/10.1080/1 7531050903273701.

Mardin, Şerif. 1989. *Religion and Social Change in Modern Turkey: The Case of Bediuzzaman Said Nursi*. Albany: State University of New York Press.

Martin, William G. 2011. 'The Rise of African Studies (USA) and the Transnational Study of Africa'. *African Studies Review* 54 (1): 59–83.

Marton, Peter. 2014. 'The New Scramble for Africa; Globalization in Africa: Recolonization or Renaissance?' *Journal of Contemporary African Studies* 32 (1): 137–40.

Mason, Robert. 2015. 'Patterns and Consequences of Economic Engagement across Sub-Saharan Africa: A Comparative Analysis of Chinese, British and Turkish Policies'. In *Working Paper Centre for International Studies (CIS)*. London: London School of Economics.

Mastanduno, Michael. 2019. 'Partner Politics: Russia, China, and the Challenge of Extending US Hegemony after the Cold War'. *Security Studies* 28 (3): 479–504.

Mbabia, Oliver. 2011. 'Ankara en Afrique: stratégies d expansion'. *Outre-Terre* 3 (29): 107–19.

McDonald, John W. 1991. 'Further Exploration of Track Two Diplomacy'. In *Timing the De-Escalation of International Conflicts*, edited by Louis Kriesberg and Stuart J. Thorson, 201–20. Syracuse: Syracuse University Press.

McKinnon, Ronald I. 2010. 'China in Africa: The Washington Consensus versus the Beijing Consensus'. *International Finance* 13 (3): 495–506.

Mclean, Wayne. 2015. 'Understanding Divergence between Public Discourse and Turkish Foreign Policy Practice: A Neoclassical Realist Analysis'. *Turkish Studies* 16 (4): 449–64.

Melissen, Jen, ed. 2005. *The New Public Diplomacy: Soft Power in International Relations*. London: Palgrave Macmillan.

Memiş, Hasan, Mehmet Kara and Lütfü Tayfur. 2010. 'Yoksulluk, Yapısal Uyum Programları ve Sahra Altı Afrika Ülkeleri'. *Mustafa Kemal Üniversitesi Sosyal Bilimler Enstitüsü Dergisi* 7 (14): 325–46.

Menkhaus, Ken. 2004. *Somalia: State Collapse and the Threat of Terrorism*. New York: Routledge.

Menkhause, Ken, Hassan Sheik, Ali Joqombe and Pat Johnson. 2009. *A History of Mediation in Somalia since 1988*. Nairobi: Interpeace.

Miller, Christopher L. and Tamer Balci, eds. 2012. *The Gülen Hizmet Movement: Circumspect Activism in Faith-based Reform*. Cambridge: Cambridge Scholar Publishing.

Minawi, Mostafa. 2016. *The Ottoman Scramble for Africa: Empire and Diplomacy in the Sahara and the Hijaz*. Stanford: Stanford University Press.

Minear, Larry and Hazel Smith, eds. 2007. *Humanitarian Diplomacy: Practitioners and their Craft*. New York: United Nations University Press

Modi, Renu, ed. 2011. *South-South Cooperation: Africa on the Centre Stage*. London: Palgrave Macmillan.

Mohan, Giles and Marcus Power. 2008. 'New African Choices? The Politics of Chinese Engagement'. *Review of African Political Economy* 35 (115): 23–42.

Montville, Joseph. 1991. 'Track Two Diplomacy: The Arrow and the Olive Branch: A case for Track Two Diplomacy'. In *The Psychodynamics of International Relationships: Unofficial Diplomacy at Work*, edited by Vamik D. Volkan, Demetrios Julius and Joseph Montville, 166–75. Lexington: Lexington Books.

Moran, Michael. 2001. 'Cyprus and the 1960 Accords: Nationalism and Internationalism'. *Perceptions: Journal of International Affairs* 6 (2): 1–9.

Morgenthau, Hans J. 1948. *Politics among Nations: The Struggle for Power and Peace*. New York: Alfred Kopf.

Murinson, Alexander. 2012. 'Turkish Foreign Policy in the Twenty-First Century'. In *Mideast Security and Policy Studies*. Ramat Gan: The Begin–Sadat Center for Strategic Studies – Bar-Ilan University.

Murphy, Craig N. 2010. 'Lessons of a "Good" Crisis: Learning in, and From the Third World'. *Globalizations* 7 (1–2): 203–15.

Murphy, Martin N. 2011. *Somalia: The New Barbary?: Piracy and Islam in the Horn of Africa*. New York: Columbia University Press.

Murphy, Teri and Auveen Elizabeth Woods. 2014. *Turkey's International Development Framework Case Study: Somalia*. Istanbul: Istanbul Policy Center.

Murrell, Peter. 1993. 'What Is Shock Therapy? What Did It Do in Poland and Russia?' *Post-Soviet Affairs* 9 (2): 111–40.

Neack, Laura. 2008. *The New Foreign Policy: Power Seeking in a Globalized Era*. Miami: Rowman & Littlefield Publishers.

Neumayer, Eric. 2003. 'What Factors Determine the Allocation of Aid by Arab Countries and Multilateral Agencies?' *LSE Research Online*.

Nien-chung, Chang-Liao. 2016. 'China's New Foreign Policy under Xi Jinping'. *Asian Security* 12 (2): 82–91.

Nye Jr, Joseph S. 2010. 'American and Chinese Power after the Financial Crisis'. *The Washington Quarterly* 33 (4): 143–53.

Nye Jr, Joseph S. 2011. *The Future of Power*. New York: Public Affairs.

O'Fahey, Rex S. 1996. 'Islam and Ethnicity in the Sudan'. *Journal of Religion in Africa* 3 (3): 258–67.

Oertel, Janka. 2014. *China and the United Nations: Chinese UN Policy in the Areas of Peace and Development in the Era of Hu Jintao*. Baden-Baden: Nomos & Bloomsbury.

Ogot, Bethwell Allan, ed. 1999. *Africa from the Sixteenth to the Eighteenth Century, UNESCO General History of Africa (Book 5)*. Berkeley: California University Press.

Öniş, Ziya. 1995. 'Turkey in the Post-cold War Era: In Search of Identity'. *Middle East Journal* 49 (1): 48–68.

Öniş, Ziya and Barry M. Rubin, eds. 2003. *The Turkish Economy in Crisis: Critical Perspectives on the 2000–1 Crises*. London, Portland: Frank Cass.

Öniş, Ziya and Mustafa Kutlay. 2017. 'The Dynamics of Emerging Middle-Power Influence in Regional and Global Governance: The Paradoxical Case of Turkey'. *Australian Journal of International Affairs* 71 (2): 164–83.

Öniş, Ziya and Şuhnaz Yılmaz. 2009. 'Between Europeanization and Euro-Asianism: Foreign Policy Activism in Turkey during the AKP Era'. *Turkish Studies* 10 (1): 7–24.

Orhonlu, Cengiz. 1974. *Osmanli İmparatorlugu 'nun Güney Siyaseti: Habes Eyaleti*. Istanbul: Istanbul Üniversitesi Edebiyat Fakültesi Matbaasi.

Örmeci, Ozan. 2011. 'Ismail Cem's Foreign Policy (1997–2002)'. *SDU Faculty of Arts and Sciences, Journal of Social Sciences* 23: 223–45.

Özbudun, Ergun. 2012. 'Turkey – Plural Society and Monolithic State'. In *Democracy, Islam, & Secularism in Turkey*, edited by Ahmet Kuru and Alfred Stepan, 61–94. New York: Columbia University Press.

Özbudun, Ergun. 2014. 'AKP at the Crossroads: Erdoğan's Majoritarian Drift'. *South European Society & Politics* 19 (2): 155–67.

Özçomak, Suphi M. and Ayhan Demirci. 2010. 'Afrika Birliği Ülkelerinin Sosyal ve Ekonomik Göstergeleri Arasındaki İlişkinin Kanonik Korelasyon Analizi ile İncelenmesi'. *Atatürk Üniversitesi Sosyal Bilimler Enstitüsü Dergisi* 14 (1): 361–74.

Özdemir, Elvan and Zehra Vildan Serin. 2016. 'Trading State and Reflections of Foreign Policy: Evidence from Turkish Foreign Policy'. *Procedia Economics and Finance* 38:468–75.

Özerdem, Alpaslan. 2019. 'Turkey as an Emerging Global Humanitarian and Peacebuilding Actor'. In *The Routledge Handbook of Turkish Politics*, edited by Alpaslan Özerdem and Matthew Whiting, 470–80. London, New York: Routledge.

Özgur, Dönmez Rasim and Enneli Pinar. 2011. *Societal Peace and Ideal Citizenship for Turkey*. Plymouth: Lexington Books.

Özkan, Güner and Mustafa Turgut Demirtepe. 2012. 'Transformation of a Development Aid Agency: TIKA in a Changing Domestic and International Setting'. *Turkish Studies* 13 (4): 647–67.

Özkan, Mehmet. 2010a. 'Turkey's Rising Role in Africa'. *Turkish Policy Quarterly* 9 (4): 93–105.

Özkan, Mehmet. 2010b. 'What Drives Turkey's Involvement in Africa?' *Review of African Political Economy* 37 (126): 533–40.

Özkan, Mehmet. 2011. 'Turkey's "New" Engagements in Africa and Asia: Scope, Content and Implications'. *Perceptions – Journal of International Affairs* 16 (3): 115–37.

Özkan, Mehmet. 2012. 'A New Actor or Passer-By? The Political Economy of Turkey's Engagement with Africa'. *Journal of Balkan and Near Eastern Studies* 14 (1): 113–33.

Özkan, Mehmet. 2012. 'Turkiye'nin Afrika'da Artan Rolu: Pratik Cabalar ve Soylem Arayislari'. *Ortadoğu Analiz* 4 (46): 19–28.

Özkan, Mehmet. 2013. 'Turkey's Religious and Socio-Political Depth in Africa: "Emerging Powers in Africa"'. *LSE IDEAS Special Report* 16:45–50.

Özkan, Mehmet. 2014. *Turkey's Involvement in Somalia: Assessments of a State-Building in Progress*. Ankara: SETA Publications.

Ozkan, Mehmet. 2018. 'Africa's Place in Turkey's Foreign Policy: From Doubts to Normalization'. *Africa e Orienti* 20 (1–2): 41–53.

Özkan, Mehmet and Birol Akgün. 2010. 'Turkey's Opening to Africa'. *Journal of Modern African Studies* 48 (4): 525–46. doi: http://dx.doi.org/10.1017/S0022278X10000595.

Özkan, Mehmet and Serhat Orakçı. 2015. 'Viewpoint: Turkey as a "Political" Actor in Africa – An Assessment of Turkish Involvement in Somalia'. *Journal of Eastern African Studies* 9 (2): 343–52.

Özoran, Beris Artan. 2014. 'Güney Afrika'da Halkla İlişkiler: Farklı bir Yol Arayışına Vaka Analizi Yoluyla Bakmak'. *İletişim Kuram ve Araştırma Dergisi* 38:74–95.

Özpek, Burak Bilgehan, and Yelda Demirağ. 2014. 'Turkish Foreign Policy after the "Arab Spring": From Agendasetter State to Agenda-Entrepreneur State'. *Israel Affairs* 20 (3): 328–46.

Öztürk, Ahmet Erdi. 2018. 'Transformation of the Turkish Diyanet Both at Home and Abroad: Three Stages'. *European Journal of Turkish Studies* 27. doi: https://doi.org/10.4000/ejts.5944.

Özyüksel, Murat. 2014. *The Hejaz Railway and the Ottoman Empire: Modernity, Industrialisation and Ottoman Decline*. London: I.B. Tauris.

Paolo, de Renzio and Jurek Seifert. 2014. 'South–South Cooperation and the Future of Development Assistance: Mapping Actors and Options'. *Third World Quarterly* 35 (10): 1860–75.

Papa, Michael J., Jeffrey Mapendere and Patrick J. Dillon. 2010. 'Waging Peace through Improvisational Action: Track-Two Diplomacy in the Sudan-Uganda Conflict'. *Southern Communication Journal* 5 (4): 349–69.

Pape, Robert A. 2005. 'Soft Balancing against the United States'. *International Security* 30 (1): 7–45.

Parlar Dal, Emel. 2014. 'On Turkey's Trail as a "Rising Middle Power" in the Network of Global Governance: Preferences, Capabilities, and Strategies'. *Perceptions – Journal of International Affairs* 19 (4): 107–36.

Paul, T. V. 2005. 'Soft Balancing in the Age of U.S. Primacy'. *International Security* 30 (1): 46–71.

Peacock, A. C. S. 2012a. 'The Ottomans and the Funj sultanate in the sixteenth and seventeenth centuries'. *Bulletin of the School of Oriental and African Studies* 75 (12): 87–111.

Peacock, A. C. S. 2012b. 'Suakin: A Northeast African Port in the Ottoman Empire'. *Northeast African Studies* 12 (1): 29–50.

Peacock, A. C. S. 2018. 'The Ottomans in Northeast Africa'. *African History*. doi: 10.1093/acrefore/9780190277734.013.190.

Pease, Kelly-Kate. 2016. *Human Rights and Humanitarian Diplomacy*. Manchester: Manchester University Press.

Pelt, Mogens. 2014. *Military Intervention and a Crisis Democracy in Turkey: The Menderes Era and Its Demise*. London: I.B. Tauris.

Pieterse, Jan Nederveen. 2011. 'Global Rebalancing: Crisis and the East–South Turn'. *Development and Change* 42 (1) :22–48.

Princeton, Lyman. 2006. 'China's Involvement in Africa: A View from the US'. *South African Journal of International Affairs* 13 (1): 129–38. doi: 10.1080/10220460609556790.

Putnam, Robert D. 1988. 'Diplomacy and Domestic Politics: The Logic of Two-Level Games'. *International Organization* 42 (03): 427–60.

Quadir, Fahimul. 2013. 'Rising Donors and the New Narrative of "South–South" Cooperation: What Prospects for Changing the Landscape of Development Assistance Programmes?' *Third World Quarterly* 34 (2): 321–38.

Quataert, Donald. 2005. *The Ottoman Empire, 1700–1922*. Vol. 34. Cambridge: Cambridge University Press.

Randall, German. 2009. 'Financial Order and World Politics: Crisis, Change and Continuity'. *International Affairs* 85 (4): 669–87.

Rathbun, Brian. 2008. 'A Rose by Any Other Name: Neoclassical Realism as the Logical and Necessary Extension of Structural Realism'. *Security Studies* 17 (2): 294–321.

Ravenhill, John. 1998. 'Cycles of Middle Power Activism: Constraint and Choice in Australian and Canadian Foreign Policies'. *Australian Journal of International Affairs* 52 (3): 309–28.

Régnier, Philippe. 2011. 'The Emerging Concept of Humanitarian Diplomacy: Identification of a Community of Practice and Prospects for International Recognition'. *International Review of the Red Cross* 93 (884): 1211–37.

Ripsman, Norrin M. 2017. 'Neoclassical Realism'. In *Oxford Research Encyclopedia of International Studies*, edited by Nukhet Sandal and Renée Marlin-Bennett. Oxford: Oxford University Press.

Roberts, Jonathan M. 1988. 'The Importance of Individual and Role Variables'. In *Decision-Making during International Crises*, edited by Jonathan M. Roberts, 160–80. London: Palgrave Macmillan.

Robins, Philip. 2003. *Suits and Uniforms: Turkish Foreign Policy Since the Cold War*. London: Hurst & Co.

Rose, Gideon. 1998. 'Neoclassical Realism and Theories of Foreign Policy'. *World Politics* 51 (1): 144–72.

Rosecrance, Richard. 1986. *Rise of the Trading State: Commerce and Conquest in the Modern World*. New York: Basic Books.

Rossiter, Ash and Brendon J. Cannon. 2018. 'Re-examining the "Base": The Political and Security Dimensions of Turkey's Military Presence in Somalia'. *Insight Turkey* 1–22. doi: 10.25253/99.2019211.09.

Rotberg, Robert I., ed. 2003. *State Failure and State Weakness in a Time of Terror*. Washington: Brookings Inst. Press.

Rubin, Lawrence. 2014. *Islam in the Balance: Ideational Threats in Arab Politics*. Stanford: Stanford Security Studies.

Rudincová, Kateřina. 2014. 'New Player on the Scene: Turkish Engagement in Africa'. *Bulletin of Geography. Socioeconomic Series* (25): 197–213.

Rupesinghe, Kumar. 1997. *The General Principles of Multi-track Diplomacy*. Durban: ACCORD.

Rupesinghe, Kumar and Sanam Naraghi Anderlini. 1998. *Civil Wars, Civil Peace: An Introduction to Conflict Resolution*. London, Sterling: Pluto Press.

Rutland, Peter. 2013. 'Neoliberalism and the Russian Transition'. *Review of International Political Economy* 20 (2): 332–62.

Saggiomo, Valeria. 2014. 'Rebuilding the State from Below: NGO Networks and the Politics of Civil Society in Somalia'. In *Informal Power in the Greater Middle East: Hidden Geographies*, edited by Luca Anceschi, Gennaro Gervasio and Andrea Teti, 129–42. Abingdon: Routledge.

Şakı Aydın, Oya. 2005. 'Afrika'da Sinema Serüveni ve Cinéma Beur Akımı'. *Galatasaray Üniversitesi İleti-ş-im Dergisi* 2:89–103.

Sally, Razeen 2010. 'The Shift to the East'. *Economic Affairs* 30 (3): 94–104.

Salzman, Rachel S. 2019. *Russia, BRICS, and the Disruption of Global Order*. Washington: Georgetown University Press.

Sancar, Gaye Aslı. 2014. 'Turkey's Public Diplomacy: Its Actors, Stakeholders, and Tools'. In *Turkey's Public Diplomacy*, edited by Philip Seib and Senem B. Çevik, 13–42. New York: Palgrave Mavmillan.

Santini, Ruth Hanau. 2017. 'A New Regional Cold War in the Middle East and North Africa: Regional Security Complex Theory Revisited'. *The International Spectator* 52 (4): 93–111.

Saraçoğlu, Cenk and Özhan Demirkol. 2015. 'Nationalism and Foreign Policy Discourse in Turkey Under the AKP Rule: Geography, History and National Identity'. *British Journal of Middle Eastern Studies* 42 (3): 301–19.

Sayari, Sabri. 2000. 'Turkish Foreign Policy in the Post-cold War Era: The Challenges of Multi-regionalism'. *Journal of International Affairs* 54 (1): 169–82.

Sazak, Onur and Auveen Elizabeth Woods. 2017. 'Thinking Outside the Compound: Turkey's Approach to Peacebuilding in Somalia'. In *Rising Powers and Peacebuilding*, edited by Charles T. Call and Cedric de Coning, 167–89. London: Palgrave Macmillan.

Schiff, Amira. 2010. 'Quasi Track-One Diplomacy: An Analysis of the Geneva Process in the Israeli–Palestinian Conflict'. *International Studies Perspectives* 11 (2): 93–111.

Scholvin, Sören, ed. 2015. *A New Scramble for Africa? The Rush for Energy Resources in Sub-Saharan Africa*. Abingdon: Routledge.

Schudel, Carl J. W. 2008. 'Corruption and Bilateral Aid: A Dyadic Approach'. *Journal of Conflict Resolution* 52 (4): 507–28.

Schuett, Robert. 2010. *Political Realism, Freud, and Human Nature in International Relations*. Basingstoke: Palgrave Macmillan.

Schweller, Randall L. 2003. 'The Progressiveness of Neoclassical Realism'. In *Progress in International Relations Theory: Appraising the Field*, edited by Colin Elman and Miriam Fendius Elman, 311–47. London: MIT Press.

Schweller, Randall L. 2004. 'Unanswered Threats: A Neoclassical Realist Theory of Underbalancing'. *International Security* 29 (2): 159–201.

Schweller, Randall L. and Xiaoyu Pu. 2011. 'After Unipolarity: China's Visions of International Order in an Era of U.S. Decline'. *International Security* 36 (1): 41–72.

Shaw, Timothy M., Andrew F. Cooper and Gregory T. Chin. 2009. 'Emerging Powers and Africa: Implications for/from Global Governance?' *Politikon: South African Journal of Political Studies* 36 (1): 27–44.

Shinn, David. 2015a. *Hizmet in Africa: The Activities and Significance of the Gülen Movement*. Los Angeles: Tsehai Publishers

Shinn, David. 2015b. *Turkey's Engagement in Sub-Saharan Africa: Shifting Alliances and Strategic Diversification*. London: Chatman House. The Royal Institute of International Affairs.

Sinha, Shakti. 2016. *Rising Powers and Peacebuilding: India's Role in Afghanistan*. New Delhi: VIJ Books India PVT.

Siradag, Abdurrahim. 2013. 'The Making of the New Turkish Foreign and Security Policy towards Africa'. *Africa Insight* 43 (1): 15–31.

Sıradağ, Abdurrahim. 2018. 'Turkey–Africa Alliance: Evolving Patterns in Security Relations'. *African Security Review*. doi: 10.1080/10246029.2018.1550429.

Smith, Steve, Amelia Hadfield and Tim Dunne, eds. 2012. *Foreign Policy: Theories, Actors, Cases*. Oxford: Oxford University Press.

Solberg, Anne R. 2007. 'The Role of Turkish Islamic Networks in the Western Balkans'. *Southeast Europe Journal of Politics and Society* 55 (4): 429–62.

Sönmezoğlu, Faruk. 1994. *Türk Dış Politikasının Analizi*. Istanbul: Der Yayınları.

Sørensen, Georg. 2006. 'What Kind of World Order?: The International System in the New Millennium'. *Cooperation & Conflict* 41 (4): 343–63.

Southall, Roger and Melber Henning, eds. 2009. *A New Scramble for Africa? Imperialism, Investment and Development*. South Africa: University of Kwazulu-Natal Press.

Sözen, Ahmet. 2010. 'A Paradigm Shift in Turkish Foreign Policy: Transition and Challenges'. *Turkish Studies* 11 (1): 103–23.

Sözen, Ahmet. 2011. 'A Paradigm Shift in Turkish Foreign Policy: Transition and Challenges'. In *Islamization of Turkey under the AKP Rule*, edited by Birol Yesilada and Barry M. Rubin, 101–21. Abingdon: Routledge.

Stein, Aron. 2015. *The Rise and Fall of the AKP's Foreign Policy: In Pursuit of a New Regional Order.* London: Routledge.

Stephen, Matthew D. 2017. 'Emerging Powers and Emerging Trends in Global Governance'. *Global Governance* 23 (3): 483–502.

Stoddard, Abby, Adele Harmer and Victoria Di Domenico. 2009. 'Providing Aid in Insecure Environments: 2009 Update'. In *Humanitarian Policy Group.* London: Overseas Development Institute.

Stuenkel, Oliver. 2015. *The BRICS and the Future of Global Order.* Lanham: Lexington Books.

Sucuoğlu, Gizem and Onur Sazak. 2016. 'The New Kid on the Block: Turkey's Shifting Approaches to Peacebuilding'. *Rising Powers Quarterly* 1 (2): 69–91.

Sylla, Ndongo Samba. 2014. 'From a Marginalised to an Emerging Africa? A Critical Analysis'. *Review of African Political Economy* 41 (1): 7–25.

Tabak, Hüsrev. 2015. 'Broadening the Nongovernmental Humanitarian Mission: The IHH and Mediation'. *Insight Turkey* 17 (3): 193–217.

Taliaferro, Jeffrey W., Steven E. Lobell and Norrin M. Ripsman. 2009. *Neoclassical Realism, the State and Foreign Policy.* Cambridge: Cambridge University Press.

Tank, Pinar. 2013. *Turkey's New Humanitarian Approach in Somalia.* Oslo: Peace Research Institute Oslo.

Taş, Hakkı. 2018. 'A History of Turkey's AKP–Gülen Conflict'. *Mediterranean Politics* 23 (3): 395–402.

Taspinar, Omer. 2005. *Kurdish Nationalism and Political Islam in Turkey: Kemalist Identity in Transition.* New York: Routledge.

Tausch, Arno. 2003. 'Social Cohesion, Sustainable Development and Turkey's Accession to the European Union: Implications from a Global Model'. *Turkish Journal of International Relations* 2 (1): 1–41.

Taylor, Ian. 2006. 'China's Oil Diplomacy in Africa'. *International Affairs* 82 (5): 937–59.

Taylor, Ian. 2016. 'Dependency Redux: Why Africa Is Not Rising'. *Review of African Political Economy* 43 (147): 8–25.

Tedeschi, Salvatore. 1973. 'Note Storiche Sulle Isole Dahlak'. *Proceedings of the Third International Conference of Ethiopian Studies*, Addis Ababa.

Tee, Caroline. 2016. *The Gülen Movement in Turkey: The Politics of Islam and Modernity.* London, New York: I.B. Tauris.

Telci, Ismail and Tuba O. Horoz. 2018. 'Military Bases in the Foreign Policy of the United Arab Emirates'. *Insight Turkey* 20 (2):308–25.

Tepeciklioğlu, Eiem Eyrice. 2012. 'Afrika Kıtasının Dünya Politikasında Artan Önemi ve Türkiye-Afrika İlişkileri'. *Ankara Üniversitesi Afrika Çalışmaları Dergisi* 1 (2): 59–94.

Terzioglu, Aysecan, Cenk Ozbay, Maral Erol and Z. Umut Turem, eds. 2016. *The Making of Neoliberal Turkey.* London: Ashgate.

TİKA. 2013. *2012 Annual Report.* Ankara: Turkish Development and Coordination Agency.

Tocci, Nathalie, E. Fuat Keyman and Michael Werz. 2017. *Trends in Turkish Civil Society.* Washington: Center for American Progress.

Tüfekçi, Özgür. 2017. *The Foreign Policy of Modern Turkey: Power and the Ideology of Eurasianism*. London: I.B. Tauris.

Tugtan, Mehmet Ali. 2016. 'Kulturel degiskenlerin dis politikadaki yeri: Ismail Cem ve Ahmet Davutoğlu'. *Uluslararasi Iliskiler* 13 (49) :3–24.

Turam, Berna. 2007. *Between Islam and the State: The Politics of Engagement*. Stanford: Stanford University Press.

Uchehara, Kieran E. 2008. 'Continuity and Change in Turkish Foreign Policy Toward Africa'. *Akademik Bakış* 2 (3) :43–64.

Ufiem, Maurice Ogbonnaya. 2016. 'Terrorism, Agenda 2063 and the Challenges of Development in Africa'. *South African Journal of International Affairs* 23 (2) :185–99.

Ülgen, Sinan. 2010. 'A Place in the Sun or Fifteen Minutes of Fame?: Understanding Turkey's New Foreign Policy'. Carnegie Endowment for International Peace, Carnegie Europe.

Ulrich, Krotz and James Sperling. 2011. 'Discord and Collaboration in Franco–American Relations: What Can Role Theory Tell Us?' In *Role Theory in International Relations: Approaches and Analyses*, edited by Sebastian Harnisch, Cornelia Frank and Hanns W. Maull, 213–33. Abingdon, New York: Routledge.

Üngör, Ugur Ümit. 2011. *The Making of Modern Turkey: Nation and State in Eastern Anatolia, 1913–1950*. Oxford: Oxford University Press.

Uzer, Umut. 2011. *Identity and Turkish Foreign Policy: The Kemalist Influence in Cyprus and the Caucasus*. London: I.B. Tauris.

Uzer, Umut. 2018. 'Glorification of the Past as a Political Tool: Ottoman History in Contemporary Turkish Politics'. *The Journal of the Middle East and Africa* 9 (4): 339–57.

Vali, Nasr. 2009. *Forces of Fortune: The Rise of the New Muslim Middle Class and What It Will Mean for Our World*. New York, London: Free Press.

VanderLippe, John M. 2005. *The Politics of Turkish Democracy: Ismet Inonu and the Formation of the Multi-Party System, 1938–1950*. Albany: State University of New York Press.

Verhoeven, Harry. 2015. 'Africa's Next Hegemon: Behind Ethiopia's Power Plays'. *Foreign Affairs*. URL: https://www.foreignaffairs.com/articles/ethiopia/2015-04-12/africas-next-hegemon.

Verhoeven, Harry. 2018. 'The Gulf and the Horn: Changing Geographies of Security Interdependence and Competing Visions of Regional Order'. *Civil Wars* 20 (3): 333–57.

Vidino, Lorenzo, Raffaello Pantucci and Evan Kohlmann. 2010. 'Bringing Global Jihad to the Horn of Africa: al Shabaab, Western Fighters, and the Sacralization of the Somali Conflict'. *African Security* 3 (4): 216–38. doi: https://doi.org/10.1080/19392206.2010.533071.

Villanger, Espen. 2007. *Arab Foreign Aid: Disbursement Patterns, Aid Policies and Motives*. Bergen: Chr. Michelsen Institute.

Walker, Stephen G., ed. 1987. *Role Theory and Foreign Policy Analysis*. Durham: Duke University Press.

Walls, Michael and Steve Kibble. 2010. 'Beyond Polarity: Negotiating a Hybrid State in Somaliland'. *Africa Spectrum* 45 (1): 31–56.

Walt, Stephen M. 1987. *The Origins of Alliance*. Ithaca: Cornell University Press.

Wang, Hongying and Erik French. 2013. 'Middle Range Powers in Global Governance'. *Third World Quarterly* 34 (6): 985–99.

Warde, Ibrahim. 2000. *Islamic Finance in the Global Economy*. Edinburgh: Edinburgh University Press.

Ware, Glenn T. 1997. 'The Emerging Norm of Humanitarian Intervention and Presidential Decision Directive'. *Naval Law Review* 44:1–58.

Wasuge, Mahad. 2016. *Turkey's Assistance Model in Somalia: Achieving Much with Little*. Mogadishu: Heritage Institute for Policy Studies.

Weiss, Linda. 1997. 'Globalization and the Myth of the Powerless State'. *New Left Review* 225:3.

Wendt, Alexander. 1999. *Social Theory of International Politics*. Cambridge: Cambridge University Press.

Wesseling, Henk L. 1996. *Divide and Rule: The Partition of Africa, 1880–1914*. Westport: Praeger Publishers.

Wheeler, Tom. 2011. 'Ankara to Africa: Turkey's Outreach since 2005'. *South African Journal of International Affairs* 18 (1): 43–62.

Wiley, David. 2012. 'Militarizing Africa and African Studies and the U.S. Africanist Response'. *African Studies Review* 55 (2): 147–61.

Williams, Paul D. 2018. *Fighting for Peace in Somalia: A History and Analysis of the African Union Mission (AMISOM), 2007–2017*. Oxford: Oxford University Press.

Williamson, John. 1989. 'What Washington Means by Policy Reform'. In *Latin American Readjustment: How Much Has Happened*, edited by John Williamson. Washington: Institute for International Economics.

Williamson, John. 2012. 'Is the "Beijing Consensus" Now Dominant?' *Asia Policy* 13:1–16.

Wohlforth, Curtis. 2008. 'Realism and Foreign Policy'. In *Foreign Policy: Theories, Actors, Cases*, edited by Steven Smith, Amelia Hadfield and Tim Dunne, 31–48. Oxford: Oxford University Press.

Woods, NGaire. 2008. 'Whose Aid? Whose Influence? China, Emerging Donors and the Silent Revolution in Development Assistance'. *International Affairs* 84 (6): 1205–21.

Wu, Fulong. 2010. 'How Neoliberal Is China's Reform? The Origins of Change during Transition'. *Eurasian Geography and Economics* 51 (5): 619–31.

Yagci, Mustafa. 2016. 'A Beijing Consensus in the Making: The Rise of Chinese Initiatives in the International Political Economy and Implications for Developing Countries'. *Perceptions – Journal of International Affairs* 21 (2): 29–56.

Yalvaç, Faruk. 2014. 'Approaches to Turkish Foreign Policy: A Critical Realist Analysis'. *Turkish Studies* 15 (1): 117–38.

Yanık, Lerna K. 2011. 'Constructing Turkish "Exceptionalism": Discourses of Liminality and Hybridity in Post-Cold War Turkish Foreign Policy'. *Political Geography* 30 (2): 80–9.

Yankaya-Péan, Dilek. 2017. 'Étude des reconfigurations patronales de la dérive autoritaire en Turquie entre contestation, domination et crise'. *Mouvements* 90 (2): 38–47.

Yavuz, Hakan M. 2003. *Islamic Political Identity in Turkey*. Oxford, New York: Oxford University Press.

Yavuz, Hakan M. and John L. Esposito, eds. 2003. *Turkish Islam and the Secular State: The Gülen Movement*. New York: Syracuse University Press.

Yesilyurt, Nuri. 2017. 'Explaining Miscalculation and Maladaptation in Turkish Foreign Policy towards the Middle East during the Arab Uprisings: A Neoclassical Realist Perspective'. *Center for Foreign Policy and Peace Research, İhsan Doğramacı Peace Foundation* 6 (2): 65–83.

Yilmaz, Muzaffer Ercan. 2010. 'Conceptual Framework of Turkish Foreign Policy in the AK Party Era'. *Turkish Review* 1 (1): 68–73.

Yorulmazlar, Emirhan and Ebru Turhan. 2015. 'Turkish Foreign Policy towards the Arab Spring: Between Western Orientation and Regional Disorder'. *Journal of Balkan and Near Eastern Studies* 17 (3): 337–52.

Zalewski, Piotr. 2010. 'The Self-appointed Superpower: Turkey Goes It Alone'. *World Policy Journal* 27 (4):97–102.

Zhao, Suisheng. 2014. 'A Neo-Colonialist Predator or Development Partner? China's Engagement and Rebalance in Africa'. *Journal of Contemporary China* 23 (90): 1033–52.

Zimmermann, Felix and Kimberly Smith. 2011. 'More Actors, More Money, More Ideas for International Development Cooperation'. *Journal of International Development* 23 (5): 722–38.

Zürcher, Erik J. 1998. *Turkey: A Modern History*. London, New York: I.B. Tauris.

Zürcher, Erik J. 2010. *The Young Turk Legacy and Nation Building: From the Ottoman Empire to Ataturk's Turkey*. London, New York: I.B. Tauris.

Index